day trips® series

day trips® from los angeles

first edition

>>> getaway ideas for the local traveler

laura kath & pamela price

gpp®
travel

Guilford, Connecticut

D0249711

All the information in this guidebook is subject to change. We recommend that you call ahead to obtain current information before traveling.

To buy books in quantity for corporate use or incentives, call **(800) 962-0973** or e-mail **premiums@GlobePequot.com**.

Day Trips is a registered trademark.

Editor: Amy Lyons
Project Editor: Heather Santiago
Layout: Kevin Mak
Text Design: Linda R. Loiewski
Maps: Design Maps, Inc. © Morris Book Publishing, LLC.
Spot photography throughout © David M. Schrader/Shutterstock

Library of Congress Cataloging-in-Publication Data is available on file.

ISBN 978-0-7627-6079-4

Printed in the United States of America
10 9 8 7 6 5 4 3 2 1

To Allen, Artie, Tony, and Harris Lechtman

—Pamela Price

To Anna Hubble Kath, my intrepid ninety-plus mom

—Laura Kath

about the authors

Coauthors Laura Kath and Pamela Price have more than sixty years combined travel and life experience in sunny Southern California. They are the coauthors of *Fun with the Family Southern California* (Globe Pequot Press, now in its seventh edition).

Pamela resides in Palm Springs when she is not globe-trotting and writing or broadcasting about her adventures. She is the author of *100 Best Spas of the World* (Globe Pequot Press, now in its third edition).

Laura is the author of seventeen nonfiction books and president of Mariah Marketing, her Santa Barbara County–based consulting business founded in 1989. She is a member of the International Food, Wine & Travel Writers Association and the Society of Incentive Travel Executives.

This dynamic duo blends comprehensive travel experience with the latest tourism information—making this guidebook an essential read for Los Angeles area residents and visitors alike.

acknowledgments

Researching, compiling, editing, and selecting our favorite day trips from Los Angeles certainly could not have been accomplished without the comprehensive and invaluable assistance of many generous individuals and organizations. From bleary eyes and achy fingers pounding our laptop keyboards, we gratefully acknowledge the many (and do apologize if we've neglected to mention anyone): Brian Hart, Amtrak; Anaheim/Orange County Visitor & Convention Bureau; Dan McKernan, Big Bear Lake; California Travel & Tourism Commission; Steve Wilson, BWR Public Relations; Frank Tysen & Marilyn Will, Casa Cody Country Inn Palm Springs; Catalina Island Chamber of Commerce; Disneyland Resort; Jeff Hocker Public Relations; Hollywood Chamber of Commerce; Pasadena Convention & Visitors Bureau; Joshua Tree National Park; LA Inc.—the Los Angeles Convention & Visitors Bureau; Long Beach Area Visitors & Convention Bureau; Oxnard Convention & Visitors Bureau; Bob Bogard, Palm Springs Art Museum; Palm Springs Bureau of Tourism; Palm Springs Desert Resorts Convention and Visitors Bureau; Tracy Conrad, Palm Springs Preservation Foundation; Mary Byrd, Santa Barbara Car Free Project; Shannon Brooks, Santa Barbara Conference & Visitors Bureau; Mary Harris, Santa Ynez Valley Visitors Association; Tracy Farhad, Solvang Conference & Visitors Bureau; Universal Studios; and Ventura Visitors & Convention Bureau.

Pamela would especially like to thank Barbara Beckley, a fellow desert denizen for her invaluable editorial assistance, as well as Mark Farley, Elite Land Tours, for his expertise in exploration; Jackie Olden (*The Jackie Olden Show,* KNWZ-970 AM/KNWQ-1140 AM, Morris Desert Media); and Janet Newcomb, Newcomb Public Relations, for their friendship and support—and certainly her sons Anthony Grant and Artie Lechtman for their patience and advice.

Laura appreciates her supportive Kath family members and dear friends who are always eager to share their favorite travel adventures with her. She gratefully acknowledges her amazing "author care team" during ankle reconstruction surgery recuperation (which occurred concurrently with writing this book) including Jane Baxter, Rev. Dr. Sandra Cook, Beverly Johnston, Thomas Keough, William Morton; her sister, Shirley Nixon; Barbara Tuch, Peggy Wentz, Lee Wilkerson and so many others that there's not enough space to name.

Last, but never least, we acknowledge Amy Lyons at Globe Pequot Press for giving us the opportunity to write about these trips!

contents

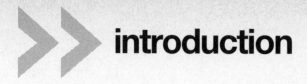

introduction

Pull out a traditional paper map of Southern California and place an old-school compass on downtown Los Angeles—no matter what direction the needle swings, you'll find something amazing to see, do, or taste! There is just no way we can include every worthy place for you to experience in a volume of this limited size. However, we do believe that this guidebook will give you a fantastic sampling of day trips within a 2-hour driving radius of downtown Los Angeles. Plus, we've included some places for you to stay since we just know you'll want to spend more time in these environs!

Both of us, along with our families and friends, have traveled thousands of miles by trains, planes, automobiles, horses, and aching feet to discover the best trips around greater Los Angeles. We are rather proud of our adopted home state—Pamela originally hails from Minnesota, and Laura is from Michigan—and have spent more than sixty combined years as journalists researching and describing life here in the Golden State. We are delighted to share our experiences with you!

We believe the most important element to enjoying your day trips is time. Be sure you allow yourself plenty of it. Be sure to carefully select the day trips that appeal to your own unique tastes. Distances around here are very deceptive. Five miles does not necessarily mean 5 minutes away—especially during rush hours on Los Angeles's infamous freeways. It's probably why those of us who live here never say something is only X miles away—we say, "it's about X minutes depending on when you try to go." For all our love of cars and whining about traffic, there are alternative transportation options aplenty in Los Angeles, and we urge you to use them to explore the bounty and beauty surrounding *El Pueblo de la Reina de los Angeles* (The Town of the Queen of the Angels).

Our day trips from the City of Angels will provide you with options ranging from the Pacific Ocean and its awesome beaches to the mountain ranges, inland valleys, rivers, freshwater lakes such as Big Bear and Arrowhead, and the deserts such as Palm Springs and Joshua Tree.

How about recreation? Participant or spectator, you can experience it all here. Teams such as basketball's Los Angeles Lakers and Clippers, hockey's Mighty Ducks of Anaheim, baseball's L.A. Dodgers and Los Angeles Angels of Anaheim offer the thrill of professional action. Needless to say, waterfront activity should rate high on your list when visiting this area—boating, fishing, sailing, sunbathing, surfing, and swimming are what California dreams are made of. If you visit between December and April, whale watching along the Pacific is an absolute must-see thrill. Of course, biking and hiking trails abound to explore, yet they preserve all the area's natural beauty. You can visit natural parks full of wildlife and

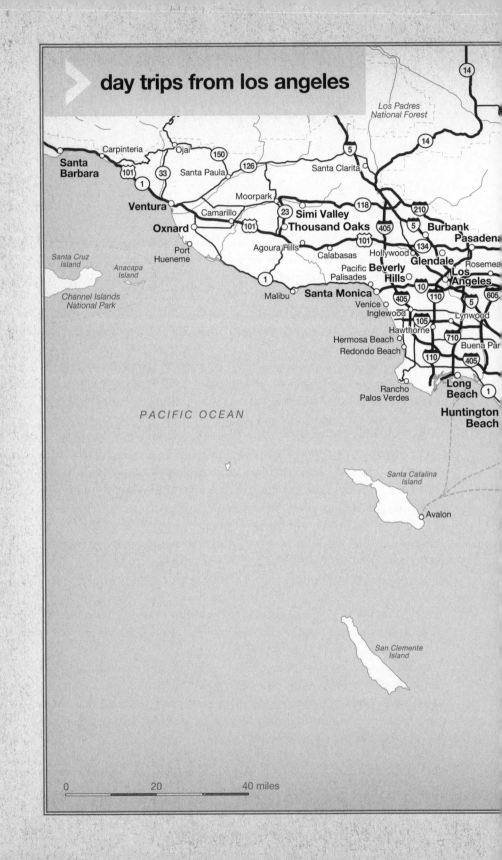

day trips from los angeles

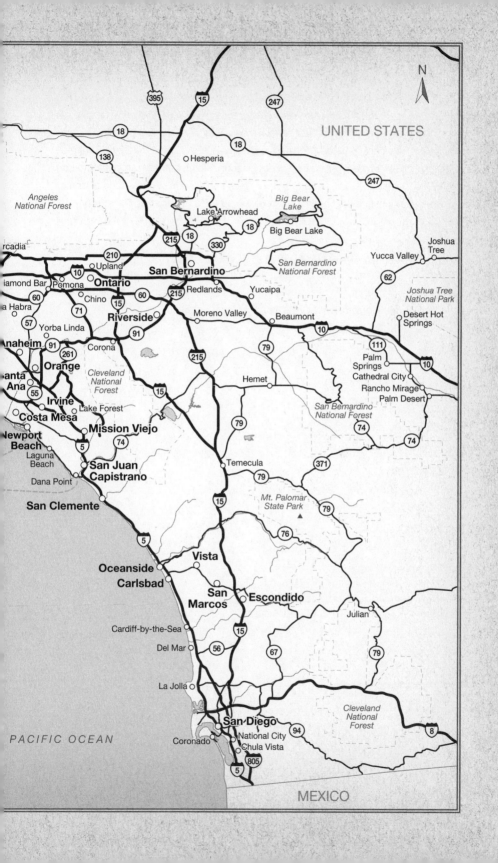

sea life or human-made amusement parks stocked with thrills. Local museums are filled with hands-on displays of fun things from archives to outer space. Be certain to include the magnificent J. Paul Getty Museum as well as the Ronald Reagan Library. California's history, rich with Native American, Spanish, and Mexican influences, provides plenty of cultural-diversity education, not to mention the thrill of deciphering foreign names—such as San Luis Obispo, Port Hueneme, and Ojai. Greater Los Angeles is blessed with hundreds of annual special events—starting with January's immensely popular Rose Parade in Pasadena, right through holiday lighted boat parades all along the coast. We've put some of the highlights in a special appendix for your easy reference.

We think that tripping around Los Angeles is like an endless vacation. Where else can you travel from the desert to a futuristic metropolis to some snow-covered mountain before, finally, taking in the sunset at the beach—all in one day? Would you expect anything less from the birthplace of Hollywood and Disneyland? Enjoy your trips!

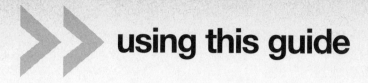

using this guide

All our day trips from Los Angeles originate from (or use as a starting point) historic **Los Angeles Union Station** (LAUS), 800 North Alameda St., in the heart of downtown Los Angeles. LAUS is the transportation hub for the city, including national Amtrak and Amtrak California passenger trains, Metrolink commuter trains, MetroRail subways, Metro buses, and shuttles. Despite living in car-crazy Southern California, we do believe in alternative transportation—so car-free options will be included wherever applicable in our day trips. Opened in 1939, Los Angeles Union Station was the last post–World War I "grand terminal" of its kind to be built in the United States. Its architecture is a successful merging of Spanish Mission, Moorish, and streamline modern styles often used as movie and TV filming locations (think of scenes in *Union Station, Silver Streak, Blade Runner, Speed, Star Trek: First Contact, 24,* and *NCIS: Los Angeles*). Step outside Union Station and you're across the plaza from Olvera Street, where the city of Los Angeles was established in the late eighteenth century, and adjacent to New Chinatown, a historic Chinese district. Just walking around this area can be a festive cultural day trip in itself!

Our day trips are listed geographically—starting closest to downtown Los Angeles and radiating outward—clockwise around the compass (North, Northeast, East, Southeast, South, Southwest, West, and Northwest).

hours of operation, credit cards

Always remember to call ahead! In the interest of accuracy and because they are subject to change, hours of operation and attraction prices are given in general terms. You can assume that all establishments listed accept major credit cards unless otherwise noted. If you have any concerns, please be sure to contact the establishments for specifics.

pricing key

Rates for Accommodations: This price code reflects the average cost of a double-occupancy guest room during a peak-price period (not including hotel tax or fees). Always ask if any special packages or discounts are available during your preferred dates—there generally are!

$ . . . . . . up to $100
$$ . . . . . $100 to $199
$$$ . . . . $200 and up

Rates for Restaurants: This price code reflects the average price of an entree per person (generally dinner unless only breakfast or lunch is served) and does not include wine, beer, cocktails, appetizers, desserts, tax, or tips.

$ . . . . . . up to $10
$$ . . . . . $10 to $20
$$$ . . . . $20 and up

driving tips

In California, the driver and all passengers must wear their seatbelts at all times when traveling in a car. Any child too small to be protected by a seatbelt must be secured in a child safety seat.

Driving times in Greater Los Angeles are completely dependent upon time of day. Rush hours are generally weekdays from 6 to 9 a.m. and 3 to 7 p.m. and are to be avoided. We recommend the following times (and our day trips are based upon these assumptions):

- Driving on weekdays before 6 a.m., between 9 a.m. and 3 p.m., or after 7 p.m.

- Driving on weekends anytime, but traffic is generally unpredictable due to regionalized patterns and known bottlenecks (for example, US 101 south from Santa Barbara on Sunday) and will be advised when available for specific day trips).

highway designations

Perhaps no other area in the world has embraced the automobile as passionately as we have in Southern California (traditionally meaning Los Angeles, Orange, Ventura, Santa Barbara, San Bernardino, Riverside, and San Diego Counties). Generally, interstates are prefaced by "I" (such as I-5, one of the major north/south routes in California. U.S. highways are two and/or three lane roads (sometimes divided) that are prefaced by "US" or "Highway" (for example, US 101 or Highway 101—a major north/south artery). State Routes (SR) are real mixed bags of asphalt here—all are paved, some are undivided two-lane roads, others are divided four lanes!

Just as in many major cities, our Los Angeles–area freeways have names that are often distinct from the official state or federal highway number that they are assigned. We Southern California residents generally refer to freeways with just the number; for example, Interstate10 is also known locally as the just "the 10," or the "I-10," or its direction—the Santa Monica Freeway or the San Bernardino Freeway. However, traffic reporters and highway signs can refer to a freeway by its full descriptive name or not—which can be very confusing! And to make matters even more confusing, a "named" freeway might include portions of two or more differently numbered routes; for example, the Ventura Freeway consists of portions of Highway 101 and SR 134 (technically it's SR 134, but locally it's known as just the 134). Here are just a few basics:

Interstate 5 is known as:

- **San Diego Freeway** from downtown San Diego to the El Toro Y in Orange County

- **Santa Ana Freeway** from the El Toro Y in Orange County to the East L.A. Interchange

- **Golden State Freeway** from the East L.A. Interchange to Wheeler Ridge

Interstate 10 is known as:

- **Santa Monica Freeway** from Santa Monica to the East L.A. Interchange (downtown)

- **San Bernardino Freeway** from the East L.A. Interchange to San Bernardino (center of the Inland Empire—the area that encompasses Riverside and San Bernardino Counties—it is a common term of usage here)

U.S. Highway 101 is known as:

- **Hollywood Freeway** from downtown's Four Level Interchange to the junction with SR 134 (locally known as the 134)

- **Ventura Freeway** from the junction with the Hollywood Freeway to Santa Barbara County line

leaving the driving to somebody else

Riding the rails—it's the green alternative to driving on your day trips through greater Los Angeles. **Amtrak, Metrorail,** and **Metrolink** all have excellent routes in the region—as well as connections to convenient bus services through and around your destination cities. It's the best way to circumvent the traffic as well as reducing congestion and air pollution. For complete details, call Amtrak at (800) USA-RAIL or visit www.amtrak.com, or Metro (Los Angeles County Metropolitan Transportation Authority) at (800) COMMUTE, (323) GO-METRO, or www.metro.net. And here's an added incentive: **Metro Destinations Discounts** is a program for Metro riders to save money at popular destinations, sporting events, concerts, museums, theme parks, shops, and more around Los Angeles County simply by using Metro public transit. For example, at press time, you could save $3 on adult admission and $2 on child admission to the Los Angeles Zoo in Griffith Park. Discounts change from month to month; visit www.metro.net/around/destination-discounts for current savings. If you have a:

- **Metro Pass**—just show your valid Metro pass to receive discounts. This includes Metro Weekly, Monthly, College/Vocational, Student (grades K through 8 or 9 through 12), and Senior/Disabled.

- **Day Pass/Metro Rail Ticket**—the Day Pass/Rail ticket is only valid on the date of purchase for a discount.

Elite Land Tours offers dozens of guided, full-service day trips from greater Los Angeles. Owner Mark Farley specializes in discovery through exploration, providing an insider's tour of attractions with intel that will fascinate you from beginning to end. You can concentrate on your experience and forget about the GPS and roadmaps because these details are handled by your guide and driver. Door-to-door service signifies that Elite Land Tours will pick up you and your group of up to six passengers and return you to your hotel or home base in one of their customized Hummers. For example, if you have only a day to visit the Palm Springs desert resort area, they can customize your tour according to whether you want to delve into architectural tourism or get up close and personal with Joshua Tree National Park. More examples of Elite Land Tours include their Calico/Deep Space experience, which combines a visit to a "living ghost town" with a tour of one of only three deep space communication complexes in the world. This experience adds up to 12 hours of nonstop adventure that would be challenging to plan on your own—because of security and clearance issues—all of which Elite Land Tours handles for you. Their California Mission Tour takes you back to the era of Spanish padres and Indians, and can include visiting romantic San Juan Capistrano (remember the swallows, they return here every spring). For details, pricing and schedules; call (800) 514-4866 or visit www.elitelandtours.com.

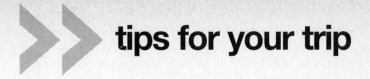

tips for your trip

Area Codes: There are more than a dozen telephone area codes in the Greater Los Angeles/Southern California region—all listings in this book will include the three-digit code and the seven-digit phone number.

Attire: In dress, as in most other respects, Los Angeles style is comfortable and casual, though evening wear may be dressier in some places. Throughout the region, you'll be most comfortable if you layer your clothing. Early mornings, evenings, and nights may be cool enough for a jacket or sweater, but daytime temperatures in the oceanfront areas and the drier, hotter inland regions are comfortable enough for short sleeves pretty much year-round.

Banking: Bank-card, bank-cash, and automated teller machines (ATMs) are located throughout the region. Members of participating banking networks and credit-card companies can obtain U.S. currency by using an ATM card or credit card and a personal identification number (PIN). Bank hours with teller services are generally Mon through Fri from 9 a.m. to 5 p.m., with limited branches open on Saturday.

Drinking Age: It is illegal in California for anyone under twenty-one years old to consume alcohol in any quantity. To purchase alcohol in a bar, restaurant, or retail establishment, you must be able to produce photographic identification that proves your age. Driving while under the influence of alcohol or drugs (DUI) is a serious offense in California. A person is considered legally drunk when the concentration of alcohol in his or her blood is at or above 0.08 percent.

Emergencies: For any and all life-threatening medical, fire, and police emergencies, call 911 from any phone anywhere.

Sales Tax: The minimum sales tax in the state of California is 8.25 percent; however, supplementary sales tax may be added (via voter approval) by cities, counties, service authorities, and various special districts. For example, at press time, the city of Los Angeles has a combined 9.75 percent sales-tax rate. Please be certain to ask if you have any questions before making a purchase.

Smoking: California law prohibits smoking in restaurants, bars, theaters, auditoriums, museums, and most other public buildings. Please be cautious and courteous if you must light up!

Time Zone: Los Angeles is in the Pacific standard time zone, eight hours behind Greenwich mean time. Daylight savings time is observed from the second Sunday in March (spring ahead one hour at 2 a.m.) to the first Sunday in November (fall back one hour at 2 a.m.) from standard time.

north

day trip 01

north

hooray for h-town:
hollywood

hollywood

If downtown is the historic center of the City of Angels, then Hollywood has to be its heartbeat. For millions around the world, Hollywood *is* Los Angeles, an illusion promoted by the movie studios, prop houses, sound stages, lighting companies, musicians, recording outlets, and casting agencies that remain very much alive in this district situated 10 miles northwest of downtown. As one of the few officially designated districts within the sprawling city of Los Angeles, Hollywood does not have its own municipal government but does have an honorary "Mayor of Hollywood" appointed by the Hollywood Chamber of Commerce for ceremonial purposes. Perhaps the golden age of Hollywood is long gone, but the 50-foot-high HOLLYWOOD sign up in the Mount Lee foothills is an icon of the entertainment capital of the world. Built in 1923 to advertise a burgeoning housing development called Hollywoodland that never materialized, today it is protected and promoted by the Hollywood Sign Trust (www.hollywoodsign.org), a nonprofit group that physically maintains, repairs, and secures its place in history.

getting there

From downtown, it's super easy and saves potential parking/traffic hassles (not to mention air pollution) to take the Metro Red Line subway operated by the Los Angeles County Metropolitan Transportation Authority (LACMTA; www.metro.net/around). Hop on at Union

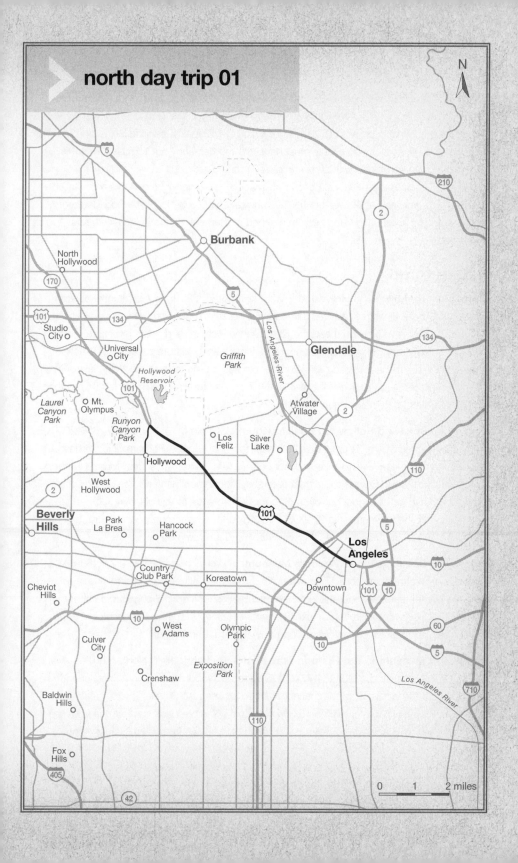

Station (the starting point for all five Metro Rail lines) and exit at Hollywood/Vine (eastern side of the Boulevard) or Hollywood/Highland (western end of the Boulevard) You can easily walk just about everywhere you want to visit in Hollywood—and frankly, strolling Hollywood Boulevard is one experience you simply must have! It's the best way not to miss the fantastic people watching combined with star- and navel-gazing!

If you simply must have your car in Hollywood, drive north from downtown via US Highway 101 and exit at Gower or Highland to make your way to Hollywood Boulevard. Movie stars, glamour, palm tree–lined streets, and excitement always in the air—hooray for Hollywood!

where to go

El Capitan Theatre. 6838 Hollywood Blvd.; (323) 468-8262; www.elcapitantickets.com. Disney and Pacific Theatres restored this historic theater in 1989. Originally opened in 1926, it is now an exclusive first-run theater for Walt Disney Pictures and hosts live stage shows, world premieres, and other special events that have helped restore showmanship to Hollywood Boulevard. The restored 4/37 Wurlitzer pipe organ—known as the "Mightiest of the Mighty Wurlitzers"—is just one of the jewels of this architectural masterpiece. It is across the street from Mann's Chinese Theatre.

Hollywood Bowl and Hollywood Bowl Museum. 2301 North Highland; (323) 850-2000; www.hollywoodbowl.org. The summer home of the Los Angeles Philharmonic Orchestra, this bowl is a terrific place to take in a concert. *Pollstar* magazine's Best Major Outdoor Venue, the Hollywood Bowl is the largest natural outdoor amphitheater in the United States. Pack a picnic to get the most out of an outdoor performance at this gleaming Los Angeles landmark. Visit the museum—it's free! Oct through June, Tues through Sat, 10 a.m. to 4:30 p.m., and July through Sept, Tues through Sat, 10:30 a.m. to 8:30 p.m.

Hollywood Guinness World Records Museum. 6764 Hollywood Blvd.; (323) 463-6433; www.guinnessattractions.com. The museum showcases offbeat testimonials to a wide variety of facts, feats, and incredible achievements. It is located in Hollywood's first movie house, the Hollywood. Hands-on exhibits involve subjects such as technology, space adventures, and natural phenomena. Open daily 10 a.m. to midnight.

Hollywood Museum in the Historic Max Factor Building. 1660 North Highland Ave. at Hollywood Boulevard; (323) 464-7776; www.thehollywoodmuseum.com. Housed in the edifice where the wizard of movie makeup worked his magic on motion-picture stars, here is where today you'll find more than 10,000 pieces of show business memorabilia from one hundred years of Tinseltown. The museum features displays from Elvis, Marilyn Monroe, Johnny Depp, *High School Musical, Twilight: New Moon, Hannah Montana,* and *Star Trek,* Hannibal Lector's jail cell, and even Cary Grant's Rolls Royce. Open Wed through Sun, 10 a.m. to 5 p.m.; closed Mon, Tues, and most holidays.

reeling through hollywood's history

*Native Americans had long occupied the lands we now call Hollywood, and with the arrival of Spanish explorers followed by Mexican soldiers and ranchers, the area continued as a flourishing agricultural community. In 1886, H. H. Wilcox bought some acreage of Rancho La Brea to build a residential subdivision, and one legend has it that his wife christened it **Hollywoodland** (there's still a dispute about this more than a century later, but we'll go with this version for now). The area became a prestigious and prosperous community and incorporated in 1903. Hollywood's city status was short-lived since a lack of water and sewers forced annexation in 1910 to the city of Los Angeles, where it remains today.*

*Drawn by the open spaces and warm, moderate year-round climate, the New Jersey–based Centaur Company opened Hollywood's first film studio in 1911 at 6121 Sunset Blvd., at the corner of Gower; it was called the **Nestor Company.** The company's subsequent financial success attracted dozens more studios and accompanying businesses. By 1920, Hollywood had become world famous as the center of the United States film industry. **KTLA,** the first commercial television station west of the Mississippi River, signed on the air in Hollywood on January 22, 1947, and is still broadcasting. On Vine Street just north of Hollywood Boulevard, the famous circular **Capitol Records Building** that looks like a stack of 7-inch vinyl records (aka 45s) was built in 1956. It houses offices and recording studios that are not accessible to the public.*

*In 1958, the **Hollywood Walk of Fame** was created as a tribute to artists working in the entertainment industry—did you know that the first star embedded on the sidewalk honors actress Joanne Woodward? In the 1970s and '80s the luster of Hollywood faded, and some blight replaced light. A revitalization plan began to emerge, and in 1985, the **Hollywood Boulevard Commercial and Entertainment District** was officially listed in the National Register of Historic Places— thereby protecting the area's important buildings and assuring that the significance of Hollywood's past would always be a part of its future—which definitely has experienced a renaissance in the twenty-first century.*

Hollywood's RockWalk of Fame. 7425 West Sunset Blvd., in the Hollywood Guitar Center; (323) 874-1060; www.rockwalk.com. Inductees include Black Sabbath, Elvis Presley, Johnny Cash, Bo Diddley, the Doobie Brothers, Jimi Hendrix, and Eddie Van Halen, just to name a few, with handprints on the sidewalk. RockWalk offers three different interactive tours: the memorabilia tour, virtual handprints (an indoors exhibit offered as an alternative to hanging out on the sidewalk to view the actual handprints), and an archives tour. Call for times and special events. Open Mon through Fri 10 a.m. to 9 p.m., Sat 10 a.m. to 6 p.m., and Sun 11 a.m. to 6 p.m. Free.

Hollywood Wax Museum. 6767 Hollywood Blvd.; (323) 462-8860; www.hollywoodwax museum.com/hollywood. Located in the historic Embassy Nightclub building, this wax museum has displayed 200-plus life-size renditions of celebrated film stars, political leaders, and sports greats since 1965. Open daily from 10 a.m. to midnight, 365 days a year.

Kodak Theatre. 6801 Hollywood Blvd., anchor of the Hollywood & Highland entertainment complex; (323) 308-6300 or (323) 308-6363 (box office and guided-tour information); www .kodaktheatre.com. Be sure you don't miss this chance to step behind the velvet rope and personally experience the glamour of the permanent home of the Oscar ceremonies. During your tour, you'll see an Oscar statuette, visit the exclusive George Eastman VIP Room (where stars party), view twenty-six Academy Awards images, learn where this year's Oscar nominees sat (and maybe sit there, too), and gain an insider's view of behind-the-scenes production from friendly, knowledgeable actors/tour guides. Be sure to call for tickets in advance since tours fill quickly, with only twenty people allowed per group. Children under twelve must be accompanied by an adult/guardian. Since opening in November 2001, the theater has hosted a range of prestigious artists and events, including the Academy Awards ceremonies, Celine Dion, Prince, Elvis Costello, Barry Manilow, American Ballet Theatre, ESPY Awards, and even the *American Idol* finals. Daily thirty-minute guided tours are offered from 10:30 a.m. to 2:30 p.m. (subject to change depending on events scheduled). Call to confirm ticket prices.

Madame Tussauds Hollywood. 6933 Hollywood Blvd.; (323) 798-1670; www.madame-tussauds.com. Right next door to Grauman's Chinese Theatre—you are guaranteed to "meet" almost one hundred celebrities at Hollywood's newest wax-figure attraction. Check them out on movie-blockbuster sets spread over three floors and take plenty of photos to impress your friends since these folks are really lifelike, really! Open daily at 10 a.m., 364 days of the year, only closed the day of the Academy Awards.

Mann's (aka Grauman's Chinese Theatre). 6925 Hollywood Blvd.; (323) 461-3331; www.manntheatres.com/chinese. Hollywood doesn't get any more Hollywood than at this unofficial emperor's palace of Tinseltown. Revel at the sight of what looks like the entrance to a Chinese imperial palace. But the main attractions here are in the theater's forecourt, where the handprints, footprints, and signatures of Hollywood celebrities dating from 1927 are quite literally cast in stone. VIP backstage tours are offered by reservation only seven days a week (323-463-9576).

On busy street corners along Hollywood Boulevard, and particularly in front of Mann's Chinese Theatre, you might spot tanned young men and women wearing sun visors and holding clipboards. If they don't approach you, make a point of approaching them: They have passes for movie previews at area studios, and sometimes you are paid to see them. It's a way the studios get audience feedback before films are released and a way for you to learn about an important, if little known, aspect of the entertainment industry.

Ripley's Believe It or Not! Odditorium. 6780 Hollywood Blvd.; (323) 466-6335; http:// hollywood.ripleys.com. No problem finding the place; there's a giant *Tyrannosaurus rex* poking his mighty head and substantial torso out of the rooftop. The Odditorium claims to have the world's most outstanding collection of the bizarre and unusual, and it probably does. Open 10 a.m. to 10 p.m. daily, later on weekends and during the summer.

The Studios at Paramount. 5555 Melrose Ave.; (323) 956-1777; www.paramountstudios .com. This is the only remaining "big name" studio lot still located and operating in Holly- wood. If you want an inside, historic look at a real working studio, Paramount is the place for a very special experience. Two-hour guided back-lot tours are given Mon through Fri for ages twelve and up by advance reservations only. Walk in the footsteps of legends and get an intimate, sneak peek behind the scenes of your favorite movies and TV shows in a small group led by Paramount Studio guides. To arrange tickets for TV shows taping at Paramount (such as *Dr. Phil*), contact the authorized ticket agency Audiences Unlimited at www.tvtickets.com.

Walk of Fame. Hollywood Boulevard from Gower Street to La Brea Avenue, and along Vine Street from Yucca to Sunset Boulevard; www.hollywoodchamber.net. In Hollywood, even the sidewalks have stories to tell. There is no admission charge to stroll along the sidewalks with more than 2,000 terrazzo-and-brass stars etched into them. Some stars' famous side- walk addresses are: 1644 Hollywood Blvd. (Marilyn Monroe), 1719 Vine St. (James Dean), 1750 Vine St. (John Lennon), and 6777 Hollywood Blvd. (Elvis Presley). Contact the Holly- wood Chamber of Commerce for the latest inductees and specific locations. (See Regional Information Appendix for more details.)

where to shop

Hollywood & Highland (H&H) Center. 6801 Hollywood Blvd., corner of Hollywood Bou- levard and Highland Avenue; (323) 817-8220, or call the Visitors Center at (323) 467-6412; www.hollywoodandhighland.com. Located in the thumping heart of Hollywood, this enor- mous complex is a must-see that's sure to please. Opened in 2001, and hosting more than 15 million visitors annually, the center features over sixty top retailers, some of L.A.'s finest restaurants and nightclubs, Lucky Strike Lanes—and the famous Kodak Theatre, home of

save with hollywood citypass

CityPASS *(888-330-5008; www.citypass.com) is the best way to enjoy Hollywood at one low price (up to 43 percent savings off tickets purchased separately). With CityPASS, you get to choose four admission tickets to famous attractions, including Madame Tussauds Hollywood, Starline Movie Stars' Home Tours of Hollywood, Red Line Behind-the-Scenes Tour, and your choice of Kodak Theatre Guided Tour or the Hollywood Museum in the Historic Max Factor Building. CityPASS is good for nine days from first day of use.*

the Academy Awards as well as other notable awards shows, concerts, and events. (See separate listing under Where to Go.)

Hollywood Toys and Costumes. 6600 Hollywood Blvd.; (323) 464-4444; www.hollywoodtoys.com. Here's where you'll find that monster mask or that conversation-starter costume perfect for next Halloween. There are tiaras in all shapes and sizes and novelties too numerous to describe. In town since 1950, this has to be the biggest supermarket of Hollywood-inspired memorabilia and trinkets. Open daily.

Samuel French Inc. Books. 7623 Sunset Blvd.; (323) 876-0570; www.samuelfrench .com. This is the ultimate bookstore for entertainment-industry-related publications. It has an extensive selection of works on the theater, movies, television, and the other performing arts. This is your chance to add an educational whirl to the puffery purveyed by Hollywood's ubiquitous PR spin doctors. Open Mon through Fri 10 a.m. to 6 p.m., Sat 10 a.m. to 5 p.m.

where to eat

Dan Tana's. 9071 Santa Monica Blvd., West Hollywood; (310) 275-9444; www.dantanasrestaurant.com. This vintage landmark celebrity hangout specializes in great steaks and chops served by waiters who probably have been there since the place opened in 1964. Open daily 5 p.m. to 1:30 a.m. $$$.

Musso & Frank Grill. 6667 Hollywood Blvd.; (323) 467-5123. A Hollywood institution where movers and shakers have "done deals" over classic flannel cakes, steaks, and Thurs-only chicken potpies since 1919. Whether you go for the atmosphere or the food, you simply must go to say you've been! For kicks, request table number one in the West Room, which was Charlie Chaplin's regular spot. Although there's no official website, the "fan site" at www.mussoandfrankgrill.com is rich. Open Tues through Sat 11 a.m. to 11 p.m. (sometimes later on Fri and Sat); closed Sun and Mon. $$–$$$.

The Palm Restaurant West Hollywood. 9001 Santa Monica Blvd., West Hollywood; (310) 550-8811; www.thepalm.com. Since this branch of the famous steak house opened here in 1975, it fast became and still is a "movie industry crowd" place to see and be seen and make the scene. Lunch weekdays and dinner every night. Call for hours. $$$.

Pink's. 709 North La Brea Ave. (corner of Melrose and La Brea); (323) 931-4223; www .pinkshollywood.com. You can't miss the line that has wrapped around this pink building since it opened in 1939, where they serve probably the best chili dog in L.A. Chili dogs, chili fries, chili burgers, turkey dogs, burrito dogs—every imaginable presentation of the wiener can be found here. No matter what time of day or night, you will find yourself standing in line with tourists, corporate climbers, and celebrities. Open 9:30 a.m. to 2 a.m. daily (sometimes later). Cash only. $.

where to stay

Renaissance Hollywood Hotel & Spa. 1755 North Highland Ave.; (323) 323-856-1200; www.renaissancehollywood.com. This hospitality cornerstone of the stunning Hollywood & Highland Center retail-and-entertainment destination features 632 sumptuously appointed rooms and suites with elegant, midcentury modern decor and green, eco-conscious amenities. Love the view from the rooftop outdoor pool (and the views from most of the guest rooms are pretty righteous as well—especially of the Hollywood Hills). All the luxury essentials are here including 24/7 room service, concierge, valet, business center (like you'd want to work!), and Spa Luce for relaxation. $$$.

hollywood homes of the famous (and still mostly rich)

If you want a guided tour past Hollywood celeb homes, here are some choices:

- *Hollywood Tours. 7095 Hollywood Blvd., #705; (800) 789-9575; www.holly woodtours.us. Air-conditioned minivans, open-air trolley, or double-decker buses. Dozens of itineraries including options to see the HOLLYWOOD sign up close.*

- *Starline Tours. (323) 463-3333 or (800) 959-3131; www.starlinetours.com. The company promises forty celebrity homes on the 2-hour tours in Beverly Hills and Bel Air, and offers excellent value on more than twenty other Hollywood/L.A. itineraries. They've been in business with their infamous double-decker red buses since 1935 (with other buses, vans, and limos, too!).*

worth more time

West Hollywood "WeHo." Considered one of the concentrated creative centers of metro Los Angeles, the city of West Hollywood (incorporated in 1984), encompasses just 1.9 square miles but has plenty of action. Bordered by Hollywood to the east and Beverly Hills on the west, West Hollywood has a trendy, unpredictable, and irreverent vibe since denizens work and play by their own rules (of which there aren't many). For your dining pleasure, choose from over 150 restaurants including Morton's, Il Sole, Lucques, La Boheme, BOA, Katana, and Mel's Diner (you saw it in the film *American Graffiti*). Check out the vibrant nightlife at landmark clubs such as the Whisky a Go Go, Troubadour, Key Club, Viper Room, and House of Blues. No slouch as a shopping mecca, visit stores such as Herve Leger, Halston, Maxfield, Anna Sui, D&G, and Tracey Ross, just to mention a few.

Few drives in Los Angeles are as exhilarating as **Sunset Boulevard,** which bisects West Hollywood. Originating downtown, Sunset winds up at the Pacific Ocean, and zipping along its famous curves in Beverly Hills, you'll see stunning mansions and gorgeous gardens at every turn. But the most famous stretch, convertible tops down, is the **Sunset Strip,** directly adjacent to Beverly Hills in West Hollywood. The heart of the action, the 1.2-mile portion between numbers 8221 and 9255, is the epicenter of L.A. nightlife. Celebrities are sighted so often here that they hardly raise eyebrows, lips, or chins. After cruising Sunset (preferably in a convertible), park your car at number 8600, Sunset Plaza, an open-air retail/office mall (home to one of Laura's favorite Chinese restaurants, Chin Chin). From here you can see the entire city of L.A. teeming during the day and twinkling at night below you.

day trip 02

north

lights, camera, action:
burbank, griffith park

burbank

Bordered by Glendale to the east, Toluca Lake on the west, Griffith Park to the south, and accessible from Hollywood via US Highway 101/134 (Hollywood Freeway), Burbank straddles two distinct geographical areas. Its downtown and civic center are nestled on the slopes and foothills that rise into the Verdugo Mountains, and its other areas are located in flatlands at the eastern end of the San Fernando Valley, 12 miles north of downtown Los Angeles.

The city was named after David Burbank, a New England–born dentist and entrepreneur who bought 9,200 acres of ranch land for $9,000 in 1867 and parlayed his holdings into a vibrant community that achieved "cityhood" in 1911. The motion picture business arrived in Burbank in 1926, when First National Pictures (later taken over by the four Warner brothers) bought a seventy-eight-acre site on Olive Avenue, which included Dr. Burbank's original ranch house. Walt Disney's company, which had outgrown its Hollywood headquarters, bought fifty-one acres and built a multimillion-dollar studio on Buena Vista Street that opened in 1939.

Brothers Allan and Malcolm Loughead, founders of the Lockheed Aircraft Company, opened a Burbank manufacturing plant in 1928, and a year later famed aviation expert Jack Northrop built his historic Flying Wing airplane in his own plant nearby, thus establishing the aircraft industry in Burbank. In 1930, United Airport (now Bob Hope Airport) opened—the

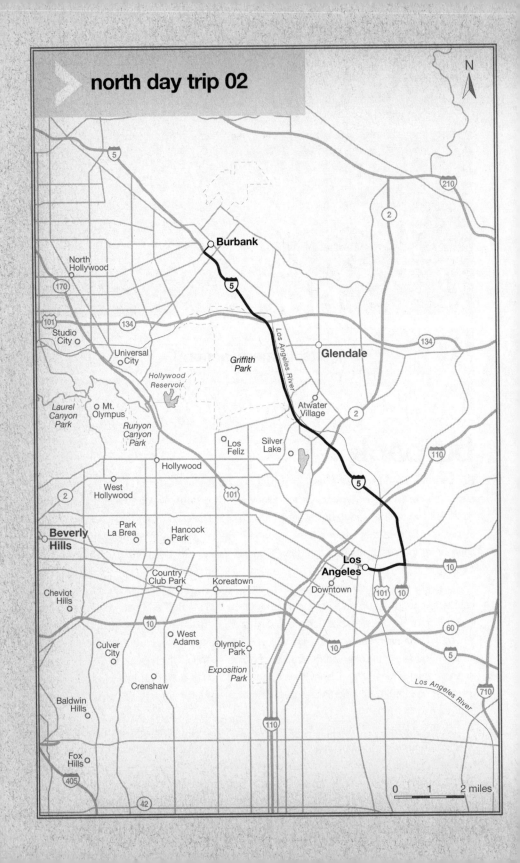

north day trip 02

largest commercial airport in the Los Angeles area until Los Angeles International Airport (LAX) opened in 1946 near El Segundo.

By the 1960s and '70s, more of the Hollywood entertainment industry was relocating to Burbank with its large tracts of available land, water, and easy airport access. Today, dubbed "Media Capital of the World," Burbank is home to companies including ABC, Cartoon Network, Dick Clark Productions, NBC Studios, New Wave Entertainment, Nickelodeon, Technicolor/Thomson, the Walt Disney Company, Warner Bros. Studio, and Warner Music Group. Many jokes have been made on television shows that emanate from here, such as *Laugh-In* and *The Tonight Show,* about "beautiful downtown Burbank," but you know you want to visit those TV studios to experience the lights, cameras, and all the action personally!

getting there

From downtown L.A. you can take I-5 (Golden State Freeway) north to the Burbank Boulevard exit (this takes you east around Griffith Park). The car-free alternative is to board a Metrolink train at Union Station and disembark at the Burbank Metrolink Station, sometimes referred to as the Burbank Transportation Center (served by Metrolink's Antelope Valley and Ventura County Lines). It's important to note that Amtrak trains do not stop at the downtown Burbank station; instead, they stop at the Bob Hope Burbank Airport station, only 120 yards from the terminal—which makes train/plane connections incredibly easy.

where to go

NBC/Universal TV Studios. 3000 West Alameda Ave.; (818) 840-3537 (guest relations) or (818) 840-4444 (main switchboard). Escorted 70-minute walking-only tours are generally available on a first-come, first-served basis with limited availability, Mon through Fri, every hour on the hour between 9 a.m. and 3 p.m. The guest relations bungalow opens at 8:30 a.m. If you're lucky, you might see Jay Leno on the lot! Be sure to call for current tour schedules and fees, as many NBC shows are now filming at Universal Studios (owner of NBC).

Warner Bros. Studio VIP Tour. VIP Tour Center, 3400 Riverside Dr., Gate 6; (818) 972-8687; www.wbstudiotour.com. The studio is located at the intersection of Olive Avenue, Pass Avenue, and Barham Boulevard, just a few blocks southeast of Disney Studios and northeast of Universal Studios. After parking at Gate 6, go to the VIP Tour Center just outside the studio entrance at Gate 5 to check in. This is an intimate insider's look since only about 120 people a day are allowed at this very busy and famous motion picture and television studio—past and present. The tour begins with a short film highlighting the movies and television shows created by Warner Bros. talent. Then, via electric tour carts to and from the Warner Bros. Museum, you visit back-lot sets, soundstages, and craft/production shops. Remember the line from the classic *Casablanca* where Humphrey Bogart tells Ingrid Bergman, "We'll always have Paris"? Those Paris flashback scenes were shot on a mock

"French street" here on the Warner Bros. back lot, and chances are you'll get to see it for yourself! However, routes change from day to day to accommodate production on the lot, so no two tours are exactly alike—you never know what shows or movies and stars you

filmed before a live studio audience

Greater Los Angeles and Burbank in particular are definitely the places to see the television industry in action. Live studio audiences are always needed, and tickets are free. Don't ever pay for TV-show taping tickets! They are given out free, always by production companies and studio representatives. Remember, very little to no taping is done during the summer months because shows are on hiatus. There are age requirements for attending most TV show tapings. Most sitcom tapings require audience members to be at least age eighteen, but game shows and children's variety shows sometimes set the age requirement at age twelve. This rule is strictly enforced, so be sure to check in advance. Not all shows use audiences (e.g., most soap operas). The more popular the show, the harder it is to get tickets. Comedies shoot a few times a month, usually from September to March. Besides having to show up early to get through security, most tapings last 3 to 6 hours, so allow yourself plenty of extra time. Soundstages generally have bleacher-type seating, and it's sometimes hard to see the action even though you're right in front of the stage, so most stages have video monitors that show what's going on. Most scenes are shot several times, and this can get boring occasionally. To help pass the down times between shooting, a comic often entertains the audience. Soundstages are notoriously cold, so bring a sweater—the lights only heat up the actors, not you, the "guest."

- *Here are some of the best sources for those free tickets. **Audiences Unlimited, Inc.** www.tvtickets.com. More than forty sitcom, pilot, and talk-show tickets are usually available. Tickets are offered online starting approximately thirty days prior to show date. This is an excellent website and a good source of information about what to expect, along with maps on how to reach each of the studios.*

- ***Audience Associates, Inc.** (www.tvtix.com) and **Hollywood Tickets** (www .hollywoodtickets.com) both offer tickets to a wide variety of game shows, talk shows, specials, and sitcoms on their easy-to-use websites. You can search by date and/or the show you want to see—and print out your ticket selection right away.*

will see filming that day—or maybe meet! Your VIP Tour lasts approximately 2 hours and is held generally Mon through Fri 9 a.m. to 3 p.m., with expanded hours in summer. Call for the schedule; reservations are required. There also is a 5-hour Deluxe Tour where you really get an in-depth look behind the scenes—literally and figuratively—plus you'll enjoy lunch in the Studio Commissary—it's not inexpensive, but it's a peak experience that could be the highlight of your day trip from L.A.!

where to shop

Burbank Town Center. 201 East Magnolia; (818) 566-8556; www.burbanktowncenter .com. Opened in 1991 and continually evolving—check out the new Backlot Adventure children's play area with a soft-sculpted design that's easy on the tots as well as our eardrums! There are three levels of interior shopping, anchored by Macy's, Mervyn's, and Sears; outdoor shopping anchored by IKEA, Loehmann's, and Office Depot; plus an AMC Theater with fourteen movie screens. Multitudes of dining options include Baja Fresh Mexican Grill, California Pizza Kitchen, Chevy's Fresh Mex, Corner Bakery Café, Haagen Dazs, Johnny Rockets, Maui Wowi Hawaiian Coffees and Smoothies, Mongolian Grill, and P. F. Chang's China Bistro.

where to eat

Bob's Big Boy. 4211 Riverside Dr.; (818) 843-9334; www.bobs.net. Built in 1949, this iconic restaurant is the oldest remaining Bob's Big Boy in America and was honored in 1993 as a "California Point of Historical Interest." The towering 70-foot BOB'S sign is an integral part of the building design and still is its most prominent feature. Breakfast at Bob's is served anytime you want it. Sometimes you just hunger for a Big Boy—the original double-decker hamburger with two all-beef patties on a grilled sesame-seed bun with crisp shredded lettuce, American cheese, special dressing, and relish—or a Bob's milk shake made 1950s-style with real ice cream and served with a silver tin goblet that comes with your order. Yum. Open 24 hours. $.

where to stay

Marriott Burbank Airport Hotel & Convention Center. 2500 Hollywood Way; (818) 843-6000; www.marriottburbankairport.com. Located across the street from the Burbank Bob Hope Airport (the closest to Hollywood, NBC/Universal Studios, and ABC). Free airport shuttle service every 10 minutes. An excellent home base for exploring greater L.A., it has 488 comfortable rooms and 77 suites with PUR improved air-quality amenities; two large heated pools; whirlpool and spa; fitness center; business center; gift shop; and self and valet parking that is very convenient. **The Daily Grill** restaurant serves breakfast, lunch, and dinner featuring American fare and libations. **Starbucks** is in the lobby, and the friendly hotel staff seems always at the ready to assist with your travel plans. $$–$$$.

griffith park

Located just west of the I-5 (Golden State Freeway), roughly between Los Feliz Boulevard on the south and SR 134 (Ventura Freeway) on the north, with over 4,120 acres, Griffith Park (4730 Crystal Springs Dr., Los Angeles; 323-913-4688; www.laparks.org/dos/parks /griffithpk) is one of the largest urban wildernesses in the United States.

Freeway off-ramps leading to the park from I-5 are Los Feliz Boulevard, Griffith Park (direct entry), and Zoo Drive. Approaching the park on SR 134 eastbound, take either the Forest Lawn Drive or Victory Boulevard off-ramps. From SR 134 westbound, take Zoo Drive or Forest Lawn Drive. After leaving the freeways, follow the signs into the park.

The park is named for its former owner, Colonel Griffith J. Griffith, who emigrated to the United States from south Wales in 1865. He made a personal fortune in California gold mines and settled in Los Angeles, purchasing a 4,071-acre portion of the Rancho Los Feliz, one of the original Spanish land grants in California. In 1896, Griffith bequeathed 3,015 acres of his estate as a Christmas gift to the people of Los Angeles to be used as parkland.

Thanks to Griffith's benevolence and stewardship of the Los Angeles Recreation & Parks Department, you'll discover some incredibly amazing attractions and activities here, including the Autry National Center; Greek Theatre; a merry-go-round; Griffith Observatory; L.A. Equestrian Center; L.A. Live Steamers Railroad Museum; L.A. Zoo; pony rides; and Travel Town Museum. In most developed areas of the park, games and sports are played frequently by groups. There are also special areas set aside for soccer, badminton, baseball, and softball. Children's playgrounds, in addition to the main area off Griffith Park Drive in Park Center, are found at various locations in the acreage, usually near plentiful picnic grounds. Open to the public from 6 a.m. to 10 p.m. daily. Bridle trails, hiking paths, and mountain roads are closed at sunset. Call for current special events and activities.

where to go

Autry National Center. 4700 Western Heritage Way; (323) 667-2000; http://theautry.org. Celebrating the American West through three important institutions—the Museum of the American West, the Southwest Museum of the American Indian, and the Institute for the Study of the American West—the Autry was established in 2003 following the merger of the Southwest Museum, the Women of the West Museum, and the Museum of the American West (formerly the Autry Museum of Western Heritage that opened in 1988). Thousands of Old West artifacts and hands-on exhibits are here, including many designed with children in mind. Special exhibits explore America's western heritage, including Native American culture, early tourism, and weaving. Check out the Golden Spur Café for great grub. Open Tues through Sun 10 a.m. to 5 p.m.

The Greek Theater. 2700 North Vermont Ave.; (323) 665-5857 or (323) 665-1927; www .greektheatrela.com. This premiere outdoor theater is secluded in the picturesque, tree-enclosed setting of Griffith Park and hosts some of the biggest names in entertainment, from pop to classical, reggae to rock, such as the Who, Sting, Alicia Keys, Pearl Jam, José Carreras, Marc Anthony, Tina Turner, Elton John, Santana, the White Stripes, the Gipsy Kings, and even the Russian National Ballet. This deceptively intimate 5,801-seat venue has state-of-the-art acoustics combined with excellent site lines—making for one of our favorite outdoor amphitheaters in Southern California. Call for current schedule and tickets.

Griffith Observatory. 2800 East Observatory Rd.; (213) 473-0800; www.griffithobserva tory.org. Admission to the observatory building and grounds is free. There is a nominal charge to see shows in the Samuel Oschin Planetarium. Colonel Griffith J. Griffith certainly had a clear vision for the public observatory that bears his name—specifying in his will that it be located in a prominent hilltop location on Mount Wilson and offer free public telescopes, a science theater, and exhibits featuring the best of new and classic astronomical wonders. Check out the **Samuel Oschin Planetarium,** now with a new dome, star projector, digital laser projectors, seats, sound system, and lighting, especially the show "Centered in the Universe," which is scheduled every hour. Public telescopes, both optical and solar, are offered for free public viewing each day and evening when skies are clear and the building is open. Roughly seven million people have looked through the observatory's 12-inch Zeiss telescope, more than have gazed through any other telescope on Earth. The triple-beam solar telescope is one of the largest-such public instruments in the world.

The new **Robert J. and Suzanne Gottlieb Transit Corridor** is a humongous 150-foot-long, 10-foot-wide glass-walled passageway depicting the motions of the sun, moon, and stars across the sky, and demonstrates how these motions are linked with time and the calendar. You can refresh yourself at the Café at the End of the Universe during your visit. Frankly, we think the observatory has some of the most magnificent naked-eye views of Los Angeles and the famous Hollywood sign.

Los Angeles Zoo. Griffith Park, 5333 Zoo Dr., Golden State Freeway (I-5) at Ventura Free- way (SR 134); (323) 644-6400; www.lazoo.org. Go ahead, run wild in this 120-acre setting that harbors more than 1,100 mammals, birds, amphibians, and reptiles representing more than 250 different species (29 of which are endangered). In addition, the zoo's botanical collection comprises several planted gardens and over 800 different plant species with over 7,400 individual plants. Check out the Chimpanzees of Mahale Mountain, and World of Birds, all accessible via a tram around the zoo's perimeter. Opened in 2008, a new $19 million habitat for six African lowland gorillas, Campo Gorilla Reserve, provides the gorillas with an environment that closely resembles their native west African homeland. There are seven cafes located throughout the zoo that feature a wide variety of meals suitable for almost everyone, so nobody can get too hungry when you see the animals being fed! Open daily from 10 a.m. to 5 p.m.

Travel Town. Griffith Park, 5200 Zoo Dr.; (323) 662-5874; www.traveltown.org. Since 1952, kids of all ages have loved this outdoor transportation museum with steam locomo- tives to scramble over and Live Steamers, a large collection of miniature trains. Free admis- sion; rides at a nominal fee. Open weekdays 10 a.m. to 4 p.m., weekends 10 a.m. to 5 p.m.

day trip 03

north

adventures in entertainment:
universal city, north hollywood

universal city

When is a city not legally a city but has realistic looking cities on its premises? That would be Universal City, located in the San Fernando Valley about 15 miles north of downtown Los Angeles at the intersections of three major highways: U.S. Highway 101, the 134, and the 170 (aka SR 134 and SR 170).

Today, this unique 415-acre entertainment entity is owned by NBC Universal and includes Universal Studios, a theme park, hotels, offices, CityWalk, and Gibson Amphitheatre. Back in 1912, Carl Laemmle (pronounced lem-lee) merged his Independent Moving Picture Company of America (IMP) with five other film companies to create Universal Film Manufacturing Company, encompassing all facets of movie production, distribution, and exhibition. Laemmle also briefly operated some studios in Hollywood itself but decided he really needed more space, so he purchased 230 acres of dusty San Fernando Valley ranch land for $165,000 and called it Universal City—where his workers erected streets, facades, and buildings including a bank, post office, soda fountain, and bungalows, and set up cameras and film stages to churn out silent western movies.

In 1915, Laemmle opened Universal City to the public at the ripe admission price of 25 cents each (which included a boxed lunch) to showcase the magic of moviemaking and generate free advertising for his Universal films. Laemmle ended the studio tours in the 1920s when "talking pictures" arrived and "quiet on the set" became an absolute necessity.

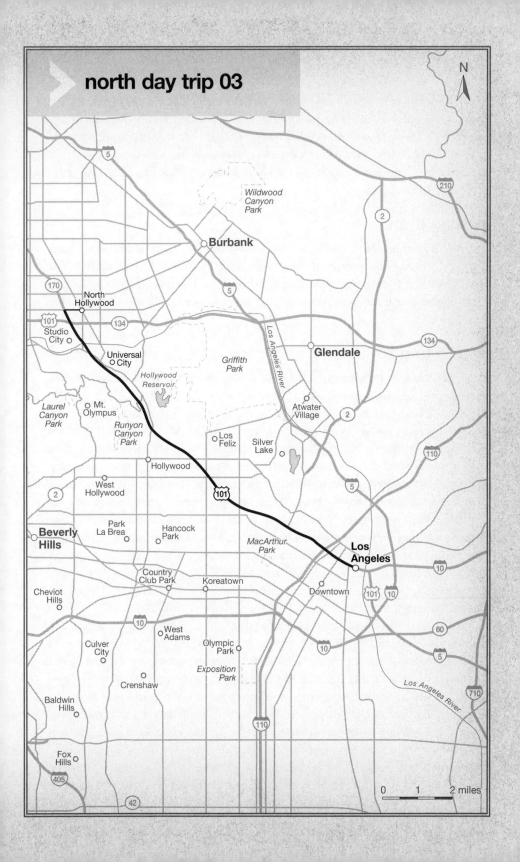

N

He sold his sprawling entertainment empire in 1936 to pay debts generated during the Great Depression. In 1950, Universal City added 140 acres and thus became the largest film factory in the world, but it didn't welcome visitors again until July 4, 1964—opening day of the Universal Studios Tour. This was followed in the ensuing decades with two hotels, an amphitheater, a cinema complex, and an urban retail park called Universal CityWalk, which opened in 1993.

getting there

For your day trip purposes, we recommend leaving your vehicle in downtown L.A. and taking the efficient Metro Red Line subway to Universal City Station to experience a galaxy of entertainment. If you simply must drive from downtown L.A., take US 101 (Hollywood Freeway) northbound and exit at Universal Studios Boulevard and follow the signs into the theme park.

where to go

Universal Studios Hollywood. 100 Universal City Plaza (Universal Center Drive or Lankershim Boulevard from Highway 101/Hollywood Freeway; (818) 622-3801 or (800) UNIVERSAL; www.universalstudioshollywood.com. Universal Studios is an integral part of L.A.'s history. And while another version is now in Florida, for us Southern Californians there is but *one* Universal Studios. They are always adding mega-attractions—some of the latest are King Kong 360/3D; blockbuster TV series–based Simpsons Ride; Universal's World of Entertainment (never-before-seen props, costumes, wardrobe, and artifacts, with special-effects displays from the latest to the earliest films amassed from Universal Pictures film library); the Adventures of Curious George, a 30,000-square-foot interactive play zone featuring three separate adventures: Curious George Flies to Space (where you can get drenched as you wait in the blast-off zone, but thankfully, there is a dry zone); Curious George Goes to the Jungle, and Curious George Visits the Zoo. Also be sure to check out the cutting-edge roller coaster Revenge of the Mummy—The Ride, Shrek 4-D, House of Horrors, Backdraft, and Jurassic Park—The Ride (you will get soaked!).

But it's the classics that make Universal a genuine blast for both kids and adults. The staple is the 45-minute tram ride (catch one every 5 to 10 minutes), during which Hollywood history and special effects cast their magical spell. You're whisked past the set from Steven Spielberg's *War of the Worlds, Jurassic Park,* and the Norman Bates House (from the movie *Psycho*), over a collapsing bridge, into a Mexican village that falls prey to a flash flood, and through a Red Sea that parts just for you. Then there's a landslide and a simulated fishing village where the naughty shark from the movie *Jaws* surfaces with a vengeance. The tram ride also takes visitors past enormous studio back lots, reminding you that this is the world's biggest film and television studio. Something is almost always in production, and chances are you'll catch a bit of the action—such as *CSI* and *Desperate Housewives.* Open daily

9 a.m. to 6 p.m.; expanded hours for summer and holidays. Always be sure to ask about special values and packages.

Plus, CityWalk Hollywood boasts nineteen movie theaters all with surround sound, plush stadium-style seating and IMAX. Open Sun through Thurs 11 a.m. to 9 p.m., Fri and Sat 11 a.m. to midnight. Free admission. For show times call (818) 508-0711 or visit www .citywalkhollywood.com/cinemas. CityWalk also connects to the **Gibson Amphitheatre** in Universal City; (818-622-4440), an outstanding concert and performance venue with no seat more than 150 feet from the stage. Visit www.citywalkhollywood.com/concerts.php or call for event schedules.

iFLY Hollywood. Universal CityWalk; (818) 985-4359; www.iflyhollywood.com. You can actually experience human flight with this unique indoor skydiving adventure in a vertical wind tunnel. No experience is necessary, but riders must be ages three and up. Open daily, call for times, flight instructions, and complete details on this adrenalin-charged adventure.

where to shop & eat

Universal CityWalk Hollywood. 1000 Universal Center Dr., Universal City; (818) 622-4455; www.citywalkhollywood.com. A three-block entertainment district featuring more than thirty places to eat, a nineteen-screen movie theater featuring an eight-story-high IMAX system, seven hot night spots including the new Jon Lovitz Comedy Club and Samba Brazilian Steakhouse & Lounge, indoor skydiving, and more than thirty retail stores with everything under the California sun. This eclectic, electric outdoor pedestrian promenade

universal studios hollywood vip experience tour

If you want to personally experience the world's largest movie and television studio as well as genuine hospitality and special treatment, treat yourself to the VIP Experience tour. You will have your own private tour escort (with encyclopedic knowledge) for the entire day (only fifteen people per group) and enjoy front-of-the-line admission and the best views and seating at all attractions and rides. Plus your tour escort will take you deep into the back lot, where you'll have special access to soundstages—many in use by your favorite stars. Best of all, instead of the huge tram, you'll have a private trolley bus that can stop and let you out to take pictures. Feel like a movie star yourself. It's expensive but worth it! For more information call (800) UNIVERSAL, option 3.

has an atmosphere made to resemble a studio back lot. There are actually two streets lined with palms and joined by a central courtyard area with fountains. But all is not so sedate: A mammoth King Kong clings to the facade of one building. Open daily, free admission. Be sure to call for hours and special events and promotions. $–$$$.

where to stay

Hilton Los Angeles/Universal City Hotel. 555 Universal Hollywood Dr., Universal City; (818) 506-2500; www.hiltonuniversal.com. Rated AAA four-diamonds, this twenty-four-story hotel high on the hilltop is located right at the main entrance to Universal Studios, central to all the action in greater L.A. Full-service property has all the amenities you expect in 482 rooms and suites with stunning views. Check out the award-winning **Café Sierra,** voted California's Number One Seafood & Prime Rib Buffet. $$$.

Sheraton Universal. 333 Universal Terrace Pkwy., Universal City; (818) 980-1212 or reservations (800) 325-3535; www.sheraton.com/universal. This glistening glass high-rise, a landmark since 1969, underwent a $30 million renovation in 2008. Enjoy 436 rooms and suites with tremendous views. Excellent packages for families. You'll appreciate the free shuttle service to Universal Studios. $$$.

Sportsmen's Lodge Hotel. 12825 Ventura Blvd., Studio City; (818) 769-4700 or (800) 821-8511; www.slhotel.com. A Valley classic since 1962, the Lodge has 200 recently renovated country-style rooms; an Olympic-size heated outdoor pool with large lounge deck; the Patio Café for reasonably priced breakfast, lunch, and dinner daily; plus free Universal Studios shuttle and discount tickets for guests. $$–$$$.

north hollywood

North Hollywood surrounds Universal City bounded on the south by Moorpark Street and US Highway 101 (known as the Ventura Freeway); on the southwest by Burbank Boulevard and Coldwater Canyon Avenue; on the northwest by Tonopah Street; on the northeast by Laurel Canyon Boulevard/Webb Avenue/Lankershim Boulevard/Sherman Way; and on the west by Clybourn Avenue. The Hollywood Freeway (the 170) runs north/south smack through the middle of North Hollywood to confuse your directional sense even further. Established by the Lankershim Ranch Land and Water Company in 1887, the community was first named Toluca, then renamed Lankershim in 1896, and finally North Hollywood in 1927.

where to go

Academy of Television Arts & Sciences. 5220 Lankershim Blvd., North Hollywood; (818) 754-2800; www.emmys.org. This Academy of Television Arts & Sciences honors prime-time programming and is comprised of twenty-six "peer groups" whose work is aired nationally and whose members are eligible to vote for the Emmy Awards. (FYI: The National Academy of Television Arts & Sciences is based in New York City and administers daytime, news, and sports Emmys.) The Emmy Award is owned jointly by the Television Academy and the National Academy, with the awards show held in September. Here at the Los Angeles area headquarters, see the 40-foot gold Emmy statue and bronze life-size statues of Lucille Ball and Johnny Carson. Call for periodic public events in the Goldenson Theatre and Conference Center.

NoHo Arts District. www.nohoartsdistrict.com. Established in 1993, this one-square mile area at Lankershim and Magnolia Boulevards is filled with an eclectic array of entertainment options for the artist as well as the lover of the arts. From downtown Los Angeles, take US Highway 101 north, merging to the 170 (SR 170), exit at Magnolia Boulevard and turn right heading to Lankershim Boulevard.

There is ample street parking. Named NoHo (short for North Hollywood and a play on SoHo in New York City), check out these venues: twenty-plus professional, award-winning theaters producing adventurous new works (the largest concentration outside of New York City); an eclectic mix of indoor and outdoor art galleries; professional dance studios; the largest concentration of music recording venues in the United States; a plethora of vintage costume and resale boutiques; more than twenty regional and international dining options, clothing, and specialty shops; and businesses that create a myriad of art forms.

worth more time

Just 25 minutes north of Universal City/North Hollywood, discover **Valencia** in the **Santa Clarita Valley**—home to the Six Flags California Entertainment Complex that will satisfy your thrill-seeking desires.

Six Flags Magic Mountain—The Xtreme Park. 26101 Magic Mountain Pkwy.; (661) 255-4111; www.sixflags.com/magicmountain/index.aspx. The complex is located off I-5, from the Magic Mountain Parkway exit. Known worldwide as a thrill-ride haven, the 260-acre theme park features sixteen roller coasters—the most on the planet—more than one hundred rides, games, and attractions for the entire family. Enjoy such exciting thrill rides as SCREAM; X (the world's first and only four-dimensional roller coaster); Déjà Vu (the world's fastest and tallest suspended, looping boomerang coaster); Goliath (the coaster giant among giants; the Riddler's Revenge (the world's tallest and fastest stand-up roller coaster); Superman the Escape (towering 415 feet in the air); Colossus; Batman the Ride; Viper; and many more. For younger guests there is Bugs Bunny World, featuring rides and attractions that provide real thrills for kids and adults alike; Goliath Junior coaster; Thomas the Tank Engine; Merrie Melodies Carousel; and Canyon Blaster Coaster for kids and parents together. In addition, meet your favorite Looney Tunes characters—Bugs Bunny, Daffy Duck, Yosemite Sam, and Sylvester. All this in one day! Open daily from Mar through Sept; weekends and holidays the rest of the year. Call for exact schedule and opening and closing hours.

Six Flags Hurricane Harbor. Next door to Six Flags Magic Mountain; (661) 255-4100; www.sixflags.com/hurricaneharborla/index.aspx. This fifteen-acre tropical-themed water-park attraction features more than twenty-two slides and attractions, including Tornado, a six-story, 75-foot funnel, with two of the tallest enclosed speed slides in Southern California; Lizard Lagoon, a 7,000-square-foot pool for teen and adult activities; Bamboo Racer, an exciting 45-foot-tall, six-lane racing attraction; Castaway Cove, an exclusive children's water-play kingdom; Shipwreck Shores, with water-play activities for the entire family; the Forgotten Sea wave pool; and the River Cruise lazy river. Way cool fun! Open daily Memorial Day through Labor Day, and weekends the rest of the year. Be sure to call for exact schedule and times.

northeast

day trip 01

northeast

>>> **of roses & gardens:**
pasadena

pasadena

Welcome to a world unto itself: vibrant Pasadena, a mere 11 miles north of downtown Los Angeles. The annual New Year's Day Tournament of Roses Parade and Rose Bowl Game, seen around the world by millions, reveal just a fraction of the action taking place in a city studded with world-class art collections, vintage landmarks, and jacaranda-lined main streets and boulevards. Welcome to a city with sixteen historical districts packed into 23 square miles!

getting there

The Pasadena Freeway (officially known as SR 110 or just the 110) connects downtown Los Angeles to Pasadena while the Foothill Freeway (I-210) links Pasadena to the north and east. Metro Gold Line light rail spans 13.7 miles, linking Union Station in downtown Los Angeles and Sierra Madre Villa in East Pasadena via Chinatown, Highland Park, South Pasadena, and Pasadena. Using the Metro Gold Line, you can expect to get from downtown Los Angeles to East Pasadena in approximately 36 minutes without the traffic hassles of the 110 or I-210 freeway logjams.

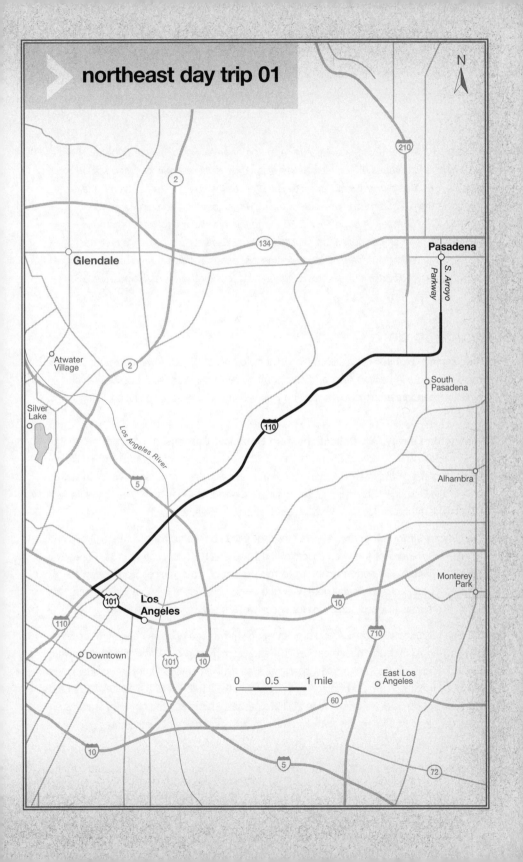

tasty tip

*Le Cordon Bleu College of Culinary Arts-Los Angeles welcomes the public to their Pasadena campus (561 Green St.) to enjoy their students' delicious coursework. The **561 Restaurant** (call 626-405-1561 for reservations) features inventive takes on California cuisine and an ever-changing menu for lunch and dinner, which is served Monday through Friday. For a more informal atmosphere on campus but with just as tasty offerings, visit the **School Café** for a bistro-style breakfast, lunch or dinner. For both restaurants, menus, prices and hours are subject to change. Additional information visit www/chefs.edu/Los-Angeles/Restaurant. $$.*

where to go

The Gamble House. 4 Westmoreland Place; (626) 395-9783; www.gamblehouse.org. Personifying the American Arts and Crafts movement, this handsome residence built in 1908 by legendary architects Charles and Henry Green is listed on the National Register of Historic Places.

Huntington Library, Art Collections, and Botanical Gardens. 1151 Oxford Rd., San Marino; (626) 405-2100; www.huntington.org. This astounding collection of art and literary classics amidst 150 acres of verdant gardens is just 2 miles from Pasadena. You will be lured to the Garden of Flowing Fragrance, where a one-and-a-half-acre lake complete with a tea house, stone bridges, and pavilions will take your breath away.

The Norton Simon Museum. 411 W. Colorado Blvd., on the corner of Orange Grove and Colorado Boulevard at the intersection of the Foothill (210) and Ventura (134) Freeways; (626) 449-6840; www.nortonsimon.org. A microcosm of masterpieces from seven centuries of European art is on display here. View the iconic paintings of Rembrandt, Picasso, Van Gogh, and Degas. Closed Tues. Call for specific hours and holiday schedules.

Old Pasadena. www.oldpasadena.org. From downtown Los Angeles head north on I-110 Freeway; I-110 Freeway becomes Arroyo Parkway; continue on Arroyo Parkway toward Colorado Boulevard and into Old Pasadena. Beautifully renovated into an entertainment district showcasing over 200 vintage buildings that take you back to the 1800s, Old Pasadena cover 22 blocks with more than 200 businesses. This revitalized hot spot features art galleries, trendy boutiques, theaters and an extraordinary choice of restaurants.

Pacific Asia Museum. 46 North Robles Ave.; (626) 449-2742; www.pacificasiamuseum .org. Once known as the historic Grace Nicholson mansion, this museum honoring the arts and culture of the Pacific and Asia is listed on the National Register of Historic Places. Call for hours.

The Pasadena Playhouse District. Main office is at 48 N. El Molino Ave., Suite 103; (626) 744-0340; www.playhousedistrict.org. The Playhouse is located at 39 S. El Molino Ave. in Old Town; (626) 737-2869; www.pasadenaplayhouse.org. The 686-seat auditorium hosts a variety of cultural and artistic events, professional shows, and community engagements each year. The official state theater of California, this Spanish-style building, built in 1917, has been designated a National Historic Landmark. From these hallowed halls emerged A-list Hollywood actors such as Dustin Hoffman and Gene Hackman.

The Pasadena Museum of California Art (PMCA). 490 E. Union St.; (626) 568-3665; www.pmcaonline.org. This is the only museum in Southern California devoted exclusively to California architecture, art, and design from 1850 to the present day. PMCA exhibitions and educational programs explore the cultural dynamics and influences unique to California that have shaped and defined art in all media. Opened in 2002, the Museum founders Robert and Arlene Oltman are long-time Pasadena residents and art collectors with a vision for preserving cultural heritage. The museum bookstore offers a wide selection of books and other media, as well as unique gifts. Open Wed through Sun from noon to 5 p.m.

South Lake Avenue Business District. Surrounded by Colorado Boulevard to the north, Mentor Avenue to the east, California Boulevard to the south, and Hudson Avenue to the west; www.southlakeavenue.org. Along ten tree-lined blocks you can explore designer stores and more restaurants than you can shake a fork or chopsticks at. This high-energy retail area has it all, and you should reserve a few hours to check it out.

Tournament of Roses House and Wrigley Gardens. 391 S. Orange Grove Blvd.; (646) 449-4100; www.tournamentofroses.com. Surrounding Tournament of Roses House are the Wrigley Gardens, which feature a 4½-acre floral display. Make a point to visit the magnificent gardens whether or not you are here for the Rose Bowl on January 1. The 1,500 varieties of roses, camellias, and annuals are a sight to behold. The gardens are open daily, and admission is free.

where to eat

There are over 500 restaurants in Pasadena ranging from chic dining rooms to cafes and diner-style eateries. Please be sure to call for hours of operation, as times can vary seasonally. Here's a good start:

Crème de la Crêpe. 36 West Colorado Blvd.; (646) 844-0007; www.cremedelacrepe.com. This touch of Paris is a casual place to spend breakfast, lunch, or dinner. Served all day; 8 a.m. to 10 p.m. $$.

haute tip: melting pot food tours

If you have limited time in Pasadena, take advantage of the tastiest 3 hours covering approximately 1.25 miles, and wear comfortable walking shoes. Melting Pot Food Tours covers a 22-block historical area bursting with one-of-a-kind shops and restaurants. Peek into colorful alleys and shops that literally spice up your journey. You will travel the culinary world without having to leave Pasadena, with stops at esoteric restaurants (Tibetan-Nepalese) and unexpected discoveries such as a Mexican tortas cafe. There's even a handmade "soap" kitchen on the route! $49 plus $2 ticket fee. For information call (800) 979-3301 or visit www .meltingpottours.com.

Mi Piace. 25 East Colorado Blvd.; (626) 795-3131; www.mipiace.com. Serving Pasadena Baking Company breads and pastries, this is the place for light and fresh New York–Italian cooking. The menu has something for everyone, from appetizers and salads to pasta and seafood. Call for hours. $$.

Pie 'n Burger. 913 East California Blvd.; (626) 795-1123; www.pienburger.com. Welcome to a Pasadena comfort-food institution, open since 1963. Burgers and fries are just the start—it will take you back to to when calories and cholesterol didn't count! Open daily; call for hours. $.

POP Champagne & Dessert Bar. 33 East Union St.; (626) 795-1295; www.popchampagnebar.com. Cutting edge concept in Old Town Pasadena, the wine list offers more than one hundred champagnes and sparkling wine. Closed Mon; call for current hours. $$$.

redwhite + bluezz. 70 South Raymond Ave.; (626) 792-4441; www.redwhitebluezz.com. Slip away to one of Pasadena's original historic buildings where the area's popular jazz artists perform. There are two sections, the Grill on the corner at Raymond Avenue open daily; and the Jazz Club, open Thurs, Fri, and Sat nights and for Sun brunch. While others in the area have either wine, music, or excellent American cuisine, all three are avaliable at redwhite + bluezz. $$.

Scarlet Tea Room. 18 West Green St.; (626) 577-0051; www.scarlettearoom.com. A perfect place to rendezvous with friends and enjoy an authentic five-course tea ceremony complete with scones and lemon curd. Open Tues through Sat. Call for lunch, tea, and dinner service hours. $$.

Smitty's Grill. 110 South Lake Ave.; (626) 792-9999; www.smittysgrill.com A good place to meet and enjoy good old American comfort-food favorites, from meat loaf to warm cherry crisp. Open for lunch and dinner. $.

where to shop

Pasadena shopping is so intensive that many serious shoppers consult a **Shopping Guru** (213-683-9715; www.urbanshoppingadventures.com) in order to maximize time. Your guide provides you with a shopping bag, bottled water, and a Simply More Value Offer Card before taking off for a 2.5-hour foray perusing fashion, gift jewelry, and antique shops. Reservations are required, be sure to call for current specials and packages. Note: Insider-guided tours of the Rose Bowl's famous flea market are also offered.

Rose Bowl Flea Market. The Rose Bowl, 1001 Rose Bowl Stadium; (323) 560-7469; www.rgcshows.com/RoseBowl.aspx. This is "America's marketplace of unusual items," so prepare yourself for a feast of fabulous finds. It is held the second Sun of every month, rain or shine. The flea market features more than 2,500 vendors and 15,000 to 20,000 buyers each month. Call for admission fees and times.

where to stay

The Bissell House Bed & Breakfast. 201 Orange Grove Ave., South Pasadena, 91030; (626) 441-3525 or (800) 441-3530; www.bissellhouse.com. The historic inn (South Pasadena Cultural Landmark No. 36) is located on the locally infamous "Millionaire's Row." This lovely residence fuses the charm and gracious hospitality of yesteryear (such as afternoon tea) with Wi-Fi and a free DVD lending library. The house's original owner was the daughter of sweeper magnate Melville Bissell. The surrounding gardens are picture-perfect and an ideal venue for quiet contemplative moments between sightseeing and shopping. There are five spacious guest rooms, each furnished with a distinctive theme. Add this to a solar-heated pool and a delicious full breakfast and you've got a perfect place to spend some more time in Pasadena.

The Langham Huntington Hotel & Spa. 1401 South Oak Knoll Ave.; (626) 568-3900; www.langhamhotels.com. A landmark since 1907, this hotel is a blast from the past with impressive touches. Its soaring ceilings and gracious gardens have hosted dignitaries, weddings, and charity balls. Guest rooms and cottages have all of the luxuries you would expect, from fine amenities to 24-hour room service. $$$.

day trip 02

northeast

an alpine paradise with hollywood connections:
lake arrowhead

lake arrowhead

This mountain community 90 miles northeast of downtown Los Angeles and a half-hour drive from San Bernardino on the Rim of the World Highway presents a panoply of sparkling water and clear blue skies. The forest setting puts you at an altitude of 5,106 feet with 782-acre Lake Arrowhead as the centerpiece. The San Bernardino Mountains offer a four-season paradise. You probably have seen Lake Arrowhead in the movies because over 300 films have been filmed here over the years. If you have seen *Gone with the Wind* or *The Bad and the Beautiful,* you have seen different scenes around Lake Arrowhead. As for the famous bald eagle, America's national symbol and one of its largest birds, know that this is their playground: The San Bernardino Mountains support one of the largest bald eagle populations in Southern California. The regal eagle can be spotted in winter, between December and March. This is the best time to catch a glimpse of the birds soaring among the mountain tops.

Lake Arrowhead Village is lakefront on Highway 189. **Blue Jay Village,** which is a 5-minute drive along the same highway, has quaint, locally owned shops. **Cedar Glen Village** is known as the gateway to **Deep Creek,** the starting point for excellent hiking; **Sky Forest** is a hideaway with restaurants and small boutiques; **Rim Forest** is yet another mountain village; and **Twin Peaks** has a historic inn. That's the basic layout of Lake Arrowhead, a pristine mountain community perfect for recreational pursuits or just sheer relaxation.

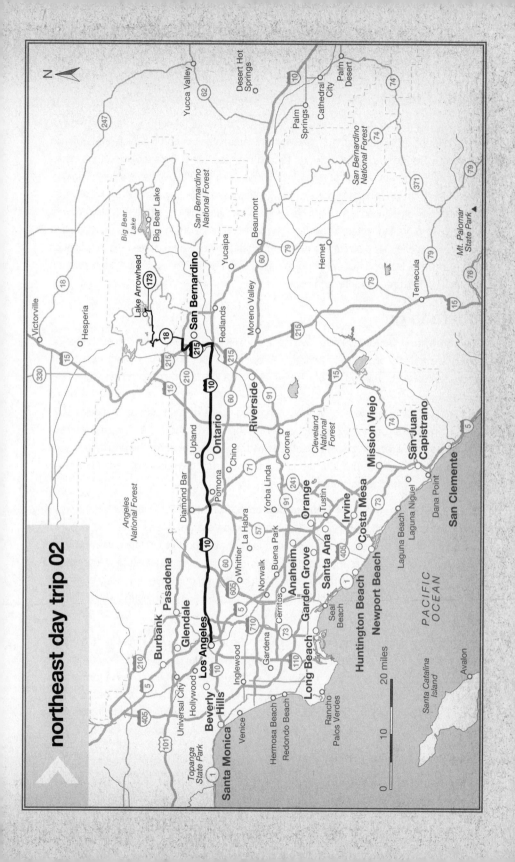

northeast day trip 02

getting there

From downtown Los Angeles, take the I-10 east to the I-215 north at San Bernardino. Then, take the I-210 east just 1.5 miles to the Waterman exit and take a left (Waterman is also known as Highway 18 aka SR 18) toward the mountains. Pass the Rim of the World High School and then turn left at Highway 173 (aka SR 173). You will see a sign stating LAKE ARROWHEAD TO THE LEFT (this is Highway 189). Once you're on Highway 189 you will arrive at this mountain-destination's "downtown," Lake Arrowhead Village, which is family and pet friendly. There are ten stores, including a few outlet stores, and, in marked contrast to Los Angeles, the parking is plentiful and free. You'll find unexpected treasures next to mountain gear. It's almost like world-class shopping on top of the world. The essentials are here, such as a post office, grocery store, and banks.

where to go

The *Arrowhead Queen*. Lake Arrowhead Village; (909) 336-6992; www.leroysboardshop .com. Buy your tickets at 28200 Hwy. 189, building C100, at the waterfront next to the *Arrowhead Queen*. This 50-minute cruise aboard a Louisiana-style paddle-wheel boat takes you by architectural points of interest and historical sites, all narrated by the ship's captain. You will be impressed with the Hollywood connection: Hundreds of movies have been filmed here since the 1920s. (We are talking about oldies such as *A Swingin' Summer*.) Many stars established homes in Lake Arrowhead. You'll hear all about this and more during this delightful cruise that provides the ideal introduction to the beauty of Lake Arrowhead and serves as a starting point for your day excursions.

The Ice Castle International Training Center. 401 Burnt Mill Rd.; (909) 337-0802; www .icecastle.us. The world-famous training center for ice skaters is also open to the public year-round for $8 plus skate rental. Aspiring skaters will find this landmark worthwhile to visit even if they can only spend a few hours here. You can even take one skating lesson, if that is all the time you have, says the staff at the skating school. These recreational lessons are $8 for the general public. Olympic medalist Michelle Kwan skated here; the rink flies the Olympic flags in tribute.

The Mountain Skies Astronomy Village. 2001 Observatory Way off Highway 18 (West of Rim of the World High School); (909) 336-1299; www.mountain-skies.org. Don't miss the informative 2-hour sessions that are scheduled throughout the year, covering topics from "Stars to Star Dust" to "Meteorites, Alien Rocks from Space" and more. You must call and reserve your preferred session in advance; they take place weather permitting. Gift shop and observation area also available. Call for current hours of operation and events.

Snow Valley Mountain Resort. 35100 Hwy. 18, Running Springs; (800) 680-SNOW or (909) 867-2600; www.snow-valley.com. Family friendly at a base elevation of 6,800 feet

mountain fishing

*One of the biggest attractions of Lake Arrowhead is the inviting lakes that cater to fishermen. It's a dream come true for those who treasure the pristine lakes amidst the fragrant pines. The well-stocked lakes and streams are waiting, but don't forget your fishing license. **Green Valley Lake** is known for trophy-sized rainbow trout and is stocked all season long by the Department of Fish and Game and the Lake Association. Some fish are up to fourteen pounds! **Silverwood Lake State Recreation Area** is known for huge striped bass, catfish, trout, and crappie. There is a marina store here; call (760) 389-2299. **Lake Gregory Regional Park** (909-338-2233) is an eighty-plus-acre mecca for anglers. **Lake Arrowhead** is operated by a private association (Arrowhead Lake Association) and open to members and guests only. Trout fishing is number one here. Sorry, there is no public fishing.*

and top elevation of 7,841 feet, this is one of the most popular local places for sledding, snowboarding and skiing. Call for the snow report and current open facilities.

where to shop

Just Browsing Gifts and Mill Creek Gallery. 28200 Hwy. 189, Suite F-140, Lake Arrowhead; (909) 337-8322; www.justbrowsinggiftstore.com. From wooden toy soldiers to wind chimes, this jam-packed store has keepsakes, gifts, and glass art galore. Plan to spend some uninterrupted time here just browsing; really, you'll be glad you did.

Lake Arrowhead Village. 28200 Hwy. 189; (909) 337-2533; www.lakearrowheadvillage .com. This shopping/dining/entertainment "village" is the nerve center of this mountain community. With fifty-some options to shop/eat/play within year-round, "The Village" is also the site of Southern California's latest free concert series that takes place every Fri, Sat, and holiday weekend May through Labor Day.

where to eat

Belgian Waffle Works. 28200 Hwy. 189, Suite E-150 in Lake Arrowhead Village; (909) 337-5222; www.belgianwaffle.com. This family-style restaurant is a tradition and serves waffles you'll remember, thanks to strawberries, blueberries, mountains of whipped cream, and dependable good service. Generally open daily at 8 a.m., but call for seasonal hours. $.

The Tea Exchange. 28200 Hwy. 189, Suite S-250 in Lake Arrowhead Village; (909) 336-5600; www.teaexchange.com. This is a serious source of tea with more than one hundred varieties of loose-leaf brewed tea mingling with gourmet tea bags! It's tea for two and a lot more. The owners Ginny and Harvey Durand have smoothies on the menu and an impressive variety of crepes, from fruit filled to spinach stuffed, to accompany any of the beverages they create individually for their customers. Check out their walk-away "strollers," a rolled-up crepe with butter and sugar, among other varieties, that serves as a perfect afternoon snack while shopping in the Village. Call for hours that may change seasonally. $$.

Woody's Boathouse. Suite B-100 in Lake Arrowhead Village,; (909) 337-2628; www .woodysboathouse.com. Another tradition here, this 200-seat dining homage to boat lovers is noisy and busy, but it doesn't deter the owners from serving comfort food in a nautical ambience. Watch out for the boats, they are even hanging from the rafters! Open daily for lunch, dinner and Sunday brunch. Call for hours. $.

where to stay

Fleur de Lac. 285 Hwy. 173, Lake Arrowhead; (909) 337-8178; www.fleurdelac.com. This is the lodging for those who think a small French château–style bed-and-breakfast is a perfect match. Built in 1915, the inn borrows its architecture from the homes of the Normandy region of France, combined with the Craftsman-style that was popular in the Los Angeles area during the turn of the century. The steep pitch of the roof and the three-story turret

paws 'n' claws, wings 'n' things at wildhaven ranch

Wildhaven Ranch in the San Bernardino Mountains is one big reason to visit Lake Arrowhead for the day. Reservations are required; call (909) 337-7389. You will be given directions to this remote location. This wildlife rehabilitation center and sanctuary is off Cedar Glen on Highway 173. Wear layered clothing and bring water and a camera. The tours are of an educational nature and are scheduled Sat between 1 p.m. and 3 p.m. The resident animals include a grey fox, red fox, two coyotes, a bald eagle, golden eagle, three female black bears, a screech owl, a great horned owl, deer, raccoons, and a bobcat.

The residents here are animals and birds that have been permanently placed into care here for the rest of their lives, for reasons determined by the U.S. Department of Fish and Game. All of the animals have been injured in some way that prevents their release back into the wild. During the tour, your guide will discuss the animals and interact with them. Wildhaven Ranch is a nonprofit organization that is also an education center for the public. Their commitment to share knowledge about wildlife, the environment, and natural resources is an enlightening experience.

are French; the coved window molding and the low ceilings are Craftsman. Every morning there is a fresh-cooked breakfast, and you can walk to the Village to shop and dine and relax lakeside. This European-style B&B is beautifully furnished with old-world decor. The property underwent an extensive restoration that brought the comfort and amenities of the twenty-first century to the inn. It's a romantic place for those who appreciate a touch of elegance in a rustic setting. $$$.

Lake Arrowhead Resort and Spa. 2984 Hwy. 189; (800) 800-6792, (909) 336-1511; www.laresort.com. This is the ideal 173-room resort where you can experience the best of Lake Arrowhead complete with a perfect location, ample free parking, outdoor swimming pool, and easy access to skiing, golf, and shopping. There is a private beach along the shores of Lake Arrowhead. The resort's **Bin189** is considered the best restaurant for fine dining in Lake Arrowhead and has an extensive wine list. The **Spa of the Pines** is a full-service spa with a fitness studio, cardio theater, Pilates, and ongoing fitness classes. Add the fresh, invigorating mountain air and you could easily turn a day trip into a longer, longevity-inspired weekend. $$$.

day trip 03

northeast

ski on the rim of the world:
big bear lake

big bear lake

Located 100 miles northeast of Los Angeles, this alpine paradise is surrounded by the majesty of the **San Bernardino National Forest,** ranging in altitude from 6,750 to 9,000 feet. Home to Southern California's premier ski resorts, this pristine dot on the map also has a sunny side, and that's during the summer when hiking, biking, and fishing attract visitors. Thanks to a superb location, this is a joyous day trip where a four-season climate creates a recreational paradise for the outdoors fans. During the spring, the welcome mat rolls out carpets of wildflowers (there are thirty varieties), and mountain biking and fishing enter the scene. During June those challenged by Southern California's "June gloom" syndrome (coastal fog, for the uninitiated) flock here because Big Bear is above the marine layers that are the culprit causing dreary, gray skies. Trailheads throughout the Big Bear Valley present fun challenges for those who treasure a pure hiking adventure. Fishing fans, especially those who prize trout, will find Big Bear Lake's water depth impressive: In 2010 it was 67 feet, a mere 5 feet from maximum capacity.

You've probably seen Big Bear in many movies and didn't know it! *Old Yeller* (1957), starring Fess Parker, was filmed here along with *Magnolia* (1999), starring Tom Cruise. If you ever chance to see vintage films such as the *Northwest Mounted Police* (1940) or *North to Alaska* (1960), you're looking at Big Bear!

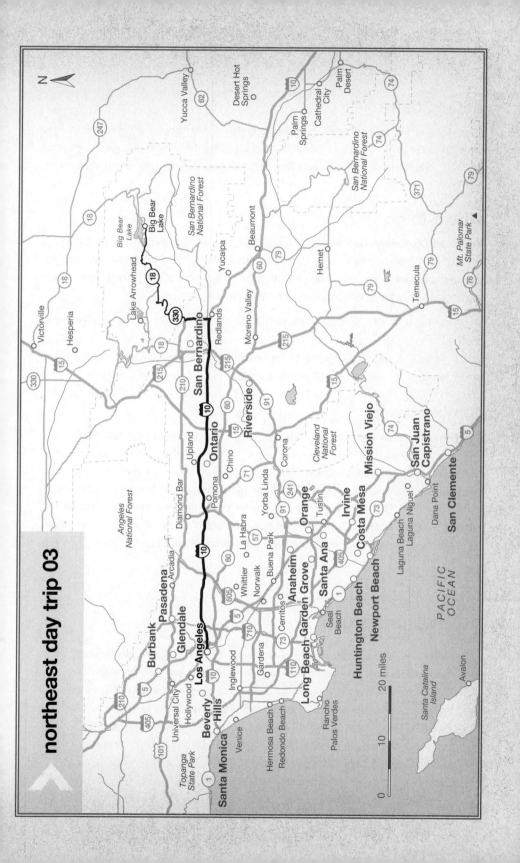

getting there

From Los Angeles, take I-10 east to the Running Springs/I-210 north exit in Redlands. Follow I-210 north to Highway 330, then to Highway 18. This 100-mile scenic journey into the mountains will take you about 2 hours (but it's wholly dependent upon time of day, week, and traffic conditions—particularly when it's snowing!)

where to go

Big Bear Discovery Center. 1288 Club View Dr.; (909) 866-3437; www.sbnfa.org. Located on the north shore of Big Bear Lake, this is the recommended starting point for exploring the area. Here you will find the latest on seasonal tours and guided hikes (which are offered at a nominal fee) and year-round educational activities.

Big Bear Lake. (800) 424-4232; www.bigbear.com. The epicenter of this vacation paradise, stunning Big Bear Lake and its 22 miles of shoreline sits above the clouds and crowds. This is where you will discover some of the best freshwater fishing in California. There is a public launch ramp and rental boats—from speedboats to canoes. The Department of Fish and Game (DFG) stocks the lake with 2,000 pounds of rainbow trout every two weeks, and that's not a fish story!

Big Bear Mountain Resorts. 800 Summit Blvd., Big Bear Lake; (909) 866-5766; www .bearmountain.com. The Park at Bear Mountain is the first full-service mountain resort in the world that is almost entirely devoted to an innovative freestyle terrain. There are two Big Bear Mountain resorts to enjoy: First, **Bear Mountain** (43101 Goldmine Dr., Big Bear Lake; 909-866-5766), which is intense and geared toward thrill-seeking youths with its 150 jumps and 80 jibs situated on 195 acres. It is also the site of the only Superpipe in Southern California. Second, there is the more family-friendly **Snow Summit** (880 Summit Blvd., Big

winter playground

*Skiing is an affordable sport at Big Bear thanks to the **Big Bear Lake Resort Association** and their seasonal deals at Snow Summit and Bear Mountain. Snow Summit is advised for everyday skiers and riders seeking a laid-back winter playground. The Park at Bear Mountain (also known as the All Mountain Terrain Freestyle Park) is ideal for every-level skills, including first-time snowboarders and skiers. It is wise to note that even when chain restrictions are in effect, roads leading to Big Bear are still open for fun in the snow. Motorists must be on high alert for driving on mountain roads during winter weather.*

Bear Lake; 909-866-2052), which has beginner-level terrain at the Family Park, intermediate level terrain at Ego Trip, or for the adventurous skiier, explore the vast interconnecting runs that wind through the park. Big Bear Mountain Resorts is proud owner of two of the largest snowmaking facilities in the world. As the staff say, "Mother Nature comes through with natural snow creating perfect powder days and terrific tree skiing and riding." If you require ski equipment, there are quality outfitters and full-service rental shops. Snow is known as "white gold"; when it rains in Southern California chances are it is snowing on Bear Mountain or Snow Summit. The resorts are open year-round. Call for current snow conditions. During warmer months, enjoy golfing, hiking, mountain biking, and sky chair rides, as well as concerts and parties.

Bear Mountain Golf Course. 43102 Goldmine Dr., Big Bear Lake; (909) 585-8002; www .bigbearmountainresorts.com/summer/big-bear-golf.php. The altitude is 7,000 feet, so you can be sure your ball will soar far. This is a 9-hole mountain-style golf course located near the base of Bear Mountain in the Moonridge meadow area. There is a pro shop, the Bear Trap restaurant, and golf club and cart rentals. This is the perfect way to take in the fragrant pine trees, blue skies, and the soft summer breezes.

Big Bear Lake Pirate Ship. Holloways Marina, 398 Edgemoor Rd.; (909) 878-4386; www .northshorelanding.com. This one-third-scale replica of a sixteenth-century Spanish galleon is complete with four masts (for landlubbers that's the sprint, fore, main, and mizzen) and has sails that are square on the first three masts. The 1.5-hour tours are narrated by the "pirate captain." Shipmates take note: The maximum number of sailors is twenty-five, so reserve in advance! Times and hours of operation vary, be sure to call ahead.

Miss Liberty Paddlewheel Tour Boat. 400 Pine Knot Ave.; (909) 866-8129; www .pineknotmarina.com. All aboard Southern California's newest and largest one-of-a-kind boat on Big Bear Lake. The 2 p.m. narrated cruise is guaranteed to depart daily for a 90-minute tour that reveals Big Bear's rich history. It's requested that you arrive at least 15 minutes prior to departure. Times and hours of operation vary,

Moonridge Animal Park. 432 Goldmine Dr.; (909) 880-4200; www.bigbearzoo.com. Check out the alpine wildlife collection of over 160 animals, which of course includes the legendary "Big Bear." Check out events throughout the year such as a Bear Country Fair in May and the Boo in the Zoo in Oct.

Goldsmith's Boardshop & Ski Rental. 42071 Big Bear Blvd.; (909) 866-2727; www .goldsmithsboardandski.com/. Snowshoeing is a major Big Bear sport, and those who want to give it a try make their way to this haven of rental snowshoes. There are miles of snowshoe trails here, and the experts say this is a terrific workout. The staff at Goldsmith recommends Bow Canyon Creek, Sand Canyon Creek, or Show Point Trail (located at the Snow Creek Forest Ski area) as a starting point.

Baldwin Lake Stables. 46475 Pioneertown Rd., Big Bear City; (909) 585-6482; www
.baldwinlakestables.com. Connect to nature during 1-, 2-, 3-, or 4-hour rides. There are
horses and mountain trails to accommodate all riding abilities.

Big Bear Charter Fishing. Holloway's Marina, 398 Edgemoor Rd., Big Bear Lake; (909)
866-2240; www.bigbearfishing.com. You can easily charter a pontoon or bass boat and fish
to your heart's desire. Fully loaded with gear, poles, reels, bait, and lures, get set to catch
trout, bass, catfish, crappie, and blue gills with a fish-friendly guide. The bass boat accommodates up to four people, and the pontoon handles up to ten people at a time.

Alpine Slide at Magic Mountain. 800 Wildrose Lane, Big Bear Lake; (909) 866-4626;
www.alpineslidebigbear.com. Custom-made for families and lots of fun, this Magic Carpet
Ride is Southern California's only authentic winter-time bobsled experience. The track is a
quarter-mile long, and during the summer there's a double water slide guaranteed to cool
you off. Making a few hours even more enjoyable are go-karts and an 18-hole miniature
golf course.

Big Bear Marina. 500 Paine Court, Big Bear Lake; (909) 866-3218; www.bigbearmarina
.com. Here's a few ways to enjoy the lake: sightseeing via comfortable pontoon boat that
accommodates up to twelve people; or by spending your day fishing from an outboard
charter boat for pinfish, trout, bass or rainbow trout. The marina also offers guide services,
Jet Ski rentals, wakeboarding, and lake tours.

Big Bear Off-Road Adventures. Big Bear Valley; (909) 585-1036; www.offroadadven
ture.com. A heavy-duty, four-wheel-drive vehicle can maneuver the toughest terrain in
this backcountry experience. An interpretive guide will accompany you on a tour that can
range from a couple of hours to a full-day adventure. The views of the San Bernardino
Mountains and Mojave Desert are spectacular. You can also visit Butler Peak, Rose Mine,
and historic Holcomb Valley. If you have only one day to spend in Big Bear, this any-season
tour is a good way to go. Off-Road will advise you on how to customize your tour. Call for
availability.

Big Bear Parasail & Watersports. 400 Pine Knot Ave.; (909) 866-4359; www.bigbear
parasail.net. A thrill ride that will take you 7,000 feet up, up, and away. The bird's-eye view
of Big Bear Valley is amazing. You'll sail right over Big Bear Lake with the clear blue sky as
a backdrop. New in 2010: New Zealand–style jet boat rides. The season is limited from late
May to mid-Sept. Call for availability and rates.

wildflowers

Wildflower hikes are a passion in Big Bear, where nearly thirty varieties flourish. Native to the region and rarely seen elsewhere, you might say you have an exclusive opportunity during the wildflower season to experience nature's wonders. Don't miss your chance as it happens only March through July. Get your hiking shoes and explore. For example, in March and April, visit the ecological preserve and pebble plains located at **Baldwin Lake,** *near the east end of the valley. During April and May head for the* **Blue Quartz Mine,** *which is on the north side of Big Bear Lake and the Holcomb Valley. Look for the Bernardino linanthus, a popular flower that blooms here. The south side of Big Bear Lake has several varieties such as Yellow Owl's Clover, found above the Performing Arts Center. Call (800) 424-4232 or visit www.bigbear.com for current reports.*

where to shop

The Christmas Mart. 652 Pine Knot Ave., Big Bear Lake Village; (909) 866-8468; www .bigbearlakevillage.com. It's Christmas year-round at this bustling shop where ornaments of every description dazzle the eye. Many visitors make this a standard stop as the selection is vast and varied with many collectibles waiting to be discovered.

Northshore Trading Company. 39130 North Shore Dr., Fawnskin; (909) 866-3414; www .gopaddleacanoe.com. Fawnskin is the quaint village where this memorable shop stocks wooden canoes, and fishing tackle with fly tying; fly-casting lessons are available. For the winter trade there are wooden toboggans, child-size sleds, and snowshoes; year-round, there's always an impressive collection of handmade jewelry from local artists. Cabin decor is on display, and there's even a selection of rowboats and fiberglass, Kevlar, and plastic kayaks!

where to eat

Jaspers Smokehouse and Steaks. 607 Pine Knot Ave., Big Bear Lake; (909) 866-2434; www.jasperssmokehouse.com. This is the home of wood-fire smoke pit, which delivers hearty portions of pork ribs, chicken, beef brisket and Texas-style ribs. Savor "sides" such as mom's baked beans, Smokehouse potato salad and southern-style coleslaw. Steaks are USDA prime and choice corn-fed midwestern Angus. It's worth driving up the mountain for the ribeye, pit porterhouse, or other mouthwatering cuts of beef. The menu lists "stressed" (desserts spelled backward), which are all homemade and terrific for stress-reduction. Open for lunch and dinner. Closed Wed. Call for seasonal hours.

Old Country Inn. 41126 Big Bear Blvd., Big Bear Lake; (909) 866-5600. Serving comfort food for over thirty years, this cozy restaurant boasts hearty breakfasts, lunches, and dinners. The cooking is home-style and you'll find it all "on the sunny side of the boulevard." This is a favorite restaurant for families and locals. Check out the patio for outdoor dining, from which you can enjoy the marvelous mountain air and get into the swing of the relaxing mountain lifestyle. Call for hours. $–$$.

where to stay

Best Western Big Bear Chateau Hotel. 42200 Moonridge Rd., Big Bear Lake; (909) 866-6666; www.bestwestern.com. The closest full-service lodging to Snow Summit and Big Bear Mountain Ski Resort is less than a mile from the slopes. There are eighty guest rooms, and the welcome mat is out for pets as well. A complimentary full breakfast is served from 7 a.m. to 10 a.m., dine-in only, at Le Bistro Restaurant (on the premises), with a buffet breakfast that is also open to the public daily. Dinner is served Fri and Sat evenings. The outdoor pool is heated and open from May through October. The steam room and hot tub are open year-round indoors. There are ski, romance, and wedding packages available. $$.

Northwoods Resort. 40650 Village Drive., Big Bear Lake; (909) 866-3121; www.north woodsresort.com. This is the largest resort in Big Bear Lake village area and has 140 comfortable guest rooms and luxurious suites, most with stunning lake and mountain views; all with Wi-Fi and complimentary coffee. The year-round heated outdoor pool (the only one in Big Bear) is a popular gathering place along with the fitness center and sauna. There is over 9,000 square feet of meeting space accommodating 10 to 400 people, making this resort a top destination for business and social events. The resort is located at the entrance to the village and is two blocks from Big Bear Lake and shopping. **Stillwell's Restaurant and Lounge,** located here, is a good choice for breakfast, lunch, or dinner. Pets are accepted; check for restrictions. $$.

east

day trip 01

east

get your kicks on route 66:
san bernardino, rancho cucamonga, riverside, redlands

san bernadino

Before the days of freeways and incessant traffic reports there was Route 66, the Mother Road and the one treasured as "America's Main Street." Capturing the spirit of the open road, Route 66 meandered across America with memorable "motor hotels," cafes, and businesses along the way. A few of those roadside reminders remain, but for the most part, shopping centers and strip malls and housing developments took over, and that nostalgic area of America's tourism nearly vanished. Today it is known as Historic Route 66, and honors its vibrant past with a few of those pop-culture icons that are still open. Take time to explore this area and stop for a cup of coffee and piece of apple pie along the way.

"San Berdoo," as it's called locally, is the gateway city to the resorts of Big Bear and Lake Arrowhead to the north, but has attractions all its own for day trippers. San Bernardino is home to year-round sports such as the Class A affiliate of Los Angeles Dodgers, the Inland Empire 66ers, and the Western Region Little League Tournament. The historic California Theater in downtown San Bernardino features Broadway plays, musicals, and cultural shows from the San Bernardino Symphony Orchestra. Visit the San Bernardino Convention & Visitors Bureau website, www.san-bernardino.org, for more info and free guides.

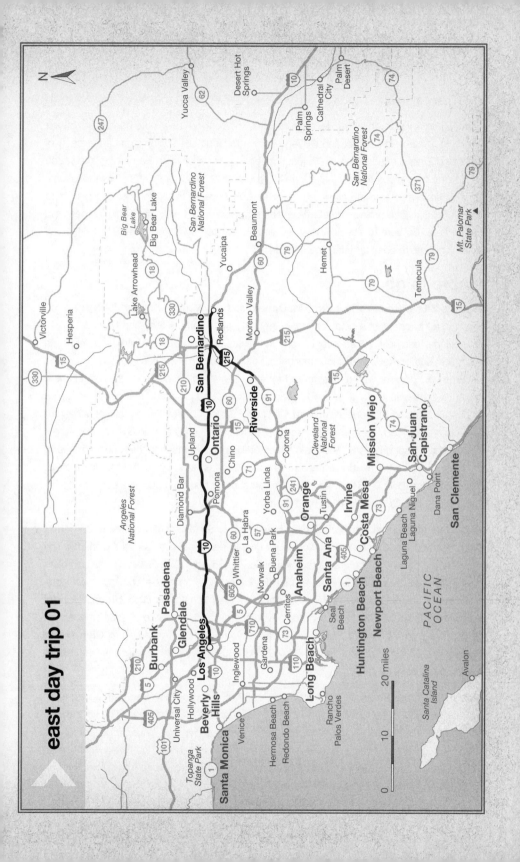

east day trip 01

getting there

Leaving Los Angeles, this 65-mile, approximately 1-hour-and-15-minute ride begins on the I-10 east toward San Bernardino County, known to Southern Californians as the heart of the Inland Empire region. At the I-15 junction, bear right toward San Bernardino and watch for several road signs that clearly state HISTORIC ROUTE 66. You can exit at these locations. This distance and time is calculated from the Los Angeles midtown business district to the City of San Bernardino, therefore be aware of rush hour traffic that could increase the driving time. Be sure to check with the California Welcome Center (909-891-1874; www .cwcinlandempire.com) for latest information.

where to go

Historic Site of the World's First McDonald's. 1398 North E St., San Bernardino (no website, no phone, just a place of pilgrimage). In 1948, brothers Dick and Mac McDonald opened their original namesake restaurant on this site on the business district loop of Route 66. It sold hamburgers, cheeseburgers, fries, soft drinks, and milk shakes at low prices and became very popular with residents and tourists. Ray Kroc encountered the restaurant in 1954 when he was working as a food-mixer salesman, and proposed and managed a plan to open franchised McDonald's around the United States. The McDonald brothers eventually sold the company to Kroc in 1961 for $2.7 million. Their original building has been razed, but there is a display of early McDonald's memorabilia—an homage to the American Dream. Ironically, it is now the headquarters for the Juan Pollo fast-food chain. Another fun factoid: Taco Tia, Taco Bell, Del Taco, and Der Weinerschnitzel fast-food chains also all started in San Bernardino. Open daily 10 a.m. to 5 p.m.

Glen Helen Regional Park. 2555 Glen Helen Pkwy., San Bernardino; (909) 887-7540 or (909) 880-6500 for concert information; www.co.san-bernardino.ca.us/Parks/glen.htm. The "jewel in the crown" of the area's regional parks, 1,425-acre Glen Helen comes complete with a half-acre swimming lagoon, a 350-foot water slide, and a beach. And proof positive that Southern Californians think big, the park also boasts the **Glen Helen Hyundai Pavilion** (909-88-MUSIC; www.hyundaipavilion.com) outdoor concert venue, the largest amphitheater in the United States (total capacity is 65,000). The adjacent **Glen Helen Raceway** (18585 Verdemont Ranch Rd.; 909-880-3090; www.glenhelen.com) features the best in motocross events.

National Orange Show. NOS Events Center, 689 South E Street; San Bernardino; (909) 888-6788; www.nationalorangeshow.com. Here's an event you'll never find in Kansas. Started way back in 1911, the show has been getting juicier ever since. Today it features fireworks, top entertainment, a rodeo, livestock shows, art exhibits, kid-friendly rides, and, of course, a broad range of oranges and orange food products. Held from Thurs through Mon (Memorial Day weekend). Admission is free.

Stater Bros. Route 66 Rendezvous. (800) 867-8366; www.route-66.org. If you're up for a healthy dose of nostalgic honky-tonk, check out this four-day affair that kicks off every year in mid-September. Southern Californians have always had a special relationship with their automobiles; what wine is to the French, cars are to us—sacred objects, worthy of adulation. This is clearly in evidence as squeaky-clean Corvettes, Cobras, and Chevys limited to 1,900 pre-1974 classics, customs, hot rods, and other vehicles receive an assigned reserved parking space for the four-day event. Vehicles cruise a 36-block area of downtown San Bernardino while visitors enjoy the beautiful cars, food, vendors, sponsor displays, and live entertainment. Drag races, an auto sound challenge, and an antique performance parts swap are also on the annual activity roster. Dozens of vendors hawk their wares, which range from antique milk caps and Elvis clocks to new stereo equipment. And to put a little honk into the tonk, celebrities come to life via ongoing Legends in Concert performances. The rendezvous, which is free to spectators, is sponsored and produced by the San Bernardino Convention and Visitors Bureau.

where to eat & stay

For a large variety of restaurants, cuisine, lodging, and shopping, check out the Hospitality Lane exit located right off the I-10. Be sure to call for hours operation first. Here's two of our favorites there:

Guadalaharry's. 280 East Hospitality Lane; (909) 889-8555. Specializing in fajitas, Guadalaharry's is also known for its fried-ice-cream dessert. Open daily for lunch and dinner and Sun brunch. Yum. $–$$.

Hilton San Bernardino. 285 East Hospitality Lane; (909) 889-0133 or (800) 445-8667; www.hilton.com. Located off I-10 at the North Waterman exit. As the street name suggests, this area of San Bernardino is visitor-friendly. The rooms come with standard amenities, and your choice of two queens or one king bed. You'll find an extensive variety of restaurants on Hospitality Lane within walking distance of the hotel. $$$$.

rancho cucamonga

Rancho Cucamonga, a city located along Historic Route 66, has a name folks love to make fun of. But there's also fun to be had in the town. There's a monument here to Jack Benny (you'll have to explain to youngsters who Jack Benny was), as he often mentioned Rancho Cucamonga on radio and television shows. For more civic information access the Chamber of Commerce at www.ranchochamber.org.

where to go

Auto Club Speedway. 9300 Cherry Ave., Fontana; (800) 944-RACE (7223), for tickets call (800) 944-7223; www.autoclubspeedway.com. Rev it up at the famous 5,680-acre

Auto Club Speedway, which opened June 20, 1997, and is still going strong. You can hear the cars getting into high gear from miles away. NASCAR returns here for major spectator events with two races a year, in Feb and Oct. Motorcycle races, such as AMA Super Bike Challenge and classic sports car races, take place here. This is recognized as "America's ultimate race place" and for good reason. The grandstand can seat 92,000, plus there are sixty-three terrace suites overlooking the pit road. For the ultimate view there are twenty-eight luxury skybox suites. As for size, 1,800 RVs can be accommodated in the infield! If you are a racing fan this is definitely a day trip you can't miss. The speedway is home of the quarter-mile NHRA-sanctioned drag strip, known to all drag fans as the Auto Club Dragway.

where to shop

Joseph Filippi Winery & Vineyards. 12467 Baseline Rd., Rancho Cucamonga; (909) 899-5755; www.josephfilippiwinery.com. This family-owned winery has produced award-winning wines (200 awards during the last thirty-five years) for over eighty years and is still going strong with wine tastings and tours. The tour gives you the history of wine making and an understanding of how it added to California's reputation as a leading wine-producing area. The wine-tasting room and gift shop are worth a visit. Hours vary, but generally are Mon from 10 a.m. to 5 p.m., Tues through Sat from 10 a.m. to 6 p.m. and Sun 11 a.m. to 5 p.m. Be sure to call to confirm, especially during harvest and holiday periods.

Victoria Gardens. 12505 North Main St., Rancho Cucamonga; (909) 463-2830; www .victoriagardensie.com. This is an ideal day trip from Los Angeles—it's an innovative shopping concept that goes beyond the expected. This is a re-creation of an old-fashioned downtown complete with retro music (think Frank Sinatra and Bing Crosby), spacious gardens, and original neon signs from vintage buildings. The modern AMC theaters feature twelve screens, and there are restaurants galore, from **Lucille's Smokehouse Barbecue** to **King's Fish House**. There is a lively schedule of entertainment at the Victoria Gardens Cultural Center Lewis Family Playhouse. Spend the day and browse at your leisure as there are over 150 specialty stores plus the Bass Pro Shops Outdoor World, considered a true sportsmen's paradise. Parking is plentiful and free. Open daily, call for specific hours and seasonal operations.

where to eat

Magic Lamp Inn. 8189 Foothill Blvd., Rancho Cucamonga; (909) 981-8659; www .themagiclampinn.com. For over half a century this landmark restaurant has lit up its neon sign, a magic lantern welcoming travelers along Historic Route 66. Many think of it as a comfortable outpost on the Mother Road. The decor is pure midcentury, comfortable and spacious, and there's dancing Wed through Sat evenings. Open Tues through Sun; call for hours. $$.

Red Hill Coffee Shop. 8111 Foothill Blvd., Suite C, Rancho Cucamonga; (909) 985-3816. Opened in 1943 and still serving massive portions of comfort food, this is authentic Route 66 roadside hospitality as it was before the onset of fast food and drive-throughs. Stop in for huge omelets or just a good cup of coffee as you're driving along this stretch of an important chapter in the development of America's travel history. Open daily, usually 6:30 a.m. to 12:30 p.m., but call to confirm as times can change. $.

Sycamore Inn. 8318 Foothill Blvd., Rancho Cucamonga; www.thesycamoreinn.com; (909) 982-7782. Built in 1848, this is Rancho Cucamonga's oldest dinner house and still a favorite for fine dining among locals and visitors. Originally a tavern and inn for weary travelers, this historic restaurant catered to many movie stars en route to Las Vegas. Their prime rib is slow roasted and hand carved and continues to bring diners to their door. Open Mon through Sat at 5 p.m., Sun at 4 p.m. Closing hours vary. Reservations suggested. $$.

Vince's Spaghetti Route 66. 8241 Foothill Blvd., Rancho Cucamonga; (909) 981-1003; www.vincesspaghettiroute66.com. This is the place where you can fill up on spaghetti without breaking the bank—one of the reasons this Italian restaurant has enjoyed such popularity. Forget those $20-a-plate gourmet pasta concoctions; this is straightforward, piping hot, and delicious. Opened over twenty-five years ago, this landmark remains a haven for home-style cooking. It started as a fruit stand, and when customers started asking for their own servings of the home-cooked lunches that were brought to Vince by his wife, it evolved into this busy restaurant that continues the tradition. Open seven days a week for lunch and dinner; call for times and holiday hours of operation. $.

where to stay

The Christmas House. 9240 Archibald Ave., Rancho Cucamonga; (909) 980-6450; www .christmashouseinn.com. Stay in the spirit of Historic Route 66 and turn back the clock. This historic turn-of-the-century Victorian home, a Rancho Cucamonga landmark since 1904, has six lovely guest rooms. A full home-cooked breakfast is served to guests, and afternoon tea is served in the parlor. Seven fireplaces and a spacious veranda pay homage to life at a slower pace, and the exquisite landscaped garden is a popular setting for weddings since opening in 1984 as an inn. $$.

riverside

You might say this was a city built on oranges! That's right; by 1895 more than 20,000 navel orange trees transformed sleepy Riverside into the nation's wealthiest city per capita! Take a walk back into time when California was young and Victorian architecture took a western curve and ended up decorating the facades of the old City Hall and the 1892 restored Heritage House. Showcasing the Victorian lifestyle with a western spin made Riverside into an important center of agriculture and trade.

where to go

Botanic Gardens at University of California–Riverside (UCR). 900 University Ave., Riverside; (951) 827-1012 or (951) 784-6962; http://gardens.ucr.edu. Located on the UCR campus, follow signs to the gardens and park in lot 13. You'll find the gardens covering forty hilly acres in the foothills of Box Spring Mountains in East Riverside. The lush gardens display more than 3,500 plant species from around the world. Bird-watchers will be impressed by the more than 200 birds that flock to the gardens. Admission is free; donations appreciated. Open daily from 8 a.m. to 5 p.m. Closed New Year's Day, July 4th, Thanksgiving Day and Christmas Day.

Castle Amusement Park. 3500 Polk St.; (951) 785-3000; www.castlepark.com. This twenty-five-acre family amusement park has a rare Dentzel carousel built in 1898, one of the oldest in America. The fifty-two hand-carved, brightly painted animals are works of art. A tri-level castle houses more than 400 state-of-the-art games, and the miniature golf course is surrounded by swaying palm trees. Admission is free, and you purchase individual tickets for the attractions. Open daily, check for hours.

where to eat

Anchos Southwest Grill and Bar. 10773 Hole St., Riverside; (951) 352-0240; www .anchos.net. Perfect for lunch or dinner, this is a rare find where you can watch tortillas being made and rotated in the warmer. There's a large enough menu so that there is something for everyone, including fresh guacamole. Open daily at 11:30 a.m., generally close at 9 p.m. (call to confirm). $.

Duane's Prime Steaks and Seafood Restaurant at the Mission Inn. 3649 Mission Inn Ave.; (951) 784-0300; www.missioninn.com/restaurants-duanes.htm. Dinner and a lavish Sun brunch are served here. Take note that Duane's has earned the only AAA Four-Diamond award in the Inland Empire. Open Mon through Sat from 5:30 to10 p.m. $$$.

where to stay

The Mission Inn Hotel & Spa. 3469 Mission Inn Ave.; (951) 784-0300; www.missioninn museum.com. This 269-room resort, a member of Historic Hotels of America, has so much history to share that it operates its own museum! Opened in 1902, this European-style national treasure reflects the era when country resorts had grand lobby areas, ornate ceilings, and the charm that only comes with time-honored traditions. Today, there's a European-inspired spa, and a Sunday buffet reminiscent of what you would find on a world-class cruise ship. No two rooms are alike, and there are five restaurants serving California classic cuisine. Plus, the **Mission Inn Foundation/Museum** has an excellent walking history tour you won't want to miss. Admission charged. $$$.

apple pickin' in oak glen

Whether its apple-picking season or just an extra day you have on your itinerary, this is the ideal place to spend some time in the country. There are several apple-picking farms, a small shopping area, and a noticeable absence of anything that reminds one of fast food and Wal-Mart.

Riley's Farm. 12261 South Oak Glen Rd., Oak Glen; (909) 797-7534; www .rileysfarm.com. If you've been thinking of picking apples, blueberries, or raspberries, or eating a piece of fresh apple pie in a country setting, drive no further than Oak Glen, home to this authentic farm where visitors can enjoy a day in the country. The cool mountain town of Oak Glen, studded with literally thousands of fruit trees, is heavenly; there isn't a parking ramp or traffic light to disturb the genuine rural ambience, which is just the way folks want it to be around here. On major holidays such as Mother's Day, Father's Day, Valentine's Day, and during apple picking season (usually October), there's a lot going on, such as great music from the 1880s and historical reenactments from the Gold Rush era and old-fashioned recreations of eighteenth-century harvest time. Riley's has a restaurant serving good old American cooking, and that means a hearty piece of fresh apple pie with or without ice cream! You can pick your apples and berries in containers purchased at the gift shop and take them home to make your own pies, too.

redlands

Quiet and quaint, this charming Southern California city was named for the color of the local soil and is home to the eponymous and highly regarded university, which is pretty as a vintage California postcard. If you have time for one detour, this is the place to take that turn off the I-10. During the nineteenth century this nook of lush hills and valleys was a mecca for midwesterners and easterners of means as being the time-honored retreat from cold, windy winters. You can drive by the mansions that for a brief spell bear witness to the Golden State's short-lived Victorian renaissance. The charming downtown, which is more of a college town, is brimming with gift shops, restaurants, and thrift shops.

where to go

Historical Glass Museum Foundation. 1157 North Orange St., Redlands; (909) 793-3333; www.glassmuseums.com. Housed in one of historic Redland's ornate Victorian homes is this twelve-room museum displaying over 7,000 pieces of American glass covering American Depression glass, Victorian art glass, early American pattern glass, and

American brilliant cut glass, among other categories. Displayed in antique and custom-built illuminated cases, each piece is meticulously described right down to maker, color, pattern, and years of production. Glassmaking is a window to the past, and this unusual museum represents over 200 years of its history. Open Sat and Sun from noon to 4 p.m.

Kimberly Crest House & Gardens. 1325 Prospect Dr., Redlands; (909) 792-2111; www .kimberlycrest.org. This six-acre estate will take you back to an era of genteel elegance. This outstanding example of turn-of-the-century architecture, where Louis XVI decor meets formal Italian gardens, is a must see. Reflecting the architecture of a French château, the estate was purchased by J. Alfred Kimberly (of Kimberly-Clark fame) and his wife, Helen, and was used seasonally. It is a California Registered Historical Landmark. You will be impressed by the view of the orange groves and the great southern magnolia tree, which was the Kimberlys' Christmas tree for many years. Generally open Thurs through Sun from 1 to 3:30 p.m., be sure to call for specific hours due to events and holidays.

San Bernardino County Museum. 2024 Orange Tree Lane, Redlands; (909) 307-2669; www.sbcounty.gov/museum. Its location midway between Los Angeles and Palm Springs makes it convenient to visit this fascinating museum. Believe it or not, this is where you will find the fifth-largest bird-egg collection in the world! There is a native plant garden, and you can picnic on the grounds. Open Tues through Sun 9 a.m. to 5 p.m. Call for specifics.

day trip 02

east

vintage hollywood, desert-style:
palm springs, desert hot springs

palm springs

This is a destination with a colorful history, and it all starts in what was once a sleepy desert town where the Agua Caliente Band of Cahuilla Indians made their home and cherished the mineral waters—eventually making this one of America's first spa destinations. As mentioned in historian Peter Moruzzi's book *Palm Springs Holiday: A Vintage Tour from Palm Springs to the Salton Sea,* he describes the back of a vintage Palm Springs postcard from the early 1930s, when this was the escape route from the prying eyes of Hollywood, with a checklist for activities. It reads "loafing, hitting the hay, hiking, playing tennis, golfing, stepping out, and celebrating." This hasn't changed much during the last seventy-five years because the desert is still a global haven for all of the above with the addition of a lot of tourism development since the good old days. Fast forward to the twenty-first century and you have the Palm Springs Aerial Tramway (an engineering masterpiece rising from the desert floor to the top of Mount San Jacinto), and a plethora of sports activities bringing everything from golf tournaments to marathon runs to motorcycling into the limelight. Consignment shopping is a favorite sport here as well, with dozens of resale shops, while art galleries exhibit internationally known and local artists and schedule openings throughout the year. A reverent preservation movement has revived the dozens of architectural gems and cozy motels from the midcentury (1950 to 1960s), and Modernism Week that takes place here every February symbolizes the fascination and commitment Palm Springs has

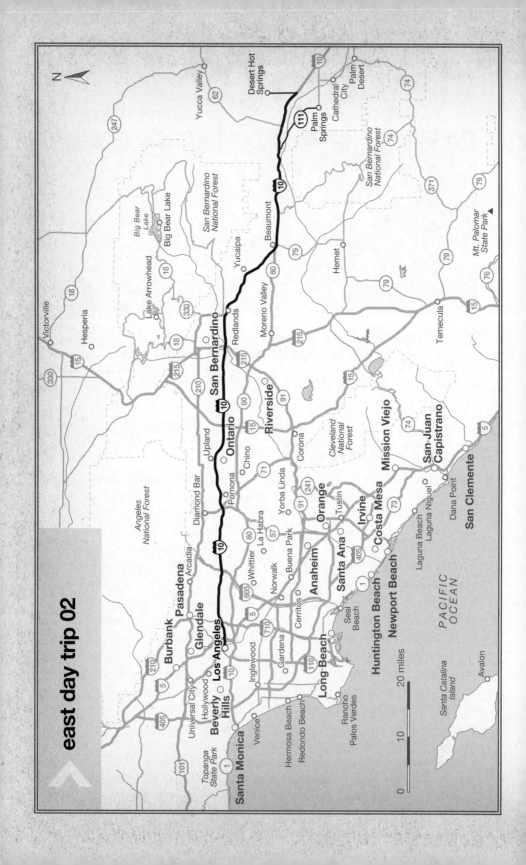

for midcentury architecture and design. Worldwide recognition and interest in the architects, photographers and designers that personify this style has attracted visitors to a year-round calendar of social, cultural and educational events celebrating modernism. While the postcard from the 1930s listed sleeping as one thing you are "doing lots of," today there's so much offered that you won't have time for dozing off!

getting here

As you head east from Los Angeles on I-10, the first glimpse of Palm Springs is rows of modern windmills, actually working wind turbines protruding sentrylike alongside the freeway. If you saw the film *Rainman* with Dustin Hoffman and Tom Cruise, you might recall this scene. Exit onto Highway 111 (officially SR 111, but no one uses that name here) and you're on a journey that takes you to Palm Springs, the gateway to the Coachella Valley—with the cities of Cathedral City, Rancho Mirage, Palm Desert, Indian Wells, La Quinta, and Indio beyond.

where to go

Elite Land Tours. 540 South Vella Rd., (800) 541-4866, (760) 318-1200; www.eliteland tours.com. There's a lot of terrain to discover in the Palm Springs area, and travelers can see it best by treading lightly. All tours are conducted in fully air-conditioned, best-in-class all-terrain vehicles—the Hummer H2—accommodating up to five passengers plus a professional guide. Owner Mark Farley and his team of expert guides can take you on a scheduled or customized tour of Palm Springs, from celebrity homes to a trek through the Indian canyons. Full- or half-day tours are available. Call for schedule and reservations.

Indian Canyons & Tahquitz Visitor Center. 500 West Mesquite, west of Palm Canyon Drive in downtown Palm Springs; (760) 416-7044; www.tahquitzcanyon.com. This is one of the most culturally sensitive areas of the Agua Caliente Indian Reservation, and you should take time for the Tahquitz Visitor Center where there is an observation deck. A narrative video reveals the legend of Tahquitz Canyon; don't miss it. The ranger-led 2.5-hour interpretive hikes give you an insider's perspective on this historic canyon. Open daily Oct through July from 7:30 a.m. to 5 p.m. and from Aug through Sept Fri through Sun from 7:30 a.m. to 5 p.m.

Knott's Soak City Water Park. 1500 Gene Autry Trail; (760) 327-0499; www.soakcityusa .com. Museums, Indian canyons, and movies stars aside, this is one of the reasons kids flock to the desert: the water! The park is an immaculately clean twenty-one-acre fantasy playground where cool water reigns supreme. There is amusement for kids of all ages, from Kahuna's Beach House and the tranquil Sunset River inner-tube ride to more than eighteen other water slides ranging from simple to simply outrageous. The Sea Snake slide is a case in point. Those who dare coast in inner tubes along a 54-inch-wide, 450-foot-long slide that at certain points takes riders through total darkness and down a 50-foot drop—yippee! Plus

shopping nirvana: desert-style

*It's not so much where to shop in Palm Springs (and even before you arrive), it's about how much time you have to take in literally hundreds of stores from budget to boutique with a frosting of haute couture. Don't slam on your brakes while driving on the I-10 east when you see a near mile-long stretch of designer boutiques; it's not a desert mirage. You have reached the **Desert Hills Premium Outlets,** and it seems like the outlet stores never end. And you may not reach Palm Springs if you try to visit all the stores. There are over a hundred shops side by side here, and overwhelming is only word that comes to mind! Consider this line up: Jimmy Choo for shoes; Judith Lieber for crystal-studded hand bags; Brighton for leather belts, shoes, and accessories—and that's just a hint of what treasures you will discover here at outlet prices. Dozens of tour buses pull up here daily before heading toward casino country, such as the **Morongo Casino Resort & Spa,** and further on I-10 east to the **Agua Caliente Casino-Resort-Spa,** so arrive early to avoid the crowd. Check www.premiumoutlets.com or call (951) 849-6641.*

*Register for a VIP card that will generate discount coupons. Tuesday is 10 percent off for those fifty years old and older. If you still have the time and strength to soldier on, continue driving and take Highway 111 into Palm Springs. You'll arrive at **Downtown & Uptown Palm Springs,** an eclectic shopping district where consignment shops, art galleries, trendy restaurants, and boutiques comingle. The stores to your left and right on Palm Canyon reveal the thriving Palm Springs modernism and midcentury architecture and style.*

*Begin your exploration at a shop that doubles as a welcome center; it's called **Just Fabulous** (515 North Palm Canyon Dr.; 760-864-1300; www.bjustfabulous .com), and it is! This is the go-to shop for those who want to know more about*

there is stand-up surfing and body boarding, as well as California's largest wave-action pool (800,000 gallons), a broad expanse of water that starts out calm but churns away every fifteen minutes to be a sort of Malibu-in-the-desert. Open daily from mid-March through Labor Day, and weekends only through Sept. Call for specific hours and promotions.

Palm Springs Aerial Tramway. One Tram Way, Chino Canyon, off Highway 111; (760) 325-1499; www.pstramway.com. You can't miss riding the world's largest glassed-in rotating tramcars that take you on a 2.5 mile ascent in 15 minutes to the majesty of Mount San Jacinto State Park. Hop on one of two eighty-passenger cars that slowly revolve from

modernism as it developed here during the mid-twentieth century; it's also a wise starting point as the shop sells the latest books on Palm Spring's architecture, focusing on desert icons such as Albert Frey, Donald Wexler, and John Lautner. You'll also find the latest books about Julius Shulman, world-renowned photographer who captured the beauty of this genre in black and white, who subsequently put Palm Spring's midcentury architecture on the map and his photographs in countless magazines and art galleries. Book signings at Just Fabulous are major events; with authors on hand they resemble "red carpet" events!

*A few steps away is **Café Chocolat of Palm Springs** (760-320-8889) where visitors are mesmerized by a stunning variety of chocolate candy from around the world. Savor the displays of chocolate from milk to dark in tempting flavors, along with a selection of chocolate gelato. If you have time, lunch is served daily. Across the corridor from Café Chocolate is **Koffi** (760-416-2244), featuring an appetizing display of freshly baked cookies, brownies, cupcakes, cinnamon rolls and everything that goes well with coffee and teas, iced and hot. You'll find mountains of local tourist publications and the local newspaper for browsing. Here, you never know who you may glimpse in their outdoor garden, sipping a frothy cappuccino. There is ample free parking.*

*Continue on Palm Canyon, now a one-way street, and you are officially downtown, a lovely area that is reminiscent of Palm Springs when it had more of a village feel during the midcentury. You'll find the 1950s-inspired art of Shag (aka Josh Agle) at **M Modern Gallery** (2500 North Palm Canyon Dr.; 760-416-3611; www.mmodern .com). His prints depict Palm Springs with pools, cocktails and tiki scenes (a spin on the "Polynesian pop" style which was popular in the '50s and '60s) and all that made the idiosyncratic midcentury lifestyle a classic era. For more information, visit www.palmcanyondrive.org.*

within, enabling everyone to take in the breathtaking 360-degree views of the valley floor. Once you arrive there are well-marked trails and, during the winter, cross-country skiing, snowboarding, snowshoeing, and even snow camping! This is pine tree country, some forty degrees cooler than the valley below. Really! What a relief in the summer! Tram rides depart on the half hour, starting at 10 a.m. Mon through Fri; 8 a.m. weekends and holidays. Last ride at 9:45 p.m. Schedules subject to change without notice. Please call ahead for times and weather conditions. No advance reservations required.

Palm Springs Air Museum. 745 North Gene Autry Trail; (760) 778-6262; www.palm springsairmuseum.com. Honoring the World War II era, this world-famous museum displays actual propeller-driven aircraft from an era today's generation knows only from the movies. It is interesting to note that many guides here who educate the public about aviation's role in winning the war are veterans, and their knowledge is at once astounding and memorable. Check the second floor for flight simulators and visit the gift shop if only to browse through books that shed light on this passage of military history. Open year-round from 10 a.m. to 5 p.m.

Palm Springs Art Museum. 101 Museum Dr.; (760) 322-4800; www.psmuseum.org. This extraordinary museum that hints of New York with its ongoing openings for world class artists, photographers, glassmakers, and architects is family friendly too, offering programs for children on the fourth Thursday of each month, free of charge. The Annenberg Theater on the lower level has ongoing plays, concerts, and lectures. Stay for lunch at the Muse Café and visit the gift shop, which locals and tourists find a fascinating art adventure with designer-inspired jewelry, gifts, and handbags. Open Oct through May. Closed Monday and major holidays. Open Tues, Wed, Fri, Sat, and Sun from 10 a.m. to 5 p.m.; Thurs noon to 8 p.m. Free admission every Thurs from 4 to 8 p.m. during downtown Villagefest.

Smoketree Stables. 2500 Toledo Ave.; (760) 327-1372; www.smoketreestables.com At the same location for over fifty years, next to the late Fess Parker's former residence (remember him as Disney's Davy Crockett in the 1950s?), there are trail rides exploring the canyons scheduled daily. It's Coachella Valley horseback riding at its best. Open year-round except July and August, 8 a.m. to 4 p.m. (when daylight is longer, hours to 6 p.m.).

where to shop

Villagefest. Palm Canyon Drive between Baristo and Amado Roads; (760) 320-3781; www .villagefest.org. This street transforms the main thoroughfare into a lively bazaar complete with street entertainers, food booths, and over 150 vendors. From custom-made canine fashions to homemade fudge and arts and crafts, this is a lively venue for strolling. It takes place every Thurs between 6 p.m. and 10 p.m.

where to eat

Sherman's Deli & Bakery. 401 East Tahquitz Canyon Way; (760) 325-1199; www.shermans deli.com. Part of the Palm Spring's deli culture, the corn beef and pastrami here are tops, and the bakery display case worthy of a painting. Constantly busy with locals and tourists, breakfast, lunch, and dinner are served daily, and the service is always friendly and efficient. You might say this is the nerve center of Palm Springs; it's been a favorite meeting place for decades. $–$$.

Tyler's. 149 South Indian Canyon Dr.; (760) 325-2990; www.tylersburgers.com. Hamburgers with personality are served here, a bustling indoor/outdoor restaurant that was once a bus station. Overstuffed chicken- and egg-salad sandwiches with a fresh strawberry milkshake put smiles on customers' faces, even if they have to wait in line to be seated. $.

Johannes. 196 S. Indian Canyon Dr., Palm Springs; (760) 778-0017; www.johannes restaurants.com. Treat yourself an authentic Weiner schnitzel—in Palm Springs, of all places! Austrian-trained chef/owner Johannes Bacher stays open year around serving "schnitzels" four ways—finished with choices such as Calvados apple cream sauce. His mother's treasured apple strudel has been on the menu since he opened. From spaetzle (housemade noodles) to seafood, there is something for everyone at this local favorite in the center of downtown Palm Springs. Open Tues through Sun for lunch from 11:30 a.m. to 2:30 p.m. and dinner from 5 to 10 p.m. Call for seasonal specials and hours. $$.

where to stay

Casa Cody Bed & Breakfast. 175 S. Cahuilla Rd., (760) 320-9346; www.casacody.com. Vintage Palm Springs at its best, this 23-room inn, surrounded by citrus-filled courtyards, spacious lawns, swimming pools and a Jacuzzi, was founded in the 1920s by Harriet Cody, cousin of Buffalo Bill Cody. Film stars flocked here over the years, from Charlie Chaplin to Lawrence Tibbett (the bon vivant Metropolitan Opera star). The adobe Tibbet loved (built in 1910) was beautifully restored with a large living room and two bedrooms. Located downtown and within walking distance of the Palm Springs Art Museum and the Thursday night Villagefest, you will experience all that has made the desert a living legend. Breakfast is complimentary. $$.

Movie Colony Hotel. 726 North Indian Canyon Dr.; (760) 320-6340; www.moviecolony hotel.com. This sixteen-room hotel was designed in 1935 by Albert Frey, a modernist architect whose name you will hear frequently in Palm Springs, especially during Modernism Week in February. The minimalist decor shows off the best of Frey, a look that is accentuated by luxurious bedding and, in most rooms, private terraces and patios. Guests flock to the complimentary wine-and-cocktail hour served poolside. It's a retro experience that is quite the opposite of the corporate mega resort hotels catering to the convention crowd. $$–$$$.

The Willows Historic Palm Springs Inn. 412 Tahquitz Canyon Way; (760) 320-0771; www.thewillowspalmsprings.com. If you want to experience historic Palm Springs in an authentic estate adjacent to the Palm Springs Art Museum, within walking distance to downtown Palm Springs, this handsome hideaway built in 1924 is a local treasure. Their gourmet breakfast served by the plunging rock waterfall is unforgettable. $$$.

triple entertaining event treats

*Three strictly Palm Springs events that you should not miss are captivating as well as cultural. Fasten your seat belts because this is where time moves backwards as well as forwards! The **Palm Springs International Film Festival** (PSIFF; www.psfilmfest.org) takes place in early January and has grown steadily during the last twenty-one years. A global headline-grabbing event with film stars walking the red carpet and the paparazzi in high gear, this event drew more than 130,000 visitors in 2010 according to Harold Matzner, PSIFF chairman. He said that attendees were invited to select from 450 screenings of 190 films from seventy countries during the fourteen-day event. Try to be here for at least a day to see what it is like when the movies take over Palm Springs!*

*The second event that has enjoyed unparallel success is the beloved **Fabulous Palm Springs Follies** (www.psfollies.com) where "everything old is new again." That's because the stunning Long Legged Lovelies and handsome Dapper Dans are for the most part eligible for Social Security. In other words the dancers that prance across the stage of the historic Plaza Theatre (it's where Camille, starring the inimitable Greta Garbo, premiered on December 12, 1936) are well over fifty years old! It's part of the glamour that has made Palm Springs "The Playground of the Stars," even those who you have thought of as being retired! Headliners have brought many stars to the Plaza's stage, from Howard Keel to Kaye Ballard. Follies themes—from "Flying Down to Rio" to "Tin Pan Alley"*

desert hot springs

A mere twenty minutes north of star-studded Palm Springs is the spa-studded Desert Hot Springs community, which you can access off I-10 at the Palm Drive exit. Thanks to a convergence of geothermal underground water, earthquake faults, the alignment of mountain peaks, and wind and sun energies, this is one of the most captivating spa destinations in the world. For more information, visit www.visitdeserthotsprings.com.

where to go & stay

This boils down to, in thermal mineral talk, a collection of boutique hotels ranging from 6 to 110 rooms, but all having one natural resource in common: healing mineral waters that flow into swimming pools of all shapes and sizes. These hotels, many built in the midcentury, have been renovated and can take you on a magic carpet ride, for example, if you choose to stay at the twelve-room El Morocco Inn & Spa. Or, to make you feel as if you are

and "Get Your Kicks," a tribute to Route 66—are performed eight times a week. Three million people have seen this outrageously inspirational show and keep coming back. If you still appreciate the music of Irving Berlin, George M. Cohan, and George Gershwin, slip back to the past for a few nostalgic hours.

*The third event for day-trippers is actually a weeklong event, but you can easily drive in for the day to attend one of over forty events planned for **Palm Springs Modernism Week** (www.psmodcom.org), where you can turn back time, architecturally speaking, every February. This homage to midcentury architecture will take your breath away! This is especially true if you visit the Elrod House where* Diamonds Are Forever *was filmed in 1971. Designed by John Lautner, this dramatic cliff hanger of a house is where Sean Connery was pitched into a swimming pool by Thumper, one of the famous Bond girls.*

"Modcom events" (Modern Committee, a preservation-oriented group dedicated to promoting and maintaining the heritage of modern architecture and design in Palm Springs and the entire Coachella Valley) defy the imagination, such as the "Vintage Airstream and Trailer Show" at the Ace Hotel & Swim Club. For those born too late to recall, these are the mobile midcentury condos on wheels that hugged those old narrow highways and byways. Also a hit in 2010 was program called "Those Fabulous Foods of the 50s and 60s" and a house tour of Frank Sinatra's Twin Palms estate designed by architect E. Stewart Williams.

in a Switzerland-style spa with Alpine-inspired mural, stay at the eleven-unit Swiss Health Resort. The diversity of these small hotels is impressive, and they attract spa-goers from around the world who flock here for the revitalizing and rejuvenating. In the European tradition a spa cure is a leisurely process, so if you have just a day, the alternative is a day pass.

Cabot's Pueblo Museum. 67616 East Desert View Ave.; (760) 329-7610; www.cabots museum.org. From Los Angeles, exit off I-10 at Palm Drive and go north 5 miles. Turn right on Desert View Avenue and continue 1 mile to the museum (on the corner of Miracle Hill). Once you've dried off from the spa waters, head for this Hopi-style museum that was once the home of Cabot Yerxa, a man of many professions, from architect and artist to world traveler. He used recycled materials to construct this unusual thirty-five-room mansion that was meant to be a tribute to Native Americans. No two rooms, windows, or doors are alike, and to mystify visitors even further there are secret rooms, hiding places, and passages galore! Yerxa is credited with discovering the hot, curative mineral water that became the basis of tourism here in the 1930s.

Today there are tree-covered picnic tables among the sheds, rustic tools, and machinery and, when in bloom, an array of native wildflowers that dazzle the eye. **Cabot's Trading Post & Gallery** opened in February 2008 on-site and is spacious, with four rooms brimming with original photography, pottery, handmade jewelry, and collectibles by local and well-known artists. Open Tues through Sun—call for seasonal schedule and hours of operation.

worth more time

If you've reserved a day trip for "taking the waters," drive no further than the twin spas of **Miracle Springs Resort & Spa** and the **Desert Hot Springs Spa Hotel** (10525 and 10805 Palm Dr.; 760-251-2069; www.Miraclespring.com; and 760-329-6000; www.dhsspa.com). Desert Hot Springs Spa opened in the 1970s and is family friendly with a children's wading pool. Miracle Springs opened in 1996 and has six natural mineral pools, one contour swimming pool, and is known worldwide for naturally flowing hot mineral waters including a spa with an 18-inch depth. The water is crystal clear and rises from aquifers measuring 300-feet deep. The temperature is delivered at a steamy temperature of 140 degrees Fahrenheit and then cooled and pumped into the pools. Enjoy the award-winning cold drinking water throughout the day that originates from the wells penetrating the 900-foot-deep aquifers. Regardless of which pool you select, the views are lovely and the hospitality welcoming. The good news is you can reserve a Special Package in advance and spend the entire day here for under $200! Helen Alexander, director of spa services, recommends the Amethyst Amor (2 hours), which includes a full-body Swedish massage and a Sothy's basic facial. If you have an extra hour, the Tranquil Turquoise adds a pedicure. Can you chill out another hour to make it three? Then go for the Sassy Sapphire and feel totally rejuvenated, as this includes the massage, facial, plus an aromatherapy scrub. If you have even more time, the Opaque Opal (4.5 hours) is slightly more but adds to the combination full-body massage and facial, paraffin body therapy, and the "Spa Essential" manicure and pedicure. There are two full-service restaurants, an excellent spa boutique, plus complete locker room facilities. This is a perfect spa day you won't want to miss at a price you would have trouble finding in Los Angeles!

day trip 03

east

>>> glitz & glamour:
rancho mirage, palm desert

rancho mirage

Rancho Mirage has attracted the rich and famous ever since midcentury millionaires and movie stars established second homes, ranches, and magnificent estates here. Today sprawling resorts, marvelous mountain hiking, private gated neighborhoods, and highly rated golf courses have filled in the vast, once-empty desert spaces. Ambassador and Mrs. Walter H. Annenberg made their home here, calling it Sunnylands. It will open in late 2011 as the Education Center at Sunnylands, with tours, a focus on mid-century architecture, and a spectacular nine-acre garden.

Celebrities have flocked to Rancho Mirage since the golden age of Hollywood; the residential legacies of Lucille Ball, Bob Hope, and Frank Sinatra recall a vintage era of film and television classics. Private and public country clubs are scattered throughout the city and attract major golf tournaments such as the Bob Hope Chrysler Classic and the Kraft Nabisco Women's Professional Golf Championship.

Many streets, all pre-Madonna and Brad Pitt, are named for vintage celebrities such as Frank Sinatra, Dinah Shore, Dean Martin, and Ginger Rogers. President Gerald Ford lived here—and his street intersects with Bob Hope Drive! A rarified collection of posh estates, many of them respected architectural statements, are well protected with security gates. As one would expect, excellent shopping abounds—one a classy shopping center that is actually built around a man-made lake!

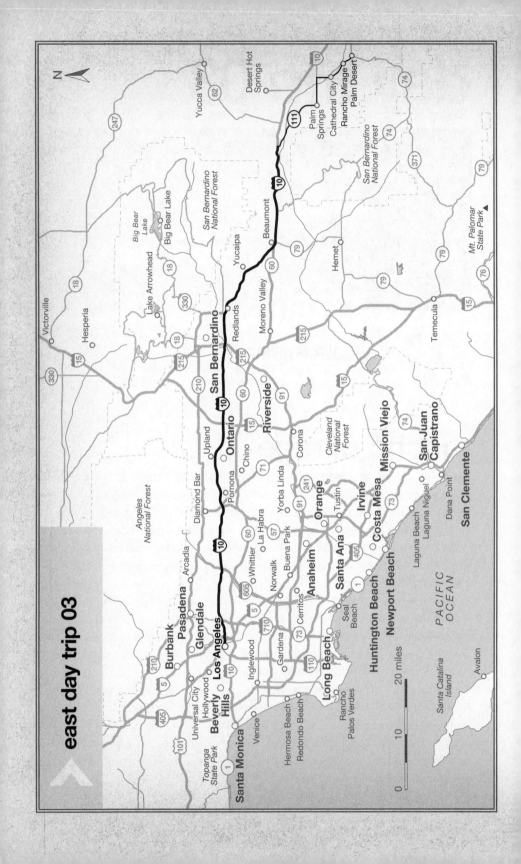

east day trip 03

Rancho Mirage is eye candy with a fusion of Native American and European cultures evident in the architecture, parks, and landscaping. Hosting over a million visitors annually, it is obvious tourism is the leading industry. Snowbirds (seasonal residents) flock here during the "season," which is generally December through May, when a bevy of social and charitable events fill the calendar. The weather is delectable, as are views of the surrounding mountains, framing all those highly rated golf courses. It's perfectly choreographed thanks to the "undergrounding" of nearly all utilities. This means picture-perfect unobstructed views from most vantage points. The city takes pride as the "Oasis of Gracious Living" in the Palm Springs Valley. Visitors enjoy the desert's casual lifestyle. The cachet generated by just mentioning Rancho Mirage adds to the glamour. The bonus of being adjacent to Palm Desert with its own list of activities makes this well worth a day trip.

getting there

The drive from Los Angeles is 120 miles east on I-10; exit at Highway 111 to begin your desert journey through the Coachella Valley. Heading east along Highway 111, first you'll pass through the cities of Palm Springs and Cathedral City, and will eventually arrive at the 24-square-mile oasis of Rancho Mirage (Palm Desert is to the east). A great place to stop and orient yourself is at the Palm Springs Desert Resorts Convention & Visitors Authority office. Not just any building—you can't miss this midcentury architectural statement at 70100 Hwy. 111; (760) 770-9000. Stop by and check out over 250 brochures; there's enough here to keep day trippers on the right track. There's free parking and an exhibit of black and white photographs depicting the desert's bygone days with celebrities galore (also listed in the Regional Information section).

where to go

The Children's Discovery Museum of the Desert. 71-701 Gerald Ford Dr.; (760) 321-0602; www.cdmod.org. This is an absolute must if you are traveling with children. The interactive hands-on exhibits are educational. Parents and kids can make a pretend pizza or dig for Cahuilla Indian treasures, depending what's on display. Open May through Dec from Tues to Sun 10 a.m. to 5 p.m. and Jan through April open 10 a.m. to 5 p.m. Closed Monday.

Tolerance Education Center. 35147 Landy Lane; (760) 328-8252; www.toleranceeducation center.org. A small space (4,000 square feet) with a big message focused on learning the impact of prejudice and intolerance, this is a worthwhile educational experience with access to films, a media room, and revolving exhibitions such as one featuring Polish artist Kalman Aron, who survived seven concentration camps. The Center was founded by Earl Greif, a Holocaust survivor. Open 9 a.m. to 6 p.m. Mon through Fri. Free admission and parking.

where to shop

The River at Rancho Mirage. 71-800 Hwy. 111 at Bob Hope Drive; (760) 341-2711; www .theriveratranchomirage.com. A thirty-acre waterfront entertainment, dining, and shopping center, the River offers a pedestrian-friendly ambience. It is considered the downtown of Rancho Mirage and is anchored by the 3,114-seat Cinemark Century Theater complex. It is the "dinner and a movie" place to go. If the shopping options here are somewhat lacking in originality, it can safely be said that the River features some of the latest desert-inspired fashions for men, women, and children, plus a variety of carts that cater to everyone from accessory divas to dog lovers. Valet parking is available. Call for seasonal hours of operation.

where to eat

Babe's Bar-B-Que Grill & Brewhouse. 71800 Hwy. 111 at the River at Rancho Mirage; (760) 346-8738. Look for the big brass pig at the entrance and then prepare to dine on authentic barbecued ribs that have made this upscale rib joint a landmark. The cobblers are freshly made, and there is a brewery on the premises. Lunch and dinner are served Sun through Thurs 11:30 a.m. to 10 p.m. and Fri through Sat from 11:30 a.m. to 11 p.m. $$.

where to stay

Agua Caliente Casino-Resort-Spa. 32-250 Bob Hope Dr.; (888) 999 1995; www.hot watercasino.com. Native American heritage gets the Las Vegas treatment at this impressive 340-room hotel that has, in addition to a chic Las Vegas–style casino, featured entertainers such as Jay Leno, Melissa Etheridge, Chicago, or Tony Bennett play to a packed house. Reserve in advance. If you are a buffet fan, the Grand Palms Buffet in the casino is the best bet, with stations set up for Italian, Asian, Mexican, and American cuisine; theme nights also are scheduled when lobster and prime rib are on the menu. If you're sensitive to smoke (we are), be aware that smoking is permitted in the casino area since federal nonsmoking regulations do not apply on tribal lands. $$–$$$.

Rancho Las Palmas Resort & Spa. 41-000 Bob Hope Dr.; (760) 568-2727. This lavish 450-room resort sports twenty-one luxury suites and a popular restaurant, the Blu Ember, where outdoor dining with fire pits lights the night and enhances incomparable views of the gardens and mountains. It's pure desert magic. $$$.

The Westin Mission Hills Resort. 71-333 Dinah Shore Dr.; (760) 328-3198; www.westin .com/missionhills. This sprawling 512-room hotel features the Pete Dye Resort Course, which is a full-length 18-hole championship course; another was designed by Gary Player. Guest rooms feature a private terrace or balcony with lovely views. $$$.

heavenly hiking trails are no mirage here

The city of Rancho Mirage offers some of the most popular hiking trails in the Coachella Valley. For a map/brochure with even more details, visit www.relaxrancho mirage.com/how-to-play/hiking_and_cycling.php.

Road Runner Trail *(easy to moderate). This trail begins just past the grassy area in front of the Mirada fountain that is located at the bottom of Frank Sinatra Drive near Highway 111. It moves off the street through a group of palm trees and continues parallel to the road. The trail crosses Frank Sinatra Drive below the currently closed Ritz Carlton hotel and continues south to the hotel entrance driveway.*

Big Horn Overlook Trail *(moderate to steep). The trail is less than ¼ mile in length with several switchbacks. At the top awaits a picnic shelter and an incredible panoramic view.*

Jack Rabbit Trail *(moderate). This trail begins on the east end of the Cancer Survivors Park and goes up into the foothills behind the park towards the Bighorn Overlook. The trail passes the overlook and continues down and parallel to Frank Sinatra Drive. It ends at Frank Sinatra Drive where it merges with the Road Runner Trail and continues up to the hotel.*

palm desert

Continue driving on Highway 111 through Rancho Mirage, and you're in Palm Desert, where 350 days of sunshine puts a glow on everything, from tennis and golf to hiking and biking. The swaying date palms are reminiscent of the Sahara, and they are omnipresent. Thanks to a vibrant Art in Public Places project, an innovative program designed to integrate art and culture throughout the community, you will find original art displayed generously within the 26 square miles of this desert city. Accentuated by modern architecture and over forty-five art galleries, you get the picture: This is a haven for culture vultures. World-class golf and spas amidst luxury resorts and impressive restaurants and shopping make this a magnet for tourists.

where to go

Palm Desert Visitor Center. 73-470 El Paseo; (760) 568-1441 or (800) 873-2428; www.palm-desert.org. Definitely make this the first place to visit. The center is brimming with maps and visitor guides. Located in the midst of El Paseo where art galleries, shopping, and dining dominate the scene, this newly opened office stocks travel brochures, hiking maps and souvenirs. A well-informed staff stands by to help you make the most of your day in Palm Desert.

The Santa Rosa and San Jacinto Mountains National Monument Visitors Center. 51-500 Hwy. 74 (3.25 miles south on Highway 111 at the base of the mountain); (760) 862-9984; www.blm.gov. Established in 2000, plan to spend a leisurely hour at the Monument's Visitor Center where you can get up close and personal with the rugged nature of the desert. Take time to explore the Ed Hastey Interpretive Garden Trail to get a better picture of the fragile ecosystem here. There are free hikes at 9 a.m. on Thurs and Sat year-round. Visitor Center is open Mon through Fri from 8 a.m. to 4:30 p.m. Be sure to call for seasonal hours, special hikes and activities in this vast 272,000-acre enclave.

The McCallum Theatre. 73-000 Fred Waring Dr.; (760) 340-2787; www.mccallumtheatre .org. At this venue you'll find a stellar roster of entertainment ranging from pop and classical to jazz, ballet, and comedy, and performers from Bob Dylan and Michael Feinstein to Lily Tomlin. There's also the Living Legends series including Englebert Humperdinck and Bernadette Peters as well as the Blue Man Group and the Broadway Blockbuster series featuring *Young Frankenstein.* Concerts could mean legendary pianist Andre Watts or a Russian opera; in short, in any given month, there is something for everyone's taste. Parking is plentiful, and there is valet service. Call for current schedule of performances.

where to shop

The Gardens on El Paseo. Located between San Pablo and Larkspur, one block south of Highway 111; (760) 862-1990; www.thegardensonelpaseo.com. The epicenter of El Paseo, which is a mile-long stretch of fine shops and restaurants, is the Gardens on El Paseo, a thriving retail hub sporting Saks Fifth Avenue, Brooks Brothers, Tiffany & Co., Ann Taylor Loft, Williams-Sonoma, Coach, Banana Republic, and more, bolstered by popular restaurants, including Pacifica Seafood Restaurant, Sammy's Woodfired Pizza, and Sullivan's Steakhouse. Tommy Bahamas Restaurant and Bar is on the second level, their boutique on the first. Throughout the season events are staged here, such as Fashion Week El Paseo in March. This is one of Southern California's most sought-after events and brings together fashionistas, boutiques, galleries, and fashion students for a star-studded week of high caliber events.

where to eat

Grill-A-Burger. 73-091 Country Club Dr., Bristol Farms Shopping Center; (760) 346-8170. A burger bonanza for those with a sense of humor. Say it fast, and it sounds like "gorilla burger." With a menu listing specialties such as the Greta Garbo, and "burger fusion" that brings more ingredients into a burger bun than you could imagine, this popular restaurant

> ## palm desert's ultimate open-air fair

Organized by the Alumni Association of the College of the Desert, this is one of the most stupendous open-air markets in the Coachella Valley, and that's due to over 340 vendors offering new merchandise for people, dogs, homes—you name, it's here. It takes place at the **College of the Desert** *at 43-500 Monterey Ave., Palm Desert. Ideal for a day trip, this popular "street fair" (it actually takes place in a parking lot) is open Sat and Sun with free parking, admission, and entertainment! Oct through May the hours are 7 a.m. to 2 p.m., and June through Sept, 7 a.m. to noon, so arrive early enough to spend few leisurely hours strolling this entirely traffic-free bonanza.*

One of the most popular areas is the farmers' market where local farmers sell everything from plump flame raisins to global-sized grapefruit, a specialty of the Coachella Valley. Sun hats, jewelry, arts and crafts, and casual desert fashions take up a lot of space along with designer-influenced eyeglass frames, garden accessories, and handbags of every description. Dog owners will find ventilated jackets for their pups—ideal for the long, hot summers! Locals and tourists like the "value for dollar" attitude and visit year after year. There is a perfect gift here for every pet, child, parent, and grandparent. Surrounded by mountain vistas and palm trees, this weekend event is a desert favorite you won't want to miss.

also serves fabulous french fries in a paper cone. Select from ten sauces to dress the fries and wash it all down with a thick chocolate shake, made the old-fashioned way: You pour it from a cool shake container, just perfect for two. Call for seasonal hours. $$.

Lucky's Cook House. The Village at University Park; 36901 Cook St. at Gerald Ford Drive (Cook Street exit off the I-10); (760) 610-6817. This new, upbeat restaurant keeps their guests smiling with house-made soups, breads, desserts and some tasty slow-cooked entrees. Food is out of the ordinary, from a frisée with caramelized onions and smoked bacon to maple bourbon-cured pork loin chops with sweet potato hash. Sides include roasted and grilled Coachella Valley veggies or cheesy mac. Add to this their state-of-the-art smoker using various woods, from maple and mesquite to cherry and hickory, for spare ribs, and you're cookin! Lucky's opens for dinner nightly at 5 p.m. $$.

where to stay

Desert Springs JW Marriott Resort & Spa. 74-855 Country Club Dr.; (760) 341-2211; www.desertspringsresort.com. Formidable with 884 rooms, this behemoth facility, complete with an 18-hole golf course and a stunning world-class spa, somehow retains a more intimate ambience thanks to the warm hospitality that emanates from a caring staff. There is a fine choice of five restaurants that cater to every taste, from Italian to American cuisine, as well as thirty-six holes of Ted Robinson championship golf, twenty multi-surface tennis courts, seventeen retail shops, a 30,000-square-foot European health spa, fitness center and gym, and waterways entwining nine swimming and whirlpools. Among the many lodging options available in the Palm Desert area, this one stands above the rest. $$$.

Mojave Resort. 73-721 Shadow Mountain Dr.; (760) 346-6121; www.resortmojave.com. For those who prefer a boutique hotel experience, this twenty-three-room hideaway is made to order. The decor is desert chic with a hint of midcentury style. From here, you are within walking distance to El Paseo shops, restaurants and nightlife. A lovely landscaped pool area and a quiet residential location make this a popular desert alternative to those who prefer a low-key yet comfortable setting. $$.

worth more time

The Living Desert. 47-900 Portola Ave., Palm Desert; (760) 346-5694; www.livingdesert .org. It's worth spending the entire day at this 1,200-acre showcase of nature, which has the distinction of being the only American zoo and botanical garden dedicated to the deserts of the world. Scenic hiking trails surround this surreal setting, which features various exhibits for animal admirers of all ages. There are tempting gift shops and a superb cactus garden with many species of desert plants for sale.

If you have at least one full day to indulge in other desert pursuits, spend it here at the Coachella Valley's home to over 450 animals and more than 1,600 varieties of plants native to the world's deserts. Take Highway 111 to Palm Desert and turn south on Portola

hark! more art!

*Art is the scene in Palm Desert with a delightful event you can attend, free of charge. It's called **El Paseo Art Walk** and it happens at twenty museum-quality galleries that stay open until 9 p.m. the first Thurs of each month from Oct to May. A kaleidoscope of visual and decorative arts comes into view as galleries serve complimentary refreshments accentuated by live entertainment. There are free docent-guided art tours of the City of Palm Desert's public art the second Sat of every month, Sept through June. Check it out at (760) 568-5240; www .palmdesertart.org*

the salton sea—saltier than the ocean!

If you're heading south from Rancho Mirage and really want to explore, visit the 35-mile-long **Salton Sea** *(760-564-4888; www.saltonsea.ca.gov), the largest body of water entirely in California and saltier than the ocean. It was formed accidentally between 1905 and 1907 when the Colorado River floodwaters filled the Salton Sink, once an ancient seabed. The sea's surface is 228 feet below sea level and is a popular area for anglers and hunters. Check out the* **Salton Sea National Wildlife Refuge** *and* **Imperial Wildlife Area** *(800-444-7275), where there are viewing stations for "bird's-eye" views of—what else—countless species of birds! According to the U.S. Fish and Wildlife Service, they can identify 295 species here.*

In the **Salton Sea State Recreation Area***, boating and saltwater fishing are the order of the day. Several campsites and nature trails are located around the "sea" shores. Call (800) 444-7274 for camping reservations and learn more details about this unusual park at www.parks.ca.gov. Also worth a visit, the* **Salton Sea History Museum** *at the historic North Shore Yacht Club honors the original architect Albert Frey, the father of midcentury modernism. Call for seasonal hours and events at (760) 393-9222. Discover more at www.saltonseamuseum.org.*

Avenue, go 1.5 miles and follow signs to the main entrance, where you will find plentiful free parking.

Open-air exhibits in this natural setting reveal how diverse the desert can be. An astounding collection of animals ranges from giraffes and bighorn sheep to golden eagles and hawks. You can slither over to the Reptile House where local snakes, lizards, and insects peacefully dwell. Kids of all ages like the Wildlife Wonders Show—a live animal show performed daily, weather permitting. And if you've never been up close to an African crested porcupine or the comical roadrunner (they are part of the desert landscape), you will now have that opportunity. Ostriches? You bet, they found a home here, too! The botanical gardens represent ten different ecosystems, from Madagascar to east Africa and the desert Southwest to Mexico.

Shopping means the Kumbu Kumbu market for African-inspired baskets, bowls, and souvenirs. At the Palo Verde Garden Center, a retail nursery, plants, trees, and shrubs ideal for desert landscaping are displayed and organized so you can easily locate your favorites. The savvy sales team can answer your questions with more than an educated guess. Gardening classes also are scheduled.

Make it a point to visit the Tennity Wildlife Hospital & Conservation Center, a 24,000-square-foot complex that has state-of-the-art facilities capable of caring for the

Living Desert's 400-plus resident animals with the latest technology This center features an interactive experience as visitors are able to witness live and videotaped animal-care procedures in surgery and in the treatment rooms. Vets can interact with visitors via micro-phones, making this an extraordinary opportunity to witness the high level of animal care here. Ask about docent-led tours visiting specific parts of the building that vary according to seasonal activities. Stay longer and explore more as there are hiking trails and enchanting wildflower gardens.

Open daily from Oct 1 through May 31, 9 a.m. to 5 p.m., last admission at 4 p.m. During the summer—June 1 through Sept 30—plan to visit between 8 a.m. and 1 p.m.; hours are shortened because the temperature rises to over 100 degrees Fahrenheit during the summer, making dehydration common. Be sure to bring sunscreen, sunglasses, and comfortable walking shoes for this desert expedition that is safer than the wilds!

day trip 04

east

nature's own rocky road:
joshua tree national park

joshua tree national park

Joshua Tree National Park is a panoply of rock formations, historic sites, and palm oases punctuated by the legendary Joshua trees. Captivating desert flora backed by gorgeous sunsets draws visitors from around the world. Approximately 1.3 million people visited Joshua Tree in 2009. Visitor centers and wayside exhibits, providing opportunities to acquaint you with park resources, are located along main roads leading into and through the park.

getting there

Joshua Tree National Park lies 140 miles east of Los Angeles and less than an hour north of Palm Springs. Head east from Los Angeles and position yourself on the I-10 not much after 6 a.m. in order to avoid the morning traffic. Joshua Tree National Park's Visitor Center is open from 8 a.m. to 5 p.m., and admission is $15 per vehicle. There are three entrances to Joshua Tree National Park: The first is accessed via Route 62 by turning right on Park Drive in Joshua Tree. The second requires you to continue on Route 62 to Joshua Tree National Park, which takes you to the Oasis Visitor Center, featuring exhibits and the information center for interpretive guided tours. If you miss the Route 62 exit, slow down and don't panic, just continue on the I-10 to the last entrance, exit 197 (Cottonwood). Drive any further and you'll end up at the Arizona state line, missing one of the most extraordinary national parks in the United States.

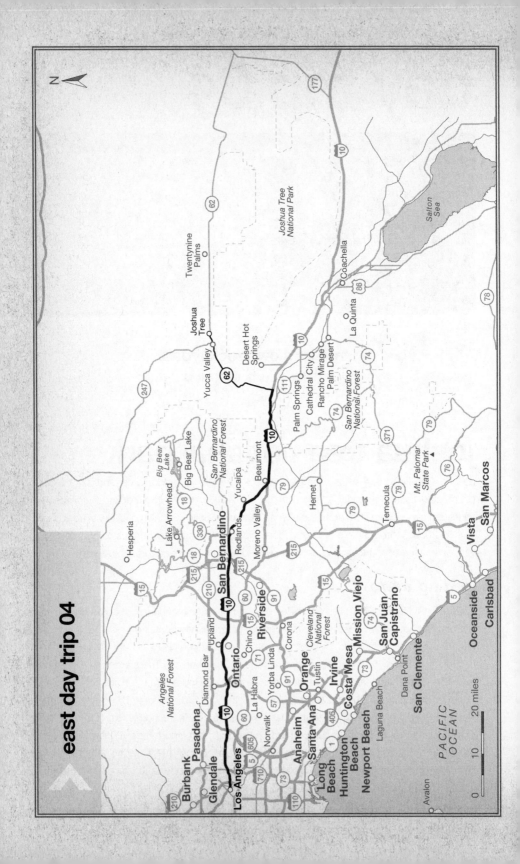

east day trip 04

> ## daunted by the drive?

The drive between Los Angeles and Joshua Tree is 138 miles, around 2 hours if you avoid the challenging traffic on I-10 during those dreaded rush hours (6 to 9 a.m. and 3 to 7 p.m.). There is a carpool lane requiring two or three passengers, depending on the time of day. If the delights of California's desert landscape beguile you, there are several esoteric inns that cater to those who resist the temptation of corporate hotels and their brand of hospitality. In other words, you aren't going to garnish any frequent-traveler points at the often idiosyncratic hotels and offbeat cafes along Historic Route 62. I have yet to see a parking valet around these parts or even a curb for your car to park against . . . giddy-up! If the prospect of visiting the park is daunting, consider driving to Palm Springs and meeting your guide at the Palm Springs Visitor Center on Highway 111 and boarding a Hummer for a personalized tour with Elite Land Tours (800-514-4866; www.elitelandtours.com); the Hummers seat up to five plus a guide. Elite's savvy guides can take you on a 3-hour (or longer) trip with stops along the way and provide an interpretive tour with insider intel you might never otherwise know. There are several stops and plenty of organic snacks along the route. Trip Advisor.com rated Elite first place for tours.

__Precautions for driving in the desert:__ The weather can change drastically in a matter of minutes, from an unexpected flash flood to extreme drops in temperature. Wear appropriate clothing and dress in layers to accommodate changing weather patterns. Wear good walking shoes or boots, protect your eyes with sunglasses, use sunscreen, and take food if you are planning to spend the day and skip dining at a restaurant. Bring your maps, a compass, and a first-aid kit. Your cell phone should be charged, and there are some areas where you may not be able to make or receive calls. Don't stray from your fellow travelers and make sure you have a full tank of gas to avoid being stranded if you wander too far off the beaten path.

where to go

Joshua Tree National Park is a destination in itself. Ansel Adams, the famous nature photographer, got it right when he praised the "sanity of nature," which gives you an idea of the majesty and simplicity of this revered national park. At an altitude of 3,000 feet, Joshua Tree National Park is known around these parts as the "high desert," which accounts for the temperature being about 10 degrees cooler than the lower desert communities in summer and 20 degrees warmer in the winter compared to the mountain communities. **Historic Route 62** (also known as the Twentynine Palms Highway) is a magical mystery tour in itself. This is an impeccably maintained highway that brings you to the two main entrances. This stretch of road gives you a bird's-eye view of the desert terrain that makes this journey one to remember, with the legendary Joshua trees (*Yucca brevifolia*) at center stage. As one road warrior said it best, "Value the journey as much as the destination."

Make a stop at the **California Welcome Center** (56711 Twentynine Palms Hwy.; 760-365-5464), approximately 19 miles off I-10 on Historic Route 62. You will pass through the communities of the **Morongo Basin,** a story unto themselves. Look for dots on the map such as **Surprise Valley, Windy Gap, Flamingo Heights,** and a place that turns back the pages of time to the Wild West, **Pioneertown.** Leave your designer labels in your suitcase, because this is cowboy country where stiletto heels have no place! A vintage community founded in 1946, Pioneertown is sequestered between the rocky peaks of the Sawtooth Range at an altitude of 4,000 feet. Does it look familiar? Several classic American movies were filmed here, such as *Gunfight at the O.K. Corral* (1954), for those who remember this vintage cowboy movie.

Look to your left and right while driving on Historic Route 62 and take in the breathtaking views of those inimitable and ancient Joshua trees found only in California, Arizona, Nevada, and Utah. They grow proudly and free on either side of Historic Route 62 and are protected and treasured in these parts, and honored in paintings, sculptures, and photographs. Look for art galleries, coffee shops, and thrift shops on either side of Route 62 selling everything from cactus creations to vintage jewelry, so prepare to make a few stops.

Historic Route 62 takes you to the city of Twentynine Palms where you can't miss the twenty or more murals depicting the area's history, flora, and fauna. They can be viewed on the exterior walls of commercial buildings, and each tells a distinctive story about this fascinating corner of the high desert. Eventually, if you turn left on Adobe Road, you reach the gates of the **United States Marine Corps Air Ground Combat Center,** the world's largest Marine Corps training base, which occupies 935 square miles and is home to approximately 12,000 active-duty marines, sailors, and soldiers—so if you hear a loud boom, take it in stride. Since your destination is the park, turn right, because that will take you on Utah Drive to the Joshua Tree National Park entrance.

The city of **Joshua Tree** is a blast to the past: population around 10,000, it comprises 96 square miles, and many of the roads are still unpaved, adding to the charm of hidden treasures that lurk off road. Homesteaders arrived here in 1911, and the West Park entrance marks the area where the Townsite Company built offices along Twentynine Palms Road nearly one hundred years ago.

If you are captivated by unusual rock formations, desert sunsets, and sweeping views, the two distinct deserts that comprise the national park's 794,000 acres will mesmerize you. First, the northwestern area of the park is in the **Mojave Desert,** a surreal area known for Joshua trees and granite rock formations. The southeastern part is a different story: This is the lower, hotter **Colorado Desert,** which is recognized as California's portion of the Sonoran Desert. You can visit both areas providing you arrive early, since there is a lot of territory to cover in one day.

when to go

The spring and fall transform the desert into a canvas of sight and sound that has inspired generations of artists and photographers. The vast open spaces and changing colors of the formations of the juxtaposed jagged and smooth rocks are a sight to behold. Stargazing here is an experience you will savor, thanks to the clear, bright skies. You will see how Mother Nature works when a light snow blankets the higher Mojave Desert, providing precious moisture for spring wildflowers. The interaction of the altitude, rainfall, and crystal clear skies is pure magic. It's one of the reasons so many tourists flock here year after year.

heaven for hikers and rock climbers

Look for the self-guided nature trails where you can get up close and personal with the desert plant and animal life, leaving ample time for the longer trails that lead to the mining sites and rocky canyons. If you've arrived with mountain bikes or a four-wheel-drive vehicle, study the extensive network of dirt roads in advance. If you are truly turned on to the countless nooks and crannies crying out to be traversed, consider the campgrounds that operate on a first-come, first-served basis. Call (800) 365-226 or try www.recreation .gov and spend a few nights under the stars at a site such as the Black Rock or Indian Cove Campgrounds.

for serious students of the desert

If you do your homework in advance, you can take one of the fascinating classes offered by the **Desert Institute** *(www.joshuatree.org); the University of California even accredits selected courses. Classes are limited to twenty or fewer students and taught by experts in their field. During the spring the wildflowers are at their peak performance, presenting the ideal time to sign on for one of the Institute's classes.*

*The **Desert Queen Ranch,** a historic ranch used for mining and milling operations that has been left in a state of "arrested decay," resembles a scene from that vintage television program* The Twilight Zone. *You can see it on a ranger-led walk by checking the park's schedule. The ranch has been abandoned, but the relics are strewn here and there to give you an idea of what family life was like in this desolate part of the desert.*

where to eat

There are several casual cafes and coffee shops on Twentynine Palms Highway in the communities of Joshua Tree and Twentynine Palms aside from the McDonald's, Taco Bell, Del Taco, Burger King, and predictable fast-food outlets. Here are some locally operated restaurants we enjoy in these parts.

Bistro Twenty Nine. 73527 Twentynine Palms Hwy., Twentynine Palms; (760) 361-2229; www.bistrotwentynine.com. This restaurant has a menu featuring steaks, seafood, chicken, salads, and specialties such as Key Lime Shrimp. The ambience is rather chic and offers some of the finest dining in the area. The wine list is impressive. Open 5 to 9 p.m. Tues through Thurs; 5 to10 p.m. Fri and Sat; closed Sun and Mon. $$$.

Country Kitchen. 61768 Twentynine Palms Hwy., Joshua Tree; (760) 366-8988; www .joshuatreevillage.com/523/523.htm. Look for the American flag and enjoy real home-cooked comfort food, from burgers to milk shakes. The entrance to Joshua Tree National Park is across the highway. Open daily from 6 a.m. to 3:30 p.m. Breakfast and lunch served all day. $.

Pappy & Harriet's. 53688 Pioneertown Rd., Pioneertown; (760) 365-5956; www.pappy andharriets.com. No reserved tables here! This is the meeting place for local desert denizens and lovers of live country western music, plates of fried chicken, and plenty of beer on tap. Established in 1972, they serve up great food entertainment Thurs through Sun 11 a.m. to 2 a.m. Local characters looking like vintage cowboys are often sitting around. There's so much going on here with dinners and western entertainment that a monthly schedule is published. $.

The Rib Co. 72183 Twentynine Palms Hwy., Twentynine Palms; (760) 367-1663; www .theribco.com. Baby back ribs crowned by house-made Jack Daniel's barbecue sauce are hard to resist. Their Exotic Sampler appetizer features kangaroo, alligator, and rattlesnake—no kidding! Serving dinner nightly, call for seasonal hours. $$.

Ricochet. 61705 Twentynine Palms Hwy., Joshua Tree; (760) 366-1898; www.ricochet joshuatree.com. If you've heard about their Cowgirl Creamery Cheeses, that's just the beginning. For local flavor try their Friday and Saturday special: Ginger Sweet Potato Waffles. For a road snack, get a sack of Bella's lemon blueberry muffins. Call for seasonal hours of operation; generally open at 7:30 a.m. $.

where to stay

The Moon Way Lodge. 5444 Moon Way in Wonder Valley, Twentynine Palms; (760) 835-9369; www.moonwaylodge.com. Ten minutes past the Joshua Tree National Park entrance on Route 62, you'll discover Wonder Valley. You will pass a small private airport (that looks like the last plane that landed here was piloted by Waldo Pepper fifty years ago). Where else would you find a museum called the Beauty Bubble, displaying beauty salon memorabilia dating to the first bobby pin and hairnet? Look around the corner from the beauty salon manned by one stylist, Jeff Hafler, and there you find an old prospector's shack transformed into a museum of vintage beauty salon memories (read: 5,000-plus artifacts), from an original baby blue Schick portable hair dryer to marvelous ads of vintage movie stars showing off their chic pageboys and "bubbles" (for those not old enough to recall, that was a midcentury hairdo!) or other raving beauties endorsing shampoos that are a mere faded memory today (remember White Rain?). There are two lovely cottages on this twelve-acre ranch adjacent to a swimming pool with 360-degree views of the Mojave Desert making this truly a "wonder" full place to spend a night in the heights of the high desert. $$–$$$.

Roughly Manor Bed and Breakfast Inn. 74744 Joe Davis Dr., Twentynine Palms; (760) 367-3238; www.roughlymanor.com. This impressive stone home built by one of area's first families is about as quiet a place as you will find near the park entrance. The Manor has two guest suites, each with its own private bath and sitting room. There are five fireplaces throughout the house, including one in each of the two suites. Historic photos and antiques bring back yesteryear. $$–$$$.

Sacred Sands. 63155 Quail Springs Rd., Joshua Tree; (760) 424 6407; www.sacredsands .com. The two-suite luxury bed-and-breakfast at the park entrance is the epitome of high desert "southwestern style" design and western-style hospitality. The desert views are spectacular and so are the luxurious linens and other fine touches that make this hideaway one of a kind—in a straw-bale home, no less. Gourmet breakfasts are innovative, healthy and delicious. $$$.

Spin and Margie's Desert Hide-A-Way. Joshua Tree, off Route 62, and ten minutes from Joshua Tree National Park; (760) 366-9124; www.deserthideaway.com. More of a hacienda with five suites within an enclosed courtyard, this is one of the most artistic boutique inns of the high desert, with a laundry list of amenities from a morning breakfast basket and stunning tiled bathrooms to portable gas grills. Hidden off a quiet side road reached via the 29 Palms Highway in Joshua Tree, this spot is chockablock with desert memorabilia. $$.

The 29 Palms Inn. 73950 Inn Ave., Twentynine Palms; (760) 367-3505; www.29palmsinn .com. This historic property has been welcoming guests to the high desert since 1928. Instead of boring hotel corridors, guests walk along sandy paths. The starlit sky will guide you to your comfortable, spacious adobe. Tour the grape arbor and fruit and vegetable gardens while as you pass frisky roadrunners, Gambel's quails, and jackrabbits along the way. Breakfast, lunch, and dinner feature fresh ingredients served daily. This is a popular place for locals as well as tourists from around the world. Try to reserve a room on Fri and Sat nights when there is entertainment; it's a classic! $$.

worth more time

Gubler Orchids. 2200 Belfield Blvd., Landers; (760) 364-2282; www.gublers.com. If you are fascinated by Joshua trees, you will be beguiled by the diversity of orchids at one of the nation's largest orchid farms, covering 50,000 square feet in the middle of the Mojave Desert! It's worth the trip just to take the 45-minute tour that reveals the diversity of the orchid world. To be precise, Gubler's showcases over 5,000 orchid hybrids in a spectacular display of color. It's all waiting for you at this rather off-the-beaten-path orchid oasis in Landers, which is reached from the I-10; exit at Route 62, north to Route 247; turn east on Reche Road and north on Belfield Boulevard. Just follow the signs! Don't worry about parking; you are somewhat in the middle of nowhere—until you feast your eyes upon some of most exquisite orchids imaginable! You've come a long way to reach this orchid extravaganza; if you bring lunch you can set out a picnic as there are indoor and outdoor picnic areas. Gubler's ships orchids throughout the world, and having established their orchid paradise here in 1975 has brought hundreds of tourists to their growing grounds. Check out their gift shop for orchid postcards, calendars, shirts, and keepsakes. Call in advance to confirm your participation on the free tours Mon through Sat 10 a.m. to 3:30 p.m. Closed Sun and major holidays.

southeast

day trip 01

southeast

**the happiest place on planet
southern california:**
anaheim and disneyland

anaheim and disneyland

Almost two centuries before Walt Disney opened his Magic Kingdom in Anaheim in 1955, Spanish explorer Gaspar de Portolá found a majestic river bringing life to a fertile valley and fields that led to the Pacific Ocean in 1769. He claimed it for Spain and named it Santa Ana. Flash forward to 1857, when German immigrants started buying farming tracts for $2 an acre and began calling their new settlement Anaheim ("home on the Ana"). With cuttings from their native Bavaria, the settlers began growing California's first grapes and making wine. In the late 1880s, the vineyards in Anaheim were devastated by blight, so the settlers decided to plant oranges and other fruits and nuts instead, creating the current moniker of Orange County. Today's fastest-growing crops in the Anaheim area are not oranges but amusement parks, sports attractions, and a galaxy of animated stars from Disney—all ready and waiting for the picking by you and your entourage. Make your first foray into Orange County at "Uncle Walt's place"—the unparalleled Disneyland Resort, which includes the original Disneyland, Disney's California Adventure, and the Downtown Disney District.

getting there

From Los Angeles, drive southeast about 25 miles on I-5 (locally known as the Santa Ana Freeway) to the city of Anaheim and its environs. Exit at Disneyland Drive (exit 110), and turn left (south). For Disney's California Adventure Park and Disneyland Park, proceed across

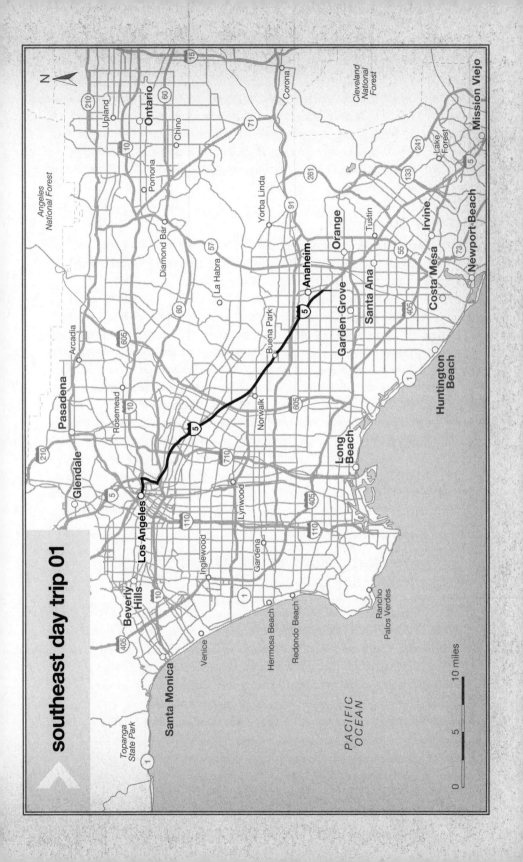

Ball Road and use the three left lanes to access the Mickey & Friends parking structure. For car-free access from Los Angeles Union Station, take Amtrak's Pacific Surfliner or Metrolink commuter trains directly to the Anaheim train station located at 2150 East Katella Ave., less than 3 miles east of Disneyland on the north side of the Angel Stadium parking lot and across from the Honda Center. Orange County Transportation Authority bus routes connect to the station, as does Anaheim Resort Transit.

where to go

Disneyland Park. 1313 Harbor Blvd. at the intersection of I-5; (714) 781-4565; www.disney land.com. Park hours are subject to change, so be sure to call ahead for exact opening and closing times on your preferred days to avoid disappointment.

Since July 17, 1955, the magic of Disneyland has existed in themed lands. With eight lands to explore, featuring sixty major attractions, fifty shops, and thirty restaurants, it can be quite daunting! Begin on **Main Street USA,** a composite of America in the 1900s. Move along to **Adventureland,** housing Tarzan's Treehouse, the Indiana Jones Adventure (one of our favorites), the Jungle Cruise, and the Enchanted Tiki Room (a good place we found to sit in a cool room for 20 minutes for the animated show). **New Orleans Square** features the classic Pirates of the Caribbean and Haunted Mansion. **Critter Country** has the wettest ride—Splash Mountain—and Many Adventures of Winnie-the-Pooh. **Fantasyland** is high-lighted by the Disney Princess Fantasy Faire (complete with options to dress up and meet royalty), Sleeping Beauty's Castle, King Arthur's Carousel, Mr. Toad's Wild Ride, Peter Pan's Flight, and the breathtaking Matterhorn Bobsleds. Next comes **Frontierland,** with the Big Thunder Mountain mine ride, and the chances to cruise on the Mark Twain Riverboat or the

anaheim resort transit—the hassle-free way to navigate the kingdom!

To navigate the Anaheim Resort Aea and avoid parking fees and traffic (and reduce air pollution), get on board ART (714-563-5287; www.rideART.org.), a sixteen-route transportation system using zero-emission electric buses and clean-fuel propane trolleys. Be sure to purchase an ART pass before you get on the bus (or you'll be charged the one-way cash fee onboard). There are convenient ticketing kiosks that accept major credit cards at all the stops, and you can also purchase online. The routes run to/from Disneyland Resort Transit Plaza/Main Entrance about every 15 to 20 minutes from all major hotels, the Honda Center, Angel Stadium, Anaheim Garden Walk, and the Amtrak/Metrolink Railway station—giving you a complete car-free option to arriving at the Magic Kingdom.

Sailing Ship Columbia around Tom Sawyer's Island. The *Fantasmic!* special-effects show is presented nightly each summer and on weekends. **Mickey's Toontown** is base camp for all your young ones' favorite Disney characters. See Mickey's and Minnie's residences and Goofy's Bounce House, and ride Roger Rabbit's Car Toon Spin and Gadget's Go Coaster. **Tomorrowland** is the launching pad for space-age attractions. Here you will thrill to classics such as Star Tours and Space Mountain, plus the Astro Orbitor, 3-D Honey I Shrunk the Audience, Buzz Lightyear Astro Blasters, and the Finding Nemo Submarine Voyage. The Disneyland Monorail, once the coolest ride in Tomorrowland, now just runs back and forth from Downtown Disney instead of around the park. The steam-engine Disneyland Railroad still circumnavigates the park with stops at various lands. We recommend you take the full 20-minute circuit for a calming respite from all the excitement!

Disney's California Adventure Park. 1313 Harbor Blvd. at the intersection of I-5; (714) 781-4565; www.disneyland.com. Hours are subject to change; call ahead for exact opening and closing times on your preferred days to visit. Admission fees are also subject to change. Many special packages and promotions are offered throughout the year.

Opened in Feb 2001 and continually adding new rides and shows, this fifty-five-acre theme park celebrates the great state of California—from Disney's imaginative perspective. You'll enter the park from the promenade area under a replica of San Francisco's Golden Gate Bridge into the Sunshine Plaza fountain area to explore four distinct lands.

Paradise Pier re-creates a beachfront amusement zone reminiscent of Santa Monica Pier or the Santa Cruz Boardwalk. Check out California Screamin'—a superfast steel roller coaster that loops you upside down around a Mickey Mouse–head icon. The interactive attraction Toy Story Mania is awesome. The 150-foot Sun Wheel Ferris wheel, Orange Stinger, Maliboomer, Mulholland Madness minicoaster, and King Triton's Carousel get fun points here, too, along with plenty of concessions and food vendors along the midway.

The second land, dubbed the **Hollywood Pictures Backlot,** has huge soundstages that hold attractions such as *Jim Henson's Muppet Vision 3-D* movie; Hyperion Theater's live hip musical/dance performances; and the Animation Center, featuring "Turtle Talk with Crush," the surfer-dude turtle from the movie *Finding Nemo.* The Twilight Zone Tower of Terror drops you thirteen stories faster than the speed of gravity (do not eat before this one, really!). Monsters, Inc.: Mike and Sully to the Rescue is another 3-D attraction that re-creates the streets of Monstropolis from the animated film. At the live show *Playhouse Disney*, kids can sing and dance along with the fun characters on stage (it's seating on the floor for 550 guests, and it gets pretty animated!).

The **Golden State** features the must-do Soarin' Over California experience, where you will hang with feet dangling as you fly like an eagle—virtually—around an 80-foot dome-shaped motion-picture screen filled with an amazing view of the best California scenery. Don't miss Grizzly River Run, a whitewater-rafting ride that swirls you down two waterfalls (and you will get wet); Bountiful Valley Farm with its demonstration veggie and fruit gardens; a working vineyard and winery complete with wine tasting options; Pacific Wharf, where you can watch Boudin's Bakery make sourdough bread and Mission-brand tortillas pop out of the bakery lines.

A Bug's Land is a fourth area including attractions inside Flik's Fun Fair. Plenty of food and beverage options abound throughout the entire park, and be prepared to spend some gold nuggets to enjoy the diverse range of fare, ranging from traditional burgers, dogs, and fries to sushi, chowder, pizza, and Chinese and Mexican cuisine. Disney's California Adventure certainly embraces Walt's original promise: "Disneyland will never be complete as long as there is imagination left in the world."

where to shop

Anaheim GardenWalk. 321 West Katella Ave. at Clementine Street, just east of Harbor Boulevard and within easy walking distance of the Disneyland Resort; (714) 635-7400; www.anaheimgardenwalk.com. First opened in 2008, this is a 440,000-square-foot outdoor shopping and dining experience set among beautifully manicured walkways and gardens. Enjoy everything from an upscale bowling lounge called 300; a fourteen-plex theater; and various establishments including Aveda, Banana Republic, Bar Louie, Chico's, Harley Davidson, Heat Ultra Lounge, White House/Black Market and XP Sports; to restaurants such as Bubba Gump Shrimp Company, California Pizza Kitchen, The Cheesecake Factory, McCormick & Schmick's Grille, P. F. Chang's China Bistro, and Roy's (Hawaiian fusion cuisine). More open every year. Open 11 a.m. to 9 p.m. daily, restaurants and nightclubs with extended hours.

cultural infusion

MUZEO. 241 South Anaheim Blvd.; (714) 956-8936; www.muzeo.org. Opened in 2007, this new model for urban cultural centers features a unique variety of changing exhibitions, special events, lectures, classes, and weekend festivals. MUZEO explores and celebrates diverse heritages, cultures, and arts through creative programming—for example, in 2010, the center offered "State of the Blues: The Living Legend of the Delta"; "Frogs: A Chorus of Colors," featuring 15 live frog habitats; and "The Holy Art of Imperial Russia: Icons from the 17th Century to the Early 20th Century." The 25,000-square-foot MUZEO complex encompasses Anaheim's original Carnegie Library (built in 1908) and a new state-of-the-art gallery space surrounded by two connecting courtyards, apartment loft living, and street-level retail outlets. Open 10 a.m. to 5 p.m. daily except holidays. Call for times and admission fees.

Downtown Disney District. (714) 300-7800; www.disneyland.com. This twenty-acre dining, shopping, and entertainment area is located precisely between Disneyland and Disney's California Adventure Parks, and encircles the three official Disneyland Resort hotels. The district is free and open to the public year-round. It features lovely landscaped gardens and promenades interspersed with 300,000 square feet of retail shops, restaurants, and twelve AMC movie theaters. Highlights include House of Blues Stage with live entertainment; ESPN Zone Restaurant, where you can catch the latest sports, dine on classic American foods, sip on ice-cold beverages, play video games, and more; Tortilla Jo's—a traditional Mexican restaurant with fresh favorites and live mariachi performances; plus plenty of other gift, souvenir, music, jewelry, and fashion emporiums.

where to eat

Within the Disneyland Resort area, there are hundreds of eating places to satisfy your every appetite. Here are a just a couple of our favorites.

Disney's PCH Grill at Disney's Paradise Pier Hotel. 1717 Disneyland Dr.; (714) 999-0990. PCH stands for Pacific Coast Highway, California's prime and celebrated coastal route. Dining in the PCH Grill for lunch and dinner celebrates all the foods and beverages that make up California cuisine. Menu maps plot your meal, course by course, and feature fresh seafood, pastas, oak-fired pizzas, burgers, and desserts. Open daily for breakfast, lunch, and dinner. Hours vary seasonally. $$$.

Goofy's Kitchen at the Disneyland Hotel. 1150 Magic Way; (714) 778-6600. Your kids, or the kid in you, will not want to miss Goofy's, one of the nine restaurants at the original Disneyland Hotel. You can dine with Disney characters (and get your picture taken), eat Disney character meals, try out the all-you-can-eat buffet, and receive a free souvenir button. Open every day—breakfast, lunch, and dinner. Call for specific hours as they vary seasonally. $$.

where to stay

Disney's Grand Californian Hotel & Spa. 1600 South Disneyland Dr.; (714) 635-2300; www.disneyland.com. Opened in February 2001, this luxurious AAA four-diamond-rated 745-room hotel with its striking California Craftsman architectural design is located on the northwest corner of Disney's California Adventure. This hotel is the only one to offer direct access straight into the park, a wonderful time-saving feature. From the moment you arrive (and are offered valet parking), you are treated with outstanding hospitality and service. Hotel dining options include 24-hour room service, the excellent Storyteller's Cafe with its tasty breakfast buffet and American cuisine for lunch and dinner daily (and visits from Disney characters such as Chip 'n' Dale), the stunning Napa Rose Restaurant (with an open exhibition kitchen), Hearthstone Lounge, and White Water Snacks poolside. Guest rooms come equipped with a choice of king, two queens, or a queen and a set of bunk beds—perfect if

doing disneyland without getting done in

It's practically impossible to do everything in one day; even one overnight and two full days can be very tricky, depending on your stamina. With three attractions—the original Disneyland (opened 1955), Disney's California Adventure, and the Downtown Disney District (both opened in 2001)—this trip can be a visual and physical overload for you and yours. We strongly advise a minimum two-night stay and three days to really enjoy everything. For first-timers, begin with the original Disneyland early in the day. Take a short break midday for lunch and probably a nap, and then return for the afternoon and evening shows (such as the fireworks over the Magic Castle). You'll need a second full day to really explore DCA (Disney's California Adventure) because many of the activities are live stage shows and movies presented at specific times. On the third day, revisit favorite attractions at either park or get in some shopping and dining or a movie at Downtown Disney. Always check park operating hours and plan your visit around a reasonable eat-sleep schedule. The best time-saving option is the FASTPASS, a computerized ticketing system that allows you to reserve a time slot for the most popular rides. When you arrive at your designated time period with your computer-generated pass, you'll go to a special line and get on within minutes. Highly recommended!

you've got the kids along! The concierge level offers extra amenities including complimentary continental breakfast and evening wine and cheese. Kick back at the Fountain Pool, or the Redwood Pool with a waterslide. The Mandara Spa provides some precious pampering and personal service. We really like this luxurious property and feel the higher room rates are justified given the ease of park accessibility combined with the outstanding amenities and service. $$$.

Disneyland Hotel. 1150 Magic Way; (714) 778-6600, reservations at (714) 956-6400; www.disneyland.com. Just west of Disneyland and connected by the futuristic Monorail, this hotel opened at the same time as the park in 1955 and has continued to evolve. This hotel is a destination within itself, and you should plan some time to enjoy all the amenities. It features 990 guest rooms and suites in three high-rise towers, including nineteen guest rooms that are highly themed to either Mickey Mouse or the regal Disney princesses. These Character Quarters each feature two twin beds and are available adjoining a standard room. They are perfect for a family. (Of course, advance reservations are required for these high-demand lodgings.) Surrounding the magical Peter Pan–themed Neverland pool complex (with water slides, bridges, and shallow play areas), there is a sandy beach with rental pedal boats, remote-control tugboats, and dune buggies. There are nine restaurants and lounges to choose from, plus four swimming pools, a hot tub, the Team Mickey Fitness Center, gift shops, and an eighty-game video arcade. Value-priced hotel and park package plans are prevalent and include early admission into both parks 1.5 hours before the regular opening; be sure to ask what's available when making reservations. Another great service is the Package Express, which delivers all your park purchases to your hotel room for free. $$–$$$.

Disney's Paradise Pier Hotel. 1717 Disneyland Dr.; (714) 999-0990 or reservations at (714) 956-6400; www.disneyland.com. This fifteen-story, full-service hotel overlooks the festive Paradise Pier area at Disney's California Adventure. Choose from 489 nicely furnished guest rooms and suites. There are four restaurants and lounges, an outdoor pool and spa deck, a game arcade, convenient indoor/outdoor parking, and gift shops. $$–$$$.

worth more time

Angel Stadium of Anaheim. 2000 Gene Autry Way; (714) 940-2000; www.angelsbaseball .com. This 45,000-seat stadium is home to Major League Baseball's Los Angeles Angels of Anaheim. Call for current schedule, tickets, and promotions.

Honda Center. 2695 East Katella Ave.; (714) 704-2400; www.hondacenter.com. Formerly known as Arrowhead Pond, this 18,900-seat enclosed arena—ranked the number-three entertainment venue in the world by *Billboard* magazine—hosts many events and concerts and is home to the National Hockey League's Stanley Cup champion Anaheim Ducks, who skate from Oct through Apr (714-704-2000; www.AnaheimDucks.com). Call for ticket prices and schedules.

day trip 02

southeast

ahoy families:
buena park

buena park

Northeast of Anaheim and Disneyland, Buena Park is another Orange County city for multifaceted family adventures with some one-of-a-kind attractions. Buena Park's entertainment district, known as the E-Zone and located along Beach Boulevard, is home to several globally popular tourist destinations including Pirate's Dinner Adventure, Medieval Times dinner and tournament show, and "America's first amusement park"—Knott's Berry Farm—and its sister water park, Knott's Soak City. There are no knights in shining armor in Buena Park's history. Founded in 1887, its roots were in agriculture (particularly dairy, wine, and fruit products) that blossomed with the development of the railroad at the end of the nineteenth century. The derivation of Buena Park's name is still a subject of conjecture, but the local historical society believes it relates to an artesian well and its parklike grounds that were once located at the modern-day intersection of Artesia and Beach Boulevards. Early Spanish settlers referred to the area as Plaza Buena, which translated into English means "good park."

Buena Park's twentieth-century development began in 1920, when Walter and Cordelia Knott and their three young children arrived and started farming on twenty acres of leased land. The Knotts set up a roadside produce stand on Beach Boulevard to sell their farm crops, and in 1932 Walter Knott started propagating a cross blend of raspberry, blackberry, and loganberry plants that he named boysenberry. In 1934, to help make ends

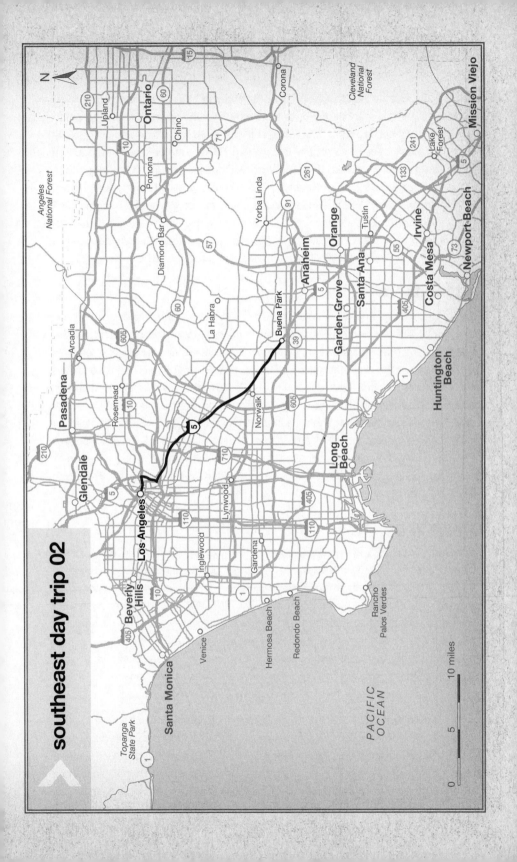

meet during the Great Depression, Cordelia Knott began serving chicken dinners on her wedding china to passing Beach Boulevard motorists for 65 cents. Very quickly, Knott's Berry Farm's boysenberry fruits, jams, jellies, and pies, along with Cordelia Knott's Chicken Dinner Restaurant, became so popular that the family decided to build something to keep all the waiting patrons amused. In 1940, Walter Knott began moving old buildings to his farm site to create a Ghost Town history display. The Calico Mine Ride followed in 1960, and a re-creation of Philadelphia's Independence Hall was constructed in 1966. In 1968, Knott's "amusement park" area was enclosed, and for the first time a general admission fee was charged. Knott's Berry Farm still forms the seed of many attractions in this commercial section of Orange County. We'll bet you all have a "berry good" time here!

getting there

From downtown Los Angeles, carefully drive perennially busy and congested I-5 (locally known as the Santa Ana Freeway) southeast for about 23 miles to the Beach Boulevard (SR 39) exit and head south toward the E-Zone. You can also take a Metrolink commuter train from Los Angeles Union Station to Buena Park (800-371-5465 for schedules and fares; www.metrolinktrains.com). Upon arrival at Buena Park's Metrolink station at 8400 Lakeknoll Dr. at Dale Street, take the Orange County Transportation Authority number 29 bus south to Beach Boulevard. (For fares and schedules visit www.octa.net). Since most hotels, restaurants, and attractions are within a short walk of each other in the E-Zone; it's possible to explore Buena Park without a car. Plus, if you're staying overnight in Buena Park, most major hotels operate a complimentary shuttle to and from Disneyland, Knott's Berry Farm, and Buena Park Mall.

where to go

Adventure City. 1238 Beach Blvd., between Cerritos Avenue and Ball Road, on the outskirts of Buena Park near Anaheim; (714) 236-9300; www.adventurecity.com. Adventure City, "the Little Theme Park That's Big on Family Fun," resembles a storybook village designed and proportioned for children ages two to twelve. For a wonderfully relaxing experience, consider visiting this two-acre park with its seventeen kid-size rides that are quiet yet still zoom and thrill, as well as hourly puppet shows, a 25-foot climbing wall, live theater, storytelling, and face painting. Parent-child interaction is made easy here because the atmosphere is very casual and low-hype. There are plenty of park benches for parental units to sit and relax on while the kids brave the Kid Coaster or the carousel.

Knott's Berry Farm. 8039 Beach Blvd. at the corner of La Palma Avenue; (714) 220-5200; www.knotts.com. Knott's Berry Farm was family owned and operated until its friendly purchase by Cedar Fair Entertainment Company back in 1997. It attracts more than five million guests each year to its entertainment park and marketplace, featuring 165 attractions, rides, live shows, restaurants, and shops. The lushly landscaped 160 acres have plenty of flowers, trees, waterfalls, and shady spots. Five theme areas include the original Ghost Town, where you can pan for gold, go for a great log ride, and take the Ghost Rider, the longest wooden coaster in the West; Camp Snoopy, the official home of the Peanuts gang, including Woodstock's air mail ride; and Fiesta Village, prowling ground for the Jaguar!—a 2,700-foot-long steel roller coaster that winds its way above the park and loops through Montezooma's Revenge (another thrilling coaster with its own 76-foot-high loop). The Boardwalk has Xcelerator, Perilous Plunge, Riptide, the Boomerang (ever been on a roller coaster that rolls backward? Definite queasy alert!), Supreme Scream (312 feet of vertical excitement), as well as Sky Cabin and Wipeout. The Mystery Lodge, located in the Wild Water Wilderness, is a magical, multisensory show focusing on Native American culture. Come here at the end of your day if you plan on riding Bigfoot Rapids. Speaking from personal experience, heed the warning signs: You will get wet on this ride—most likely drenched! It may feel great on a hot summer day, but squishy shoes and clothing can get mighty uncomfortable mighty fast. Indian Trails gives you a chance to dry off and watch Native American arts, crafts, and music. The Pony Express coaster—a horseback relay launching at a speed of 0 to 38 mph in less than 3 seconds—speeds never imagined in the Old West! Giddy-up! Be absolutely sure to call in advance for current ticket prices and schedules since all are subject to change without notice.

Knott's Soak City Orange County. 8039 Beach Blvd. at La Palma Avenue; (714) 220-5200; www.knotts.com/public/park/soakcity/orange_county/index.cfm. Across the street from Knott's Berry Farm and adjacent to Knott's Independence Hall, this California-beach-theme water park features twenty-three separate water rides and attractions, including tube and body water slides, a wave pool, a lazy river, a family fun house, restaurants, snack bars, a sand beach, a pier, and gift shops. Open daily Memorial Day through Labor Day; open Sat and Sun in May, Sept, and Oct. Be sure to check the schedule and call for current admission prices and package deals.

Medieval Times Dinner and Tournament. 7662 Beach Blvd.; (714) 521-4740 or (888) WE-JOUST; www.medievaltimes.com. You'll eat in an arena filled with more than 1,100 people—divided into six sections—wearing colored hats, waving streamers, and cheering their favorite knight on to victory over the course of a 2-hour eleventh-century show. Included is a four-course meal of twenty-first-century food (appetizer, vegetable soup, chicken, ribs, baked potato slice, and apple turnover) in medieval style (no modern knife, fork, or spoon to assist you). Make sure you bring plenty of extra cash to buy banners to wave, souvenir programs, and photos taken during dinner. Beer, wine, sodas, and coffee are included in the admission price; however, prices are subject to change and do not include gratuity for your hardworking serving wenches and serfs. Call the colorful castle for daily show times—advance reservations are required. Make sure you arrive at least an hour before your scheduled show time to navigate the parking lot with your chariot and negotiate the check-in line. This is outstanding family fun that is not to be missed—you and your kids (and/or the kid in you) can release all kinds of pent-up vocal energy as you yell for "your" knight in armor during a pageant of excellent horsemanship and tournament games of skill and accuracy. A pricey outing, but we think you definitely will agree that "your day's not over until you've seen those knights!" Open daily, call for specific times and prices.

Pirate's Dinner Adventure. 7600 Beach Blvd., immediately off the 91 Freeway interchange; (714) 690-1497 or (866) 439-2469; www.piratesdinneradventure.com. Doors open 90 minutes prior to the show for appetizers in the ship's "lounge." Showroom doors open 15 minutes prior to performance, and seating begins in an replicated eighteenth-century Spanish galleon anchored in a 250,000-gallon indoor lagoon with six "audience ships" around the perimeter—each equipped with a color-coded character pirate you are encouraged to cheer for and interact with throughout the evening. (Yes, this is very similar to Medieval Times with an "ahoy" twist.) Show is 90 minutes. Up to 750 guests can enjoy this extravaganza, featuring an astonishing display of special-effects wizardry, aerial trapeze artistry, swashbuckling swordplay, pirate fights, and dynamic duels. While all this action is going on, you'll be eating your Port of Call Feast, including garden salad, choice of beef with seafood (shrimp and scallops) or marinated chicken with seafood, West Indies yellow rice with Caribbean seasonings, and steamed vegetables, with warm apple cobbler a la mode for dessert, all washed down with a choice of soda, beer, or wine. We think the show is geared for ages ten and up, but there certainly are plenty of younger guests in attendance and participating in the pirates' activities during the show—just seemed a bit too much excitement, noise, lights, and fights for a kiddy activity. Ahoy! Open daily; call for show times and specials.

where to shop

Buena Park Downtown. 8303 On the Mall; (714) 828-7722; www.buenaparkdowntown .com. This 1.1-million-square-foot retail complex has three separate components including the **Buena Park Mall,** a 782,000-square-foot enclosed mall anchored by Wal-Mart, 24 Hour Fitness and Sport, Bed Bath & Beyond, Ross Dress for Less, DSW Shoe Warehouse, John's Incredible Pizza, and Sears; **Buena Park Place,** a 208,000-square-foot open-air center anchored by Kohl's, Office Depot, Michaels, and PetSmart; and finally, **Park Central Entertainment Center** a 137,000-square-foot open-air entertainment venue featuring the massive eighteen-screen Krikorian Metroplex Movie Theatres, plus a variety of restaurants and retail shops. Open daily, call for hours and holiday times.

Knott's California Market Place. 7662 Beach Blvd; (714) 220-5200; www.knotts.com /public/park/marketplace/index.cfm. This shopping complex includes fifteen shops and restaurants in all. From fine art and collectibles to Snoopy souvenirs at the largest Snoopy Store in the United States and Knott's famous jams and jellies, there is something for everyone and anyone, including a year-round Christmas store, an old-fashioned candy store with lots of modern varieties, or the real leather goods at the Grand Avenue Mercantile. Open daily, call for hours.

where to eat

John's Incredible Pizza Company. 8601 On the Mall at the Buena Park Downtown Mall; (714) 236-0000; www.johnspizza.com. John's serves up fun (and 800 pizzas an hour!) within 60,000 square feet of arcade-style video games and rides, and an all-you-can-eat buffet that includes a salad bar with over forty fresh vegetables, toppings, and dressings; choice of two soups, a selection of pastas and an extraordinary variety of pizzas featuring the infamous Spicy Peanut Butter Pizza, Alfredo Pizza, BBQ Chicken Ranch, Fiesta, Cheeseburger, and Garlic Pesto pies, as well as the traditional combinations like Veggie, Meat Lovers, and Hawaiian. Top this off with desserts such as home-made cookies and soft-serve ice cream. All-you-can-eat buffet prices (at press time) were only $6.99 for adult lunch; $9.49 for adult dinner; and $5.99 for children ages 7 to 12; $4.49 for ages 3 to 6; and 2 and under eat free with a paying adult. Of course, prices subject to change without notice, yet this is a great deal for any family! Open daily for lunch and dinner, call for specific hours. $.

Mrs. Knott's Chicken Dinner Restaurant. 8039 Beach Blvd. at the corner of La Palma Avenue; (714) 220-5200. Hearty American fare is served for breakfast, lunch, and dinner at very reasonable prices. We recommend eating here for lunch (go early or late to avoid crowds). Don't plan on taking any rides at the amusement park anytime near your consumption of that delicious chicken, mashed potatoes, and boysenberry pie. (We speak from experience here—trust us!) Today the Chicken Dinner Restaurant seats more than 900 guests at a time, serves more than 1.5 million guests each year, and is the largest full-service restaurant in California that serves chicken as its main course. You'll find it at Knott's California Marketplace, just outside the main entrance of Knott's Berry Farm. $$.

where to stay

Knott's Berry Farm Resort Hotel. 7675 Crescent Ave., adjacent to Knott's Berry Farm; (714) 995-1111; www.knottshotel.com. Its 320 units include a limited number of Peanuts theme rooms with nightly Snoopy character turndown service. Free Snoopy gift for kids at check-in. Outdoor kiddy pool, adult pool, whirlpool, fitness center, sauna, and steam room. Festive Italian family food at Amber Waves Restaurant with kids' menus and daily visits from Snoopy to add to the fun. Gift shops. Free parking. $$$.

day trip 03

southeast

historical anecdotes & oc options:
city of orange, santa ana,
irvine and costa mesa

city of orange

After the hype and happenings at some of the happiest places on earth, how would you like to find a slice of the traditional Americana in the heart of Orange County, California? Look no further than the historic City of Orange, sandwiched between Santa Ana and Anaheim (the two largest cities in the county). As you enter downtown Orange, tree-lined cobblestone thoroughfares take you into the intersection of Chapman and Glassell Streets, where you will discover a circular central plaza reminiscent of towns back East. In 1869, Los Angeles attorneys Alfred Chapman and Andrew Glassell received 1,385 acres of land as payment for their legal services. They quickly subdivided it into a one-square-mile town dubbed Richland with numerous ten-acre farm lots surrounding it. When attempting to register the name Richland in 1873, it was denied by the state since there already was a Richland, California, in Sacramento County. Legend has it that Alfred Chapman (who wanted the name Lemon), Andrew Glassell (who liked Orange), and two other gentlemen (who preferred Olive or Walnut) played a hand of poker, and the man that won the game named the town. Glassell, the astute poker player born in Orange County, Virginia, was the ultimate winner. The newly named small town of Orange that blossomed around its distinctive central plaza and traffic circle is still known today as the Plaza City—boasting a one-square-mile historic district, where nineteenth-century architecture is preserved and cherished, and the appeal is decidedly homespun and friendly.

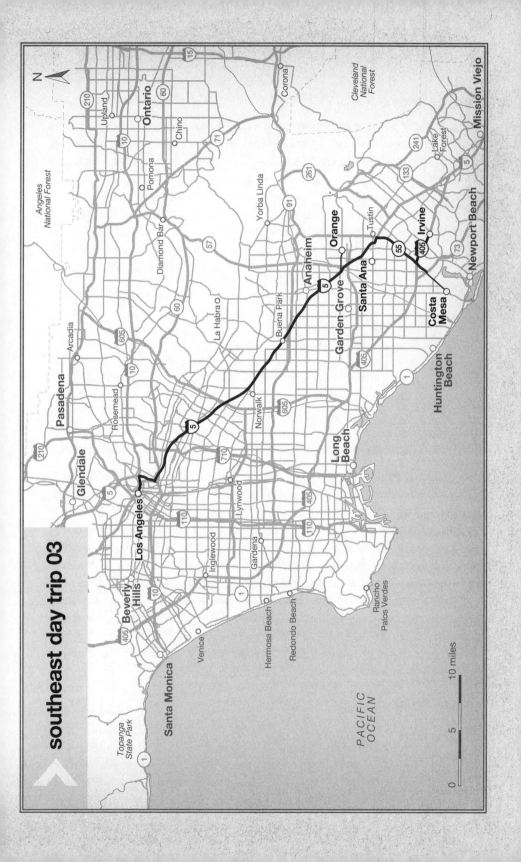

southeast day trip 03

getting there

Approximately 27 miles southeast of downtown Los Angeles, approach the City of Orange by way of I-5 (locally known as the Santa Ana Freeway or "the 5") and use exit 107B (Chapman Avenue) to reach historic Old Towne. The City of Orange is situated near many state routes—the junction of "the 5" with two state highways (SR 57, or Orange Freeway, and SR 22, or Garden Grove Freeway) is nicknamed the Orange Crush because it is one of the busiest interchanges in Southern California. From Union Station in downtown L.A., you can take Metrolink or Amtrak Pacific Surfliner trains to the Orange station at 100 North Atchison St., adjacent to the former Santa Fe depot downtown in the Historic District, also home to an Orange County Transportation Authority (OCTA) bus station for easy connections to other area cities.

where to go

Old Towne, Orange Historic District. www.otpa.org. At the intersection of Chapman and Glassell Streets, this is a vibrant commercial district filled with more than one hundred antique shops, art galleries, restaurants, and boutiques in approximately 1,300 buildings representing a diverse array of early California architectural styles. In 1997, the Historic District was listed on the National Register of Historic Places and is the largest National Register District in California. You'll feel like you are anywhere but California as you stroll around this area. The Old Towne Preservation Association is dedicated to maintaining the district.

Irvine Regional Park. 1 Irvine Park Rd., Santiago Canyon; (714) 973-6835 or (714) 973-3173; www.ocparks.com/irvinepark. Here's where you can escape to nature in the middle of Orange County. Located just 6 miles east of the City of Orange, head east from there on Chapman Avenue for approximately 5 miles and turn left on Jamboree Road for a quarter mile to the park entrance. At this 477-acre park, discover the Orange County Zoo (www.ocparks.com/oczoo), which focuses on animals and plants native to the southwestern United States; a farm animal petting zoo; nature center; lagoon; Irvine Park Railroad (www.irvineparkrailroad.com); pedal boats; bike rentals; picnic areas with barbecues; several miles of hiking, biking, and equestrian trails; plus four ball fields, a volleyball court, and eight horseshoe pits. It's great place to relax and recreate—definitely a fantastic place for you to recharge for your next trip! Fall and winter hours are 6 a.m. to 6 p.m.; spring and summer hours are 6 a.m. to 9 p.m.

where to shop

After you've hit Old Towne's famous antique malls and retro shops, if you'd like some modern fare, visit **The Village at Orange** (1500 East Village Way; 714-998-1521; www.thevillageatorange.com), with more than eighty popular name-brand stores including Ross and JCPenney; or check out insanely popular **The Block at Orange** (20 City Blvd. West, at the corner of Chapman; 714-769-4001; www.theblockatorange.com). This impressive retail and entertainment complex features hundreds of stores and outlets including Saks 5th Avenue OFF 5TH, Neiman Marcus Last Call, Off Broadway Shoes, American Eagle Outfitters, Gymboree Outlet, Nike Factory Store, Bose Factory Store, Puma, Forever 21, G by Guess, and Converse Outlet. Oh yes, you can be entertained at AMC 30 Theaters (yes, thirty screens), Dave & Buster's, Lucky Strike Lanes, and Vans Skatepark. Open daily, call for hours and special holiday times.

where to eat

Watson's Drugs and Soda Fountain. 116 East Chapman; (714) 633-1050. The best place to soak up the flavor of Orange is on a stool at a joint that has been continuously serving heaping scoops of ice cream, traditional American meals, and remedies at its Plaza Square location since 1899. The root beer floats are so frothy you will wonder how you lived this long without one; and the malts are the real deal—hand-dipped ice cream with scoop of malt and real milk. Sweet! Breakfast, lunch, and dinner daily (breakfast all day long). Go in anytime to see an authentic soda fountain in action and watch the servers in their period outfits and hairdos play soda jerks. The interior and exterior have been used in many movies and commercials, including Tom Hank's film *That Thing You Do*. Open Mon through Sat 6:30 a.m. to 9 p.m., and Sun 8 a.m. to 6 p.m. $.

where to stay

There are more than 50,000 hotel rooms in Orange County, with many concentrated in the **Anaheim Resort Area.** The City of Orange, along with other "interior" Orange County cities Santa Ana, Costa Mesa, Irvine, and Yorba Linda, all have a plethora of properties representing all major national chains to suit every taste and budget. For a complete listing, we recommend you access the database at the Anaheim/Orange County Convention & Visitor Bureau at www.anaheimoc.org.

worth more time

Nixon Presidential Library and Museum. 18001 Yorba Linda Blvd., Yorba Linda.; (714) 993-5075 or (800) 872-8865; http://nixon.archives.gov and www.nixonlibraryfoundation .org. There is a lot of political and world history depicted at this nine-acre site, first opened and dedicated on July 19, 1990. You'll begin your tour in the auditorium, which shows vintage campaign films, news footage, and historically significant television appearances by President Nixon. Then proceed to the permanent galleries displaying images, video, and artifacts related to his career, family life, and service as president—a fascinating one details the space program during the Nixon presidency, featuring an astronaut's space suit, the telephone President Nixon used to call Neil Armstrong and Buzz Aldrin on the moon, and an actual moon rock; and the 1967 Lincoln Continental limousine used by Presidents Johnson, Nixon, and Ford.

You'll also have a chance to step aboard Army One, the six-ton Sikorsky VH 3A Sea King helicopter used by Presidents Kennedy, Johnson, Nixon, and Ford. Perhaps Nixon's most famous use of the helicopter was his last, on August 9, 1974, when he resigned the presidency and flew from the White House's South Lawn to Andrews Air Force Base, where he boarded Air Force One for a flight to his private residence in nearby San Clemente, California. Check out a replica of the East Room of the White House. The exhibits portray America's thirty-seventh commander in chief right up until his death on April 22, 1994. Both President and Mrs. Nixon are buried here in the tranquil First Lady's Garden. You may visit the grave site, the reflecting pool, and the white clapboard farmhouse where Nixon was born on January 9, 1913. It remains precisely as it was when Nixon and his family lived there, right down to the bed where he was born. The intimate museum store on the premises contains commemorative souvenirs, postcards, and a selection of Nixon's books. To get there from the City of Orange, take the Orange Freeway (SR 57) north and exit at Yorba Linda Boulevard. Head east (turn right) on Yorba Linda Boulevard and proceed to the museum on the left-hand side (watch carefully for signs). Open daily; closed on Thanksgiving and Christmas Day. Call for hours and special event times.

santa ana

Orange County's largest city is also the county seat of government and home to the John Wayne/Orange County Airport (SNA) (949-252-5200; www.ocair.com). Downtown Santa Ana combines Fiesta Marketplace, a bustling Latino-style pedestrian mall with a contemporary $50 million civic center and about a hundred historic buildings that would make the Spanish explorer Portolá proud of the city he christened in 1769.

where to go

Bowers Museum of Cultural Art and Kidseum. 2002 North Main St., Santa Ana; (714) 567-3600; www.bowers.org. A significant part of Santa Ana's past is found in its first

get your adrenaline pumping!

Glacial Gardens Skating Arena (3975 Pixie St., Lakewood; 562-429-1805; www.glacialgardens.com) is the place to go if you'd rather participate than watch ice sports. Head over to this triple-rink facility (Olympic size, NHL size, and a slightly smaller training rink), complete with a pro shop, snack bar, locker rooms, and skate rentals. Open daily, with varying times and fees for open figure skating, instruction, and hockey matches.

museum, created in 1936 through a bequest from Charles and Ada Bowers to preserve the local history of Orange County. Through gifts and acquisitions, the Bowerses' collections have grown over the years, and the museum has enlarged its space three times. It is now considered one of the finest cultural arts repositories in the West. The museum specializes in the arts of the Americas, the Pacific Rim, and Africa, along with its ongoing commitment to chronicle the story of Orange County. From May through October 2008, Bowers hosted an exclusive exhibition of China's famed Terra-Cotta Warriors—the largest loan of terra-cotta figures and significant artifacts to ever travel to the United States from the enormous mausoleum of China's first emperor. The museum store has unique art treasures, cards, and gifts not readily available in traditional museum gift shops. In 1994, the 11,000-square-foot **Bowers Kidseum** opened 2 blocks away at 1802 North Main St. This amazing center has been competently designed for youth ages six to twelve as a place where children can learn about other cultures, music, art, and history through interactive, hands-on exhibits. Open Tues through Sun from 10 a.m. to 4 p.m.

Discovery Science Center. 2500 North Main St., Santa Ana, at the corner of I-5 (Santa Ana Freeway); (714) 542-CUBE; www.discoverycube.org. "The Amusement Park for Your Mind" opened in 1998 in a 59,000-square-foot multistory facility devoted to sparking natural curiosity and increasing everyone's understanding of science, math, and technology. More than 120 highly interactive exhibits make you think, search for answers, and participate in the learning process. Themed areas include Perception, Dynamic Earth, Quake Zone, Showcase Gallery, Boeing Delta III Rocket, Air & Space, Techno Arts, and Digital Lab. Our three personal favorites include the Shake Shack to experience an earthquake; lying down on a bed of nails; and dancing on the musical floor. Open daily 10 a.m. to 5 p.m.

irvine and costa mesa

The city of Irvine is the largest master-planned community in the United States. It was first developed in 1959 as a site for the University of California–Irvine on an old Spanish land grant. Billboards, overhead power lines, and TV antennas are banned here. The area is divided into thirty-eight urban villages (aka subdivisions) featuring a plethora of parks, all connected by greenbelts and bike paths. Shopping centers and services are all conveniently located nearby. The central corridor of high-rise buildings, such as the Irvine Spectrum and Koll Center, provide headquarters for plenty of Fortune 500 firms.

The adjacent city of Costa Mesa, also home to many corporations as well as a popular residential community, became a player on the Orange County shopping and entertainment scene in 1967 with the opening of South Coast Plaza: the "Ultimate Shopping Resort," a great place for you to satisfy those shopping urges.

religious headquarters

Crystal Cathedral of the Reformed Church in America. *13280 Chapman Ave.; Garden Grove; www.crystalcathedral.org. For some religious and architectural history, visit the dramatic, all-glass sanctuary designed by Philip Johnson, considered a dean of American architects. This incredible place features 10,000 glass panes covering a weblike steel frame that resembles a four-point star. The 2,890-seat cathedral hosts the annual Glory of Christmas and Glory of Easter pageants, with live animals, flying angels, and incredible special lighting reflected from the twelve-story glass walls and ceilings. Free tours are generally available Mon through Sat, but times are subject to change due to church services and events. Call the visitor center at (714) 971-4000 to check tour times, or (714) 544-5679 to reserve tickets for the extremely cherished holiday pageants. Donations appreciated.*

Trinity Christian City International. *3150 Bear St.; (714) 832-2950 or (714) 708-5405; www.tbn.org. This striking, classically inspirational building across I-405 from the South Coast Plaza Mall houses the broadcast studios of Trinity Broadcast Network (TBN) Christian television organization. All ages are welcome to tour the grounds and studios, and to view films in the Virtual Reality Theater daily. Call for current titles and show times. Tour the Demos Shakarian Memorial Building, seen regularly on international television broadcasts. On special evenings join in during a free live television broadcast of the Praise The Lord! program.*

where to go

Orange County Fair and Event Center. 88 Fair Dr., Costa Mesa; (714) 708-1567 or (714) 708-1500; www.ocfair.com/ocf. Discover a variety of events, including swap meets, automobile and motorcycle speedway races, and concerts. Each July, the Orange County Fair takes over, featuring top-name entertainment, livestock, carnival rides, rodeo, foodstuffs, arts, crafts, contests, and demonstrations.

Orange County Performing Arts Center. 600 Town Center Dr., South Coast Plaza, Costa Mesa; (714) 556-2121; www.ocpac.org. The 3,000-seat Segerstrom Hall is where major symphony concerts, operas, ballets, and Broadway musicals are presented year-round; it was joined in 2006 by the 1,700-seat Renée and Henry Segerstrom Concert Hall and the intimate Samueli Theater. It is the home of four resident companies: Pacific Symphony, the Philharmonic Society of Orange County, Opera Pacific, and Pacific Chorale. Call for specific performance times and an event schedule.

Wild Rivers Waterpark. 8770 Irvine Center Dr., Irvine; (949) 768-WILD; www.wildrivers .com. This twenty-acre park has more than forty water rides, including the Edge, the Ledge, and the Abyss; two massive wave pools; kiddy wading pools; sunbathing areas; a water slide; log flumes; picnic areas; and a video arcade to complete the mix. Open May through Sept only—call for specific days and times; subject to change without notice.

where to shop & eat

Irvine Spectrum Center. 71 Fortune Dr., Irvine, (949) 753-5180; www.shopirvinespectrum center.com. At the intersection of I-405 (exit Irvine Center Drive) and I-5 (exit Alton), this premier entertainment plaza offers twenty-one IMAX movie cinemas, world-class restaurants, nightlife, 120 specialty shops from around the globe, a 108-foot-tall Giant Wheel (Ferris wheel), and a whimsical carousel. Opened in November 1995, it was one of the first in the country to be anchored by restaurants and entertainment venues—a "lifestyle center"—setting a precedent in the shopping center industry; it attracts nearly 13 million visitors annually. Stores include Anthropologie, bebe, White House/ Black Market, Urban Outfitters, Brighton Collectibles, Ann Taylor Loft, Oakley "O" Store, Quiksilver Boardriders Club, Garys Island, Forever 21, Barnes & Noble and many more. Call for current hours of operation and special events on-site. Hours may vary seasonally and with individual stores and restaurants.

South Coast Plaza. 3333 Bristol St., at the intersection of I-405 and Bristol Street, Costa Mesa; (800) 782-8888; www.southcoastplaza.com. One of the largest retail centers in the United States, South Coast Plaza welcomes approximately 24 million visitors annually. In addition to shopping, it is also home to the Orange Lounge, a digital media-focused branch of the Orange County Museum of Art. Many ultra-luxury brands also call South Coast Plaza home including French luxury design house Chloé, Rolex, Harry Winston, Tiffany's, Cartier, Montblanc, Louis Vuitton, Versace, Prada, Dior, Valentino, Chanel, Yves Saint Laurent, Gucci, Hermès, Barney's New York Co-Op, and Nordstrom. Restaurants include Lawry's Carvery, Charlie Palmer at Bloomingdales, and Vie De France (no food courts here!). Check out the valet parking, concierge services, and hot beverage service on those infrequent cool days that make this one of the most upscale malls anywhere. For a current special-event and promotion schedule, call the concierge at (949) 435-2034 or visit the website.

day trip 04

southeast

three on the sand—the oc beach cities:

huntington beach, newport beach, laguna beach

After all your "inland" Orange County action, how about some sandy, waterside relaxation or oceanfront recreation to provide a respite? Orange County's beautiful, bountiful beaches are truly part of the defining Southern California experience, certainly immortalized by television's popular teen dramas *The O.C., Laguna Beach: The Real Orange County* and the Bravo TV reality show *The Real Housewives of Orange County* all filmed on location here. For 90 percent of your beach time, casual clothing is the way to go—be sure to pack shorts, T-shirts, cotton pants, skirts, and really comfortable walking shoes or sandals. Bring a sweater or light jacket for evenings—along the waterfront it can get nippy year-round. Don't forget your bathing suit and shades (but never fear, you can always buy the latest beachwear and gear at one of the numerous malls or surf shops). Winter brings highs of 65 degrees, and overnight lows—even in winter's darkest hours—rarely dip below 45 degrees. December through February passes for the area's "rainy season," although total annual rainfall is only 13 inches. Temperatures rise to 79 or 80 degrees in the summer. Beach babies, your days are generally sunny and mild, nights clear and cool—that's the forecast for this day trip!

getting there

Numerous auto routes are available from downtown Los Angeles to the beaches of Orange County (approximately 45 miles to the southeast). Ease of travel depends upon the time of day, traffic patterns and accidents (typical L.A. driving dilemmas), but for smooth navigating

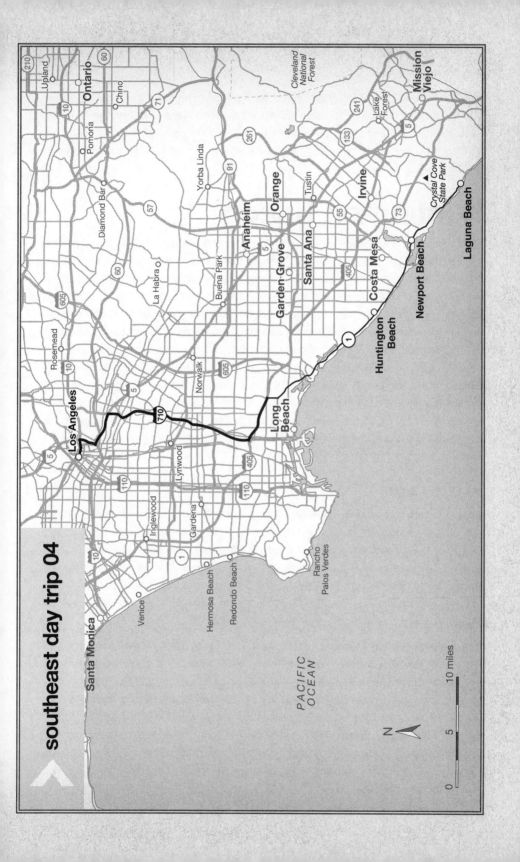

southeast day trip 04

from downtown Los Angeles here's an insider's tip: merge onto I-5 (generally just called "the 5") south; exit onto I-710 south toward Long Beach. Take the CA-1/Pacific Coast Highway (PCH) exit and follow the signs for PCH South—in just a few miles you can start savoring the ocean views. When you see Bolsa Chica, you've arrived in your first OC beach city—Huntington.

huntington beach

Orange County's third-largest city (after Santa Ana and Anaheim) has more than 8.5 miles of uninterrupted shoreline. Between Goldenwest Street and Brookhurst Street along PCH, Bolsa Chica and Huntington State Beaches provide plenty of area for safe swimming, picnicking, and surfing. Beach parking fees are charged and vary according to time and season. Huntington is the surf capital of Southern California and it has been trademarked as "Surf City USA." You can easily spend a day on the beaches of Huntington, just enjoying the beautiful surf, sand, and sea. (Do remember to use your sunscreen liberally. Ask any Huntington Beach surfer dude—sunburn is totally not cool!) The town's ambitious redevelopment efforts along Main Street, just off PCH, contain postmodern shopping plazas and condos alongside the original turn-of-the-last-century waterfront clapboards, which now house trendy clothing stores, beach shops, and bistros. Strolling the 1,856-foot municipal pier is a favorite pastime. Pier Plaza, on PCH at Main Street, hosts a farmers' market on Friday and live entertainment.

where to go

Bolsa Chica Ecological Reserve and Interpretive Center. On PCH between Warner Avenue and Goldenwest Street, just opposite the entrance to Bolsa Chica State Beach; (714) 846-1114; www.bolsachica.org. It is both relaxing and educational to walk through this 300-acre reserve, one of the largest salt marsh preserves in Southern California. The reserve supports such migratory waterfowl as avocets, egrets, plovers, and terns. A 1.5-mile walkway with explanatory signs leads the way throughout the ecosystem. Ask about the guided public tour schedule. Open daily from dawn to dusk. Free.

International Surfing Museum. 411 Olive Ave.; (714) 960-3483; www.surfingmuseum .org. An Art Deco-ish building downtown, home of radical exhibits, artifacts, and memorabilia ranging from vintage surfboards to surf wear and surf films, all preserving the heritage of "Surf City USA." Dedicated in May 1994, the **Huntington Beach Surfing Walk of Fame** marked a historic addition to Surf City. The inductees are selected annually by a panel of international surfing authorities. The winner in each category receives a granite stone placed in the sidewalk extending from the corners of PCH and Main Street. Categories include: Surf Pioneer, Surf Champion, Surfing Culture, Local Hero, Woman of the Year and the Honor

Roll. At the museum, displays, admission fees, and opening and closing hours change like the tides (well, not really that frequently!), so call ahead.

where to eat

Dwight's at the Beach. On the boardwalk, 1 block south of the Huntington pier; (714) 536-8083. Since 1932, Dwight's has been serving juicy burgers, hot dogs, ice cream, and famous cheese strips—tortilla strips and cheddar cheese topped with a secret-recipe hot sauce. Open daily; hours vary by season. $.

Lazy Dog Café. 16310 Beach Blvd., at MacDonald Avenue, just south of I-405 near Huntington Beach in Westminster; (714) 500-1140; www.thelazydogcafe.com. They're serious about quality here, but are creative with their offerings: build-your-own pizzas and even desserts served in a dog bowl are available. Open daily for lunch and dinner. $$.

where to stay

Hyatt Regency Huntington Beach Resort & Spa. 21500 PCH; (714) 698-1234; www .huntingtonbeach.hyatt.com. Garden and ocean views from 517 guest rooms and 57 suites in Andalusian-inspired style. This luxurious hotel directly across from the beach via a pedestrian walkway features three restaurants (the Californian for fine dining, Pete Mallory's Surf City Sunset Grille, and Mankota's Grill poolside), the Village shopping plaza, and the 20,000-square-foot Pacific Waters Spa. $$$.

surfing hq

Huntington Beach has lured legendary surfing icons such as Duke Kahanamoku, Corky Carroll, Pete Townend, Kelly Slater, Rob Machado and Layne Beachley over the decades with some of the most consistent surf on the West Coast. The city hosts more than 30 national and international surfing championships each year, including the **U.S. Open of Surfing** *each July—the gnarliest of North American surfing events. Many surfing industry leaders consider Huntington Beach to be their home, including Quiksilver, a worldwide clothing brand; Surfline.com, a website that monitors more than a hundred global surfing locations daily; the thirty-one-year-old Association of Surfing Professionals (ASP); and the USA Surf Team, a group of the best-of-the-best up-and-coming surfers in the country.* **Jack's Surfboards** *(www .jackssurfboards.com) and* **Huntington Surf and Sport** *(www.hsssurf.com) are legendary surf and clothing shops with headquarters in Huntington. Stop by and hang for some truly authentic culture.*

newport beach

Situated 55 miles southeast of Los Angeles and directly south of Huntington Beach along the glittering Pacific is a city of villages, islands, and private enclaves first incorporated in 1906. The Newport Beach area comprises Balboa, Balboa Island, Lido Isle, Newport Heights, Harbor Island, Bay Shore, Linda Isle, and Corona del Mar. It includes one of the West Coast's most famous yacht harbors, containing approximately 9,000 pleasure crafts. In addition, a 6-mile "inland" beach lies along the peninsula between Newport Bay and the ocean. Newport has some of the trendiest Southern California beach life, and you can taste it while you're here—championship golf courses, countless spas, world-class shopping, whale-watching and over 350 dining choices are just a few of the many activities within your grasp.

where to go

Balboa Pavilion. 400 Main St., located at the Newport Bay end of Main Street on the Balboa Peninsula; (800) 830-7744; www.balboapavilion.com. Begin your exploration of the waterfront at this classic building constructed in 1905 and now listed on the National Register of Historic Places. Here you will discover a marine recreation center offering ferries to quaint Balboa Island and Catalina Island, and charter boats for sailing, whale-watching, sightseeing, and sportfishing. The Fun Zone has a carousel, Ferris wheel, and arcade. Open daily 10 a.m. to 10 p.m.

Davey's Locker Sportfishing. 400 Main St., Balboa Pavilion, Balboa; (949) 673-1434; www.daveyslocker.com. Your headquarters in Newport Beach for harbor excursions, whale watching, and half-, three-quarter-, or full-day fishing excursions for catching yellowfin tuna, bonito, sand bass, and rockfish. Twilight fishing trips are offered in the summer, too. These folks are pros, and they will make you feel very comfortable and safe on the water. Open daily; hours vary by season.

***Pavilion Paddy* Cruises.** 400 Main St. in the Balboa Pavilion, Balboa; (949) 673-5245; www.balboapavilion.com/HarborCruise.html. At the end of the Balboa Peninsula and Pier, do not miss taking a forty-five or ninety minute sightseeing cruise aboard the old-fashioned riverboat *Pavilion Paddy*. You will wind your way through the meandering channels of Newport Harbor and see some imposing homes and dazzling yachts of the rich and famous (such as the late John Wayne and Shirley Temple Black). Tours run mostly year-round. Sunday brunch cruises are also available in season. Call for cruise times.

Hornblower Cruises & Events. 2431 West PCH, Suite 101; (949) 646-0155; www.hornblower.com. Cruises on climate-controlled large yachts are offered year-round. Excellent service from a nautically attired crew and California cuisine prepared fresh onboard make this an upscale cruising, dining, and sightseeing experience to remember. We like the

Sunday brunch cruises best. Brunch cruises sail for two hours and include an all-you-can-eat buffet with champagne for adults; children ages 4 to 12 half price. Gratuity and cocktails additional. Evening and Sunday brunch cruise schedules vary according to season and demand for private charters.

Newport Sports Museum. 100 Newport Center Dr., Suite 100; (949) 721-9333; www .newportsportsmuseum.org. This 6,000-square-foot museum features one of the world's largest collections of sports memorabilia, assembled in 15 themed rooms containing 10,000 items. Highlights include jerseys from Michael Jordan, Larry Bird, Dr. J, and Wilt Chamberlain; and autographed baseballs from every Cy Young winner. There's even a baseball park with actual seats from places such as Yankee Stadium and Wrigley Field. The collection started in 1953 when John W. Hamilton, at the age of twelve, was given a "Look All-American Football" by a family friend. Hamilton has been collecting sports memorabilia ever since, with the majority of the items personally given to him by athletes. Open Tues through Sun from 10 a.m. to 5 p.m. Free admission; donations welcome.

where to shop

Luring you away from the Newport Beach and harbor area, but with the ocean firmly in sight, is the 600-acre **Newport Center.** Located just above the Pacific Coast Highway between MacArthur Boulevard and Jamboree Road, it is an office, luxury hotel, and entertainment complex that was built in 1967. It hosts a must-stop shopping center—the trendy **Fashion Island.** The complex contains more than 200 major chain stores and regional specialty shops as well as forty restaurants in the Atrium Court. The main showpiece is the AAA-rated five-diamond **Island Hotel** (www.islandhotel.com). Call (949) 721-2000, the concierge contact number, or visit www.shopfashionisland.com, for schedules of activities, fashion shows, and great promotions.

where to eat & stay

The Newport Dunes Waterfront Resort. 1131 Back Bay Dr., just off PCH and Jamboree Boulevard; (949) 729-3863 or (800) 765-7661; www.newportdunes.com. This 100-acre "Ritz of RV Parks" is really a great waterfront resort that not only provides more than 400 hookups for recreational vehicles and campers separated by tropical vine–covered fences, but also offers twenty-four beachfront cottages and a dozen basic studio cottages inland that sleep from two to eight people, and are equipped with a kitchen and full baths. You can rent bikes, kayaks, windsurfers, paddleboats, and sailboats here for hours of fun. Lots of activities are planned for guests year-round, such as "movies on the beach" in the summer. **Back Bay Bistro** (949-729-1144), located at the resort's boat launch, overlooks the calm inland waters of Upper Newport Bay as well as all the action at the adjacent boat launch/marina. There is a casual, nautical atmosphere both indoors and out on the patio. California/American traditional foods for breakfast, lunch, dinner, and a Sunday brunch buffet are offered. $$.

The Resort at Pelican Hill. 27701 Pelican Hill Rd. South; (800) 315-8214 or (949) 467-6800; www.pelicanhill.com. Situated above the coastline between Newport Beach and Laguna Beach, the Resort's Palladian-inspired architecture from northern Italy encompasses 204 bungalow guest rooms and 128 villas (with 2, 3 or 4 bedrooms) all with panoramic views. Five dining experiences are available, including **Andrea Ristorante & Bar** (signature northern Italian cuisine); **Pelican Grill & Lounge** (California-inspired cuisine at the Golf Clubhouse); **Coliseum Pool & Grill** (for casual pool side fare); **Caffè I** (featuring pastries, light fare, gelato and rich coffee) and **Caffè II** (light refreshments and specialty at the Golf Clubhouse).

The **Spa at Pelican Hill** offers 22 private treatment rooms in 23,000 square-foot facility including warm Roman soaking pools beneath a barrel-vaulted ceiling, sauna and steam rooms; fitness center and full-service salon. **Pelican Hill Golf Club** has two championship 18-hole golf courses (Ocean North and Ocean South) designed by Tom Fazio featuring incredible ocean views from nearly every hole. You deserve the ultimate in luxury and service recognized by the AAA (five-diamond-rated) and *Conde Nast Traveler's* Hot List for 2009, ascend Pelican Hill. $$$.

laguna beach

Continuing south of Newport Beach, past the village of Corona del Mar, discover a place practically unspoiled by time or tide—the dazzling white sands of Laguna Beach. Its artist colony heritage and year-round mild climate create a unique Orange County beach resort worth your trip. When a watercolor painter named Norman St. Claire visited in 1900 and returned to his native San Francisco with tales of photolike landscapes and a perfect climate, the art world reacted and several hundred artists and patrons relocated, setting in motion the artistic bent of the village still *en vogue* today. Laguna's trio of art festivals dominate the summer OC scene—the prestigious Festival of Arts, the funky Sawdust Festival and the rival Art-a-Fair. (See Festivals & Celebrations for details.) All the major beach attractions along the Pacific Coast Highway can be found on the Main Beach downtown, in the form of art galleries, boutiques, and bistros.

where to go

Laguna Playhouse. 600 Laguna Canyon Rd.; (949) 497-2787; www.lagunaplayhouse .com. Founded in 1920, the company stages seven mainstream plays annually as well as two youth productions. Harrison Ford launched his career in this popular regional theater company.

where to eat

230 Forest Avenue. 230 Forest Ave.; (949) 494-2545; www.230forestavenue.com. Nestled in the heart of downtown Laguna, 230 is quite the "in" place. This chic sidewalk cafe has an innovative menu by chef/owner Marc Cohen, complemented by a full bar and a unique selection of California wines. Open daily for lunch and dinner. $$$.

The Cottage Restaurant. 308 North Coast Hwy.; (949) 494-3023; www.thecottageres taurant.com. This landmark "board and batten" style home has withstood the test of time and witnessed the constant changes of Laguna Beach for more than a half century. The restaurant began serving meals to the public in 1964. This is the home-style cooking we love to find—especially the Laguna Omelette with bay shrimp, snow crab, fresh dill and Swiss cheese. Call for current hours. Open for breakfast, lunch and dinner 365 days a year. $.

where to stay

Hotel Laguna and Claes Restaurant. 425 South Coast Hwy.; (949) 494-1151 or (800) 524-2927; www.hotellaguna.com. This centrally located, historic sixty-five-room property right on the sand was built in 1930. This three-story old girl has undergone several facelifts over the years, but remains a true favorite. Don't expect ultramodern furnishings, but revel in the quirky California beach atmosphere. Be sure to request a room on the ocean side, because the street side is far too noisy. Private beach access comes complete with your own beach chairs and food/drinks/towel attendant. Make this the ultimate place to people watch and create sand castles. Free continental breakfast included. Choose the Claes Restaurant or the Terrace for lunch or an early dinner (the bar gets a little hectic later on). You can dine overlooking the beach and all the action. Weddings and special events are pretty and magical at this Deco dame, too. $$–$$$.

worth more time

Crystal Cove State Park/Beach. Located off the PCH between Corona del Mar and Laguna Beach; www.crystalcovestatepark.com. In contrast to much of the glitz and glamour surrounding it, Crystal Cove is best known for its rather rustic setting. Three beach areas below the bluffs include **Reef Point** with access to two coves; **Pelican Point,** which is a 3.25-mile trail; and **Los Trancos,** which offers access to a historic district featuring 1930s style cottages. Twenty-two cottages are available for nightly rental (www.crystalcovebeach-cottages.org). Just offshore is a 1,140 acre underwater park for snorkelers and scuba divers. On the southern edge of the park is **El Moro,** a 2,200-acre chaparral canyon with 18 miles of hiking, biking and horse trails. Since the early 1920s this area has been used as a recreational refuge for people escaping the big city. A One Day Pass (good anywhere in the park) is $15. To conclude your OC beach odyssey, stop in at the Cove's **Beach-comber Café** (949-376-6900) for breakfast, lunch or dinner, or grab a famous Date Shake at **Ruby's Shake Shack** (949-464-0100). Cheers!

south

day trip 01

south

>>> **of sailing ships & queens:**
long beach

long beach

With more than 5.5 miles of shoreline, Long Beach is aptly named since life there centers on its Pacific coastal nature. Situated at the mouth of the Los Angeles River, just 22 miles south of downtown Los Angeles, Long Beach was settled by the Spaniards in 1784 and incorporated in 1888; it is the fifth largest city in California today. With an average 345 days of sunshine each year, Long Beach has been a visitor-friendly place for centuries as well as a major center of industry. Oil was discovered in 1921 on nearby Signal Hill, and Long Beach was the most productive oil field in the world at the time (and you'll still see pumps around town and shores). Long Beach has grown with the development of the high technology, aerospace, and tourism industries. Just 2 miles south of downtown Long Beach, the Port of Long Beach is ranked the second busiest in the United States and located adjacent to the top-ranked Port of Los Angeles—both major transportation hubs.

Though just a half-hour or so from downtown Los Angeles, Long Beach has a distinctly different, somewhat lower-key vibe where you'll find a variety of activities and attractions plus an array of beaches that invite sunbathing and sand-castle building. Downtown activity hustles and bustles along Pine Avenue, and a mile and a half away down Ocean Boulevard, the 15-block stretch of Second Street in the Belmont Shore area has lots of boutiques and restaurants. And of course, the venerable *Queen Mary,* one of the world's most luxurious sailing ships now in her majestic dock, rules the waterfront. Come pay her homage during your Long Beach getaway!

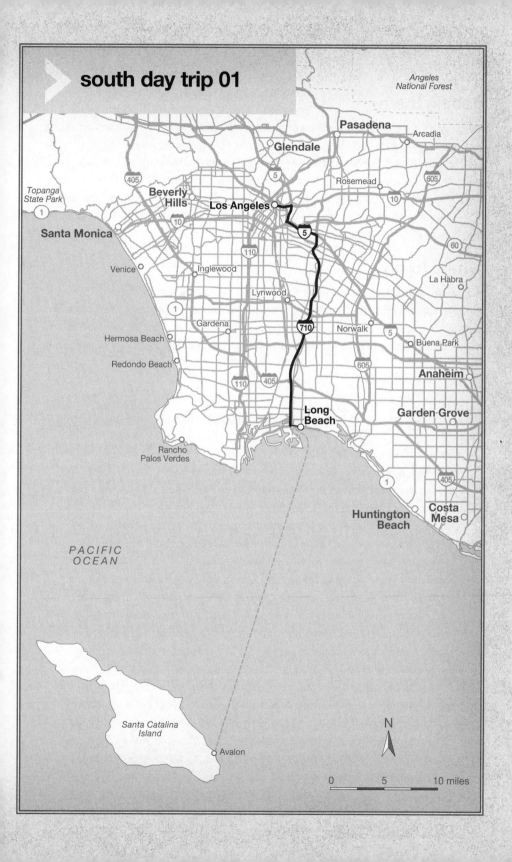

getting there

Long Beach is the southern terminus of the MetroRail Blue Line train—just hop on at Los Angeles Union Station and head south—this is a super easy and convenient way to arrive (for info call 800-266-6883 or visit www.metro.net). Driving from downtown L.A., take I-710 south (known locally as the Long Beach Freeway) over the arched Gerald Thomas Bridge across Terminal Island and the Cerritos Channel, to its terminus in downtown Long Beach. (The other distinctively green, imposing Vincent Thomas Bridge connects Terminal Island with the city of San Pedro to the west of Long Beach.)

where to go

Aquarium of the Pacific.100 Aquarium Way, off Shoreline Drive; (562) 590-3100; www .aquariumofpacific.org. This impressive 156,000-square-foot facility covers five acres and includes 550 species and 12,500 specimens in more than nineteen major habitats and thirty focus exhibits including the Sea Lion/Seal Tunnel, Baja Gallery, Wetlands Discovery

getting around long beach is pretty free & aqua easy

Whether you arrive by MetroRail Blue Line or vehicle, it's really easy to get around Long Beach. Public transportation is provided by Long Beach Transit. Beside their regular transit bus service, which charges reasonable, low fares, check out the free routes on Passport buses that shuttle passengers within the downtown zone. Passport routes A and D buses go east/west along Ocean Boulevard, linking the Catalina Landing in the west with Alamitos Bay or Los Altos via Belmont Shore in the east. Passport route B in the East Village visits museums and other points of interest. The Passport C route, serving Pine Avenue, Shoreline Drive, the Aquarium of the Pacific, and the iconic Queen Mary, connects you to downtown Long Beach's finest attractions including the AquaBus and AquaLink. The Aqua-Link is a red, yellow and purple water taxi—a 68-foot catamaran boat that comfortably ferries up to seventy-five passengers to the most popular attractions in Long Beach Harbor and on down to Alamitos Bay Landing at the marina. Fares are only $5 per person. Also, be sure to also check out the AquaBus, a bright red boat seating up to forty-nine passengers that has six "ports of call": Aquarium of the Pacific at Dock 4, the Queen Mary, Shoreline Village at Parker's Lighthouse, Catalina Landing, Pine Avenue Circle at Dock 7, and the Hotel Maya. Fare is only $1. Be certain to call (562) 591-2301 for seasonal schedules and current fares/ day passes or visit www.lbtransit.com.

Lab, Pacific Gallery, Coastal Corner, Live Coral Discovery, Lorikeet Aviary, and the Shark Lagoon. If you've got kids in tow, head for Kid's Cove, a playground and hands-on interactive aquarium experience. The focus is on feeding habits, family structures, and the lives of the exhibit specimens. Dine at the Bamboo Bistro or Cafe Scuba. Behind-the-scenes tours and 90-minute educational ocean cruises aboard *The Conqueror* are real winners, too. Open daily 9 a.m. to 6 p.m. except Christmas and during the Long Beach Grand Prix each April (which regularly reaches attendance of 200,000 people).

Gondola Getaway. 5437 East Ocean Blvd.; (562) 433-9595; www.gondolagetawayinc .com. Beginning with one boat in 1982, Gondola Getaway now has ten authentic Venetian gondolas gently cruising the enchanting canals and waterways of Naples Island near the Long Beach resort neighborhood of Belmont Shores. One-hour cruises are offered from 11 a.m. to 11 p.m., seven days a week. Reservations are highly recommended. Call for rates and special packages. Ask about all the marriage proposals on board and their 100 percent success rate!

Long Beach Museum of Art. 2300 East Ocean Blvd.; (562) 439-2119; www.lbma.org; Occupying the historic 1912 Elizabeth Milbank Anderson residence and carriage house, including oceanfront gardens plus a modern two-story pavilion that opened in 2000, the museum has a permanent collection featuring American decorative arts objects, early twentieth-century European art, California modernism, and contemporary art of California in ever-changing exhibits. Claire's at the Museum Restaurant, located on the grounds, has indoor seating in the historic Anderson house or on the outdoor patio that surrounds Claire Falkenstein's stunning water sculpture *Structure and Flow*. You'll love the unobstructed view of the *Queen Mary* and Catalina Island from here during weekday lunches and weekend brunches. Museum is open Tues through Sun 11 a.m. to 5 p.m.; closed Thanksgiving, Dec 25, Jan 1, and July 4.

Museum of Latin American Art. 628 Alamitos Ave.; (562) 437-1689; www.molaa.com. The 20,000-square-foot building was built in 1920 and houses the Robert Gumbiner Foundation collection of Latin American art (since the 1940s), galleries for rotating showings, Viva Cafe and Museum Store, a research library, and a performance area. It is the only museum in the western United States that exclusively features contemporary Latin American art. Open Tues through Fri 11:30 a.m. to 7 p.m., Sat 11 a.m. to 7 p.m., and Sun 11 a.m. to 6 p.m. Call ahead for calendar of events and exhibits.

where to shop

With dozens of neighborhoods and enclaves, you can really find just about anything you're looking for and plenty of items you hadn't even thought about in Long Beach. On **Broadway** in the East Village, discover antique shops, art galleries, and rare bookshops. Midtown's funky **Fourth Street,** between Cherry and Junipero Streets, has been dubbed the retro capital of Southern California—a vintage-clothes freak's fantasy come true.

Downtown's **Pine Avenue** and Belmont Shore's **Second Street** are also great shopping areas filled with blocks of specialty and retail stores.

A short walk from the Aquarium of the Pacific along picturesque **Rainbow Harbor,** discover two top entertainment/dining/shopping complexes. **Shoreline Village** (401–435 Shoreline Village Dr.; 562-435-2668; www.shorelinevillage.com) has the look and feel of a old-fashioned Cape Cod–style fishing village, with a boardwalk filled with dozens of specialty shops and restaurants, plus activities, and a wide variety of boat tours and cruises (including Dive Works, Marina Sailing, Offshore Watersports, the Rainbow Rocket, and Spirit Cruises) and Wheel Fun bike rentals for cyclists. **The Pike at Rainbow Harbor** (95 South Pine Ave.; 562-432-8325; www.thepikeatlongbeach.com) is Long Beach's newest attraction: a 350,000-plus-square-foot entertainment district between the Long Beach Convention Center and the Aquarium of the Pacific featuring restaurants, a multiplex movie theater, and even a Ferris wheel. For your mainstream mall fix, you can always investigate Los Altos Market Center, Marina Pacifica, Long Beach Marketplace, and the Long Beach Towne Center.

where to eat

Alegria Cocina Latina. 115 Pine Ave.; (562) 436-3388; www.alegriacocinalatina.com. When your palette craves something other than seafood, this chic restaurant serves up some of the best Latin flavors as well as live flamenco shows on Fri and Sat evenings. Chef Walter Cotta has created a menu with the foods of Spain and Latin America, rich in flavor with distinctive herbs and spices. Try the Enchiladas con Mole—soft corn tortillas filled with chicken and mixed cheeses simmered in an award-winning Oaxaca mole sauce made with a variety of eighteen Mexican spices. Serving lunch Mon through Fri and dinner seven days—call for specific hours and reservations (especially for the flamenco shows). $$.

King's Fish House. 100 West Broadway at Pine Avenue; (562) 432-7463; www.kingsfish house.com. Here are the ingredients for a popular restaurant: friendly service; comfortable wooden booths; and fair, never fishy, prices. It all adds up to a favorite "come-one, come-all" fresh, local seafood restaurant that's nearby shops and theaters. Open daily at 11:15 a.m.; closing times vary, so call to confirm. $$$.

Omelette Inn. 108 West 3rd St.; (562) 437-5625; www.omeletteinn.com. Locally owned and operated for more than two decades, serving traditional American diner food (featuring omelettes, of course) for breakfast and lunch every day from 7 a.m. to 2:30 p.m. $.

Parker's Lighthouse. 435 Shoreline Village Dr.; (562) 432-6500; www.parkerslighthouse .com. Just look for the lighthouse to find this restaurant with a terrific patio view of the *Queen Mary* and harbor. The down-to-earth menu includes fresh fish—mesquite-grilled with a choice of side sauces or blackened, seared, poached, or Cajun seasoned—as well as sushi, and an Angus burger to satisfy any carnivore. Serves lunch and dinner daily. $$$.

majestic *queen mary*

The world's largest luxury liner has been permanently retired and dry-docked since 1967 in the fifty-five-acre **Queen Mary Seaport** *at the end of the 710 Freeway in the Port of Long Beach at 1126 Queen's Hwy. This majestic vessel sailed the North Atlantic Ocean from 1936 to 1967 for the Cunard Line, served as a troop transport during World War II, and is listed on the National Register of Historic Places. Not only does the Queen Mary have a rich maritime history and authentic Art Deco decor, but there are also stunning views of the Pacific Ocean and city skyline from the beautiful restored decks, 314 staterooms, and award-winning restaurants including the signature* **Sir Winston's.** *A weekly Champagne Sunday Brunch is served in the ship's Grand Salon. The ship is open to the public for visiting daily from 10 a.m. to 6 p.m. (buy tickets and special touring packages at the wharf ticket booth at the hotel entrance).*

You can discover more about the history and mystery of the ship with the self-guided audio tour; an hour-long behind-the-scenes guided walking tour; the festive 30-minute Ghosts & Legends Show; or the guided Haunted Encounters Tour, which reveals stories of the Queen Mary's most famous reported ghosts. There are also special Attractions at Night Tours, such as Dining with the Spirits, where you'll have dinner in the five-star Sir Winston's followed by a late-night guided tour of the ship's paranormal hot spots, or the tamer one-hour guided Twilight Historical Tour at sunset. Adjacent to the Queen Mary you can also tour the docked Scorpion submarine—an authentic cold war–era Russian sub. A drink at the chic Art Deco **Observation Bar** *(the original First Class Lounge) is a popular place to enjoy the sunset and panoramas. The* **Promenade Café** *is the Queen Mary's breakfast, lunch, and dinner diner, offering American favorites such as gourmet burgers, fresh seasonal salads, and comfort-food classics. Fresh seafood served with a savory harbor view is the* **Chelsea's** *hallmark for lunch and dinner. Try the signature appetizer featuring an array of smoked salmon, chilled prawns, and crab claws served on sesame seaweed salad plus five varieties of Tobiko caviar! For a truly unique experience, we recommend that you stay overnight onboard the* **Hotel Queen Mary** *to fully experience the grandeur and ambience—be sure to ask for a stateroom with a porthole. For general information call (877) 342-0738, for hotel reservations (877) 342-0742 or (562) 435-3511; www.queenmary.com.*

where to stay

Dockside Boat & Bed. Dock 5, Rainbow Harbor, 316 East Shoreline Dr.; (562) 436-3111; www.boatandbed.com. Four private moored yachts and motor craft to stay aboard overnight (they never move except from the gentle waves lapping on the sides). All boats are fully furnished with private, functional baths, berths/beds, and fascinating indoor/outdoor spaces; continental breakfast basket provided. Next to the Aquarium of the Pacific and Shoreline Village. A highly recommended, truly one-of-a-kind lodging experience with an extraordinary perspective you'll never have in a hotel. $$.

Hotel Maya. 700 Queensway Dr.; (800) 738-7477 or (562) 435-7676; www.hotelmaya longbeach.com. Inspired by Mayan architecture, this luxury, boutique resort–style hotel reopened in 2009 after a multimillion dollar makeover. From the private balconies or patios of 195 plush guest rooms with both waterfront and garden views you'll see stunning vistas of the city skyline and the *Queen Mary*. **Fuego,** helmed by award-winning executive chef Jesse Perez, features coastal Latin cuisine, specializing in *mariscos* (fresh seafood), an extensive selection of *antojitos* (appetizers), and entrees made from both traditional and contemporary recipes. The restaurant is open for breakfast, lunch, and dinner daily and on Sun for its signature Fiesta Domingo Brunch. Viva! $$$.

worth more time

San Pedro—Port of Los Angeles. Just east and adjacent to Long Beach, San Pedro was originally settled as a commercial fishing village in the 1800s and today is home to the Port of Los Angeles, one of the world's largest deepwater commercial seaports and top-ranked container port in the United States. Here you also will find the **World Cruise Center** (located at Berths 91, 92, and 93A/B), point of embarkation for more than a million passengers annually sailing on vacations to Mexico, Alaska, Hawaii, and beyond onboard ships from such lines as Princess Cruises, Royal Caribbean, Silversea, and others. (Note that Carnival Cruise Lines docks in the adjacent Port of Long Beach.)

Located at the end of the I-110 (Harbor Freeway), San Pedro offers value-priced lodging, restaurants, and shopping options. It is easy to explore the attractions via the **San Pedro Red Car Electric Trolley** route currently stretching 1.5 miles along Harbor Boulevard and connecting the World Cruise Center to 6th Street and the L.A. Maritime Museum, Ports O' Call marketplace, and Fisherman's Wharf. Red Cars operate from noon to 9 p.m. Fri through Sun. A $1 all-day fare includes unlimited rides and is transferable for free rides on the shuttle bus to nearby Cabrillo Beach. For complete details, call (310) 732-3473 or visit www.railwaypreservation.com/page8.html.

Also worth your time in San Pedro is the **SS *Lane Victory*** at Berth 94 off Harbor Boulevard (310-519-9545; www.lanevictory.org). Open for tours daily 9 a.m. to 4 p.m., except for six daylong Sat cruises each summer. This operational World War II cargo ship with wartime armament was built in 1945 and saw service in World War II, Korea, and Vietnam.

Decommissioned and fully restored, her 455-foot length and 10,000 tons are a marvel to behold. If you are visiting the Los Angeles area in the summer, make every attempt to secure reservations on one of the day cruises, where the seamen's lives will come alive as you sail. You will even be buzzed by attacking biplanes. This ship is a living memorial to all Merchant Marines.

day trip 02

south

> a world away only 22 miles out to sea:
> santa catalina island

santa catalina island

You'll feel like you're in a different part of the world when you arrive on this Mediterranean-like island via a relaxing one-hour boat trip or scenic 15-minute helicopter flight, yet only 22 miles south of downtown Los Angeles and 22 miles out to sea. One of the chain of eight Channel Islands off the coast of Southern California, Santa Catalina Island was first discovered by a European explorer named Juan Rodriguez Cabrillo and claimed for Spain in 1542. Sixty years later, another Spanish explorer, Sebastian Vizcaino, rediscovered the island on the eve of Saint Catherine's day (November 24) in 1602 and dubbed it Santa Catalina in her honor. During the next 300 years, the island's original natives known as the Pimu of the Gabrielino tribe welcomed many "visitors," including Russian otter hunters, Yankee smugglers, British pirates, and plenty of fishermen.

The island experienced a brief gold rush in the 1860s, but little was actually found. The biggest "gold rush" came around the end of the nineteenth century when Los Angelinos sought a vacation getaway much like we do today. The first American to try to develop Catalina into a resort destination was real-estate speculator George Shatto, who purchased the island for $200,000 in 1887—his sister-in-law Etta Whitney is credited with naming the first town Avalon, taken from Alfred, Lord Tennyson's poem "Idylls of the King" about the legend of King Arthur. The Banning brothers bought the island in 1891, established the Santa Catalina Island Company and further developed some hotels and attractions, and enhanced

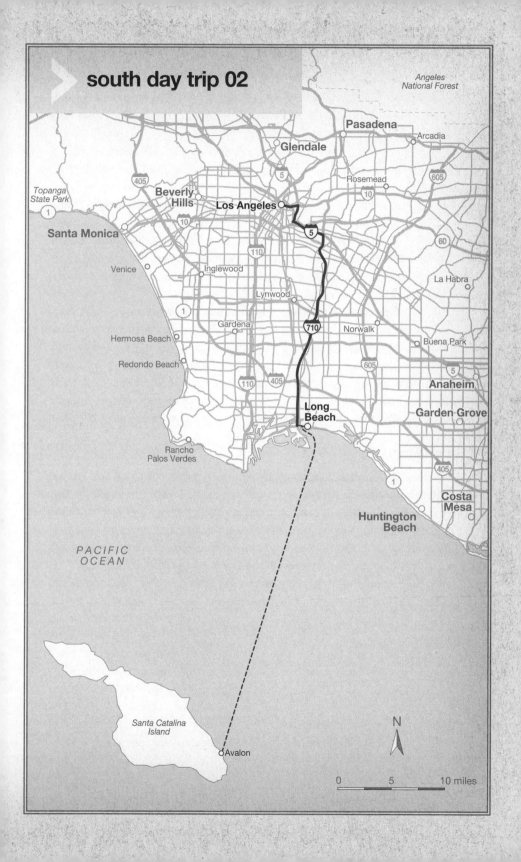

south day trip 02

the steamship line for access. After a fire and the devastating economic effects of World War I, the Banning brothers were forced to sell the island in shares by 1919—which eventually all went to chewing-gum magnate William Wrigley Jr.

Over the ensuing years, the Wrigley family further developed and enhanced most of the infrastructure and resort facilities we enjoy today. Wrigley brought his Chicago Cubs baseball team to Catalina for spring training from 1921 to 1951 (except for the war years of 1942–1945). He built Catalina's baseball field to the exact dimensions of Wrigley Field in Chicago. While only a plaque remains on the site of the field where the Cubs once practiced, their historic clubhouse remains and is now known as the **Catalina Visitors Country Club** (310-510-7404 for info and dining reservations), where the pub, decorated with local memorabilia, opens to the public Fri through Mon at 4 p.m., offering signature cocktails, beer, wine, and modern American fare for dinner.

In 1972, the **Santa Catalina Island Conservancy** (www.catalinaconservancy.org) was established by the Wrigley family as a nonprofit organization dedicated to the preservation of the flora and fauna and geographical features of this unique 22-mile-by-8-mile island. The Conservancy now owns 88 percent of the island and will maintain much of it in its present state. Day trips are very popular to Catalina (which is what locals call it), but you might want to plan to spend a couple of days on this enchanted isle, where you won't need a car for a change (since they are restricted to residents to preserve the delicate ecosystem).

getting there

Your only choices are going by sea or by air, and at a duration of 15 minutes, **Island Express Helicopter Service** flights from Long Beach or San Pedro are certainly the fastest and most exhilarating transportation to Catalina—landing at exclusive heliports in the towns of Avalon and Two Harbors, you'll see amazing panoramas as you're whisked away from the mainland. Call (800) 228-2566 or visit www.islandexpress.com for complete info on fares and schedules. Catalina's **Airport in the Sky** (AVX), was completed in 1946. The 3,250-foot runway actually sits on a mountaintop at 1,602 feet above sea level and is used for private aircraft or charters (it's a hair-raising experience to land here, trust us, but we'd do it again whenever invited!) Three boat companies provide scheduled service to Catalina with departures from the five mainland communities of Marina Del Rey, San Pedro, Long Beach, Newport Beach, and Dana Point. In our opinion, the best way to get to the island by water is aboard **Catalina Express** high-speed vessels (for current schedules and fares, call 310-519-1212 or 800-481-3470; www.catalinaexpress.com). No matter what ship you come in on, you'll arrive at the historic green Pleasure Pier in the sun-splashed city of Avalon. With its hotels, restaurants, and boutique-filled streets, and a year-round population of around 3,000, it is Catalina's biggest town and your headquarters for adventure.

where to go

Catalina Casino. 1 Casino Way, facing Avalon Bay; (310) 510-8687; www.visitcatalina island.com/avalon/poin_casino.php. Built in 1929, this round, white Art Deco structure rises the equivalent of twelve stories and is surrounded on three sides by the sea. Never actually used for gambling, the casino is famed for its ballroom. Fun fact: 6,200 people danced to the music of Kay Kyser on May 8, 1940—the largest number of dancers ever in the casino. Virtually every big band of that era played in the casino ballroom, and live broadcasts were carried over CBS radio from 1934 into the 1950s. Today the ballroom is available for special events and private parties. The casino building also houses the **Avalon Theatre,** the first specially designed for talkies in the 1920s, which seats 1,184 people. Art Deco–style murals by John Gabriel Beckman grace the interior, which also has a full-scale pipe organ. Located in the lower level of the casino, you can still see first-run movies there today. On the ground floor, visit the **Catalina Island Museum** (310-510-2414; www.catalinamuseum .com for tours and information). Founded in 1953, discover more than 7,000 years of history through dozens of engaging and visually exciting exhibits preserving the amazing cultural heritage of this fascinating island—so close to Los Angeles yet far removed from the hustle and bustle of the "mainland."

Santa Catalina Island Company's Discovery Tours. 1 Island Plaza, Avalon; (310) 510-2500 or (800) 626-1496; www.visitcatalinaisland.com. Operating since 1894 and departing from Avalon and Two Harbors, Discovery Tours by Land include the Avalon Scenic Tour, Casino Tour, Skyline Drive Tour, and Inland Motor Tour (the most comprehensive at 4 hours). Discovery Tours by Sea include Undersea Tour, Glass Bottom Boat Trip, Seal Rocks Cruise, Sundown Isthmus Cruise, and the Flying Fish Boat Trip. Plus, in 2010 the Catalina Zip Line Eco Tour was launched; the ultimate interior island tour on the only zip line in Los Angeles and Orange County drops from 500 feet to 60 feet above sea level traveling three-quarters of a mile over five consecutive zip lines at speeds pushing 45 mph. Beginning at the Hog's Back gate, high in the hills near Avalon and descending through Descanso Canyon, you will pause at several eco-stations along the way to learn about history and the eco-systems you're zipping through until you reach Descanso Beach approximately 2 hours later. Reservations are required and tickets are limited. Do not miss this if you have a spirit of adventure. Money-saving combinations are the best way to tailor the tours to your taste at discounts off regular pricing; be sure to ask about them. Reservations for all tours are recommended, especially during the busy weekends, holidays, and summer season.

Catalina Adventure Tours. On the green Pleasure Pier; (310) 510-2888; www.catalina adventuretours.com. Tours via modern air-conditioned buses include the Avalon Explorer, City Passport, City Botanical, and Inside Adventure (the most popular). On the water, tours include the SS *Nautilus* (a semisubmersible sub), *Sea View* (glass-bottom boat), Seal Rock Explorer Cruise, and a Scenic Harbor cruise. Village walking tours are also offered.

> ## on the wild side

Catalina has a 4-hour off-road tour that is ideal for an adventurous getaway. Visiting the "wild side" of the island on the **Cape Canyon Tour** *(310-510-TOUR; www.visitcatalinaisland.com), passengers ride in a open-air, twelve-passenger Mercedes Unimog—a one of a kind off-road vehicle driven by a Catalina Island Conservancy–trained guide. The tour features a scenic drive along a ridgeline overlooking coves of west Avalon, a guided tour of the American bald eagle habitat at Middle Ranch Canyon, and a ride in Cape Canyon for stunning views of the Catalina outback. Lunch is included at the famous Catalina Airport in the Sky. Reservations required.*

where to shop

Strolling around the village of Avalon, poking into courtyards and byways, is a delightful way to discover local arts, crafts, souvenirs, jewelry, and clothing. Check out this website for a current list: www.catalinachamber.com/island/shopping. Some shops are seasonal and hours of operation vary.

Open year-round is the **Metropole Marketplace** (205 Crescent Ave.; 800-541-8528; www.metropolemarketplace.com). Surrounding the Metropole Hotel, check out the Catalina Clothing Company; Bay of the Seven Moons for jewelry; the Dolphin Emporium for everything dolphin: plush animals, statues, shirts, gifts; the Stare Case with unique fashions and evening wear; Perico Gallery for fine art; Catalina Seashell Company; and more.

where to eat

Catalina Coffee & Cookie Company. 205 Crescent Ave., Avalon; (310) 510-2447; www .metropolemarketplace.com/html/body_catalina_cookie_company.html. Need a pick-me-up? Come here for an Eclipse, a fudge cookie dipped in white chocolate. Open daily at 5 a.m. year-round. Call for seasonal closing times. $.

The Cottage. 118 Catalina Ave.; Avalon; (310) 510-0726; www.menu4u.com/thecottage. Totally traditional family breakfast, lunch and dinner favorites served daily, now offering full bar service, too. The Chef's Mess omelet contains everything but the kitchen sink! Just about every breakfast item is available all day. Open every day at 6 a.m., generally closes 10 to 11 p.m. Call for specific hours. $.

Ristorante Villa Portofino. 101 Crescent Ave., Avalon; (310) 510-2009; www.ristorante villaportofino.com. For authentic Italian cuisine in a quiet, romantic dinner setting with harbor views from many tables, this could be your favorite restaurant retreat from the hubbub that can be Avalon (especially in summer season). Of course seafood and pasta specialties are on offer, and don't miss the tiramisu—accompanied by a fine selection of Italian and California wines and one of the island's only espresso bars. Call for hours of operation; reservations suggested. $$$.

where to stay

Inn on Mount Ada. 398 Wrigley Rd., Avalon; (310) 510-2030; www.innonmtada.com. Built in 1921, this gorgeous hilltop bed-and-breakfast is the former home of William Wrigley Jr. and his wife Ada. The Georgian Colonial–style inn has been meticulously restored and furnished and is listed in the National Register of Historic Places. All six rooms have private baths, fireplaces, and stunning views of the town, harbor, and ocean. Rates include gourmet breakfast and lunch, wine, appetizers, and electric golf carts to go up and down the 350-foot hill to town. Recipient of the Four-Star Award from Forbes (formerly Mobil) Travel Guide since 1991. $$$.

Pavilion Hotel. 513 Crescent Ave., Avalon; (310) 510-2500 or (800) 626-1496; www .visitcatalinaisland.com/avalon/hote_pavilionlodge.php. Formerly the Pavilion Lodge, this property re-opened after an extensive renovation in 2010, but it is still just fourteen steps from the beach. The charming two-story property now features seventy-one upscale rooms

how do you get around the island?

*Avalon, the island's principal town, is only one square mile, and everything is within easy walking distance. Your feet are the best mode of transportation around here. In car-crazy California, Avalon is the only city authorized by the state legislature to regulate the number and size of vehicles allowed to drive on city streets. Currently, there is a fourteen-year waiting list to own a car on Catalina, but you don't need one to enjoy your visit here, really! You can also rent a bicycle to go exploring or take a sightseeing tour in a comfortable motor coach or open-air tram. To enjoy the hills above the town, do what locals do—drive an electric golf cart and putt around—rental stands are all around downtown. If you want to venture beyond Avalon, the **Safari Bus** (310-510-2800) links Avalon with the village of Two Harbors, including stops at Little Harbor, Airport in the Sky, and the trailhead for Black Jack Junction. **Catalina Transportation Services** (310-510-0025) offers door-to-door taxi, shuttle, and delivery services throughout Santa Catalina Island. So relax and enjoy this picturesque place sans gas-powered vehicle!*

all facing a huge garden courtyard—with ground-floor rooms featuring private lanais as well as two ocean-view suites. $$.

Zane Grey Pueblo Hotel. 199 Chimes Tower Rd., Avalon; (310) 510-0966; www.zane greypueblohotel.com. Built in 1926, this sprawling Hopi Indian–style pueblo home located on a cliff above the harbor is the former residence of novelist Zane Grey (1872–1939), who wrote more than one hundred books in his lifetime. Choose from sixteen guest rooms named after his novels (nine rooms face the ocean, the others are mountainside—so be sure to ask for your preference). Enjoy the large decks, an arrowhead-shaped freshwater swimming pool, and the author vibes from Zane Grey's original living room with its grand piano, fireplace, and television. $–$$.

southwest

day trip 01

southwest

quintessential SoCal
marina del rey, venice beach

marina del rey

Marina del Rey is located 4 miles north of Los Angeles International Airport (LAX) and bounded on all sides by the City of Los Angeles. A friendly bit of seafaring paradise nestled on the shoreline, Marina del Rey was once the party hangout for pilots and stewardesses (back in the day when they were called stewardesses) due to its proximity to LAX. "The Marina," as it's called by the locals, today is family friendly with a splash of waterfront excitement. It's the largest man-made small boat harbor in the world, home to more than 6,000 pleasure boats and yachts. Admiralty Way is the main drag, lined with most of the city's hotels and restaurants. Avenues with names like Fiji Way and Bali Way branch off from Admiralty, providing added waterfront dining and recreational options. Prior to becoming one of the largest man-made harbors in the United States, Marina del Rey was an estuary often frequented by local duck hunters and fishermen. Just minutes away from LAX and a few miles from Venice Beach, Santa Monica, and Hollywood, Marina del Rey is a popular base for Los Angeles–area visitors due to its easy access to so many Southern California attractions.

getting there

From downtown Los Angeles, drive west on I-10, then south on the I-405 Freeway and exit west onto the SR 90 Marina Freeway for a smooth sail into Marina del Rey. From there, it's

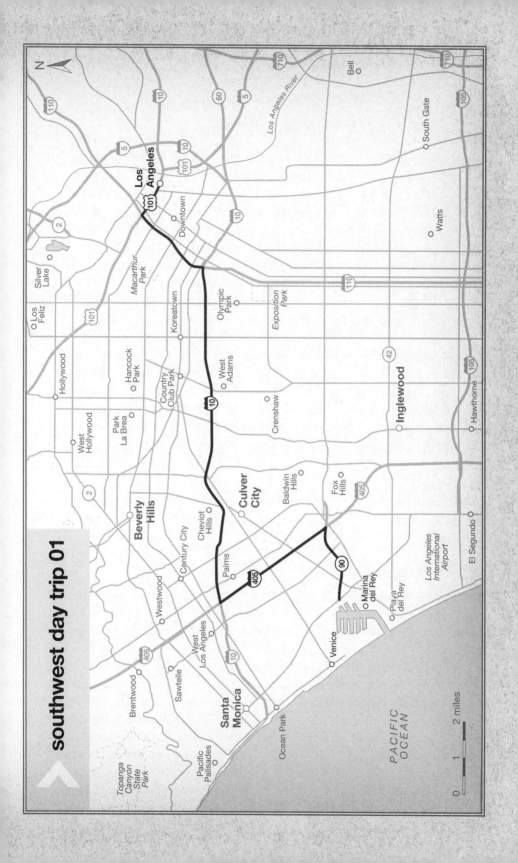

los angeles international airport (lax)

Located 10 minutes south of Marina del Rey, **Los Angeles International Airport (LAX)** *(1 World Way; (310) 646-5252; www.lawa.org/welcomeLAX.aspx), is the world's seventh busiest airport, the point of arrival for more than 56.5 million passengers in 2009. It's served by some eighty carriers including all major airlines, and had 565 daily flights to eighty-one destinations in the United States and 1,000 weekly nonstop flights to sixty-five international destinations in 2009. LAX has nine passenger terminals connected by a U-shaped two-level roadway. Curbside baggage check-in is available on the upper departure level, and baggage claim is on the lower level. The Tom Bradley International Terminal (TBIT) is currently undergoing a major renovation and expansion (completion is set for 2014), and remains open for all flights. Restaurants, including branches of favorite L.A. eateries La Brea Bakery for artisan breads and sandwiches, Pinkberry frozen yogurt, and Gladstone's 4 Fish, an oceanfront Malibu landmark; bars; gift shops; newsstands; duty-free shops for international flights; business centers; and a first-aid station are among the passenger conveniences throughout LAX. Free shuttle service runs every 12 to 15 minutes between terminals—look for the shuttle marked "A." For personal assistance, eleven information centers are located*

a short few blocks drive north to Venice Beach via Washington Boulevard west to Pacific Avenue. Turn right on Pacific Avenue, and you're in the heart of Venice, with the beach just a block away.

where to go

Fisherman's Village. 13763 Fiji Way; (310) 822-6866. With buildings designed in the New England style, this collection of shops and eateries is a scenic spot to stroll along the waterfront boardwalk, stop for an ice cream, and enjoy the panorama of the Marina's main channel. Look for mementos in the shell and souvenir shops, and stop for a bite at one of several ocean-view cafes and restaurants: El Torito (Mexican), Angler's Choice (seafood), and Sapori (Italian) offer licensed waterfront dining, whereas, Cafe Al Fresco, Thai Garden Cafe, and Lighthouse Grill offer quick gourmet meals, snacks, and drinks. This is also the departure point for many of the Marina's boat cruises offering fully catered and licensed private party harbor cruises and public cruises on weekends and for holiday celebrations. Hourly or daily rental of power, sail, and electric boats and kayaks is available seven days a week on the docks here, too. Free concerts are held on the plaza next to the lighthouse, both Sat and Sun afternoons throughout the year, weather permitting.

throughout the airport, staffed by people ready to help with airport, sightseeing, and lodging questions. LAX Ambassadors, recognizable by their straw hats, also are on hand walking throughout the airport to help with connecting-flight and surface-transportation information.

Getting to/from LAX

Vehicle-wise, LAX can be accessed from I-405 or I-110, exiting at Century Boulevard; or via the I-105 Freeway, exiting at Sepulveda Boulevard. **LAX FlyAway** *(866-435-9529; www.lawa.org), has daily bus service from three locations: Union Station Downtown at Bus Stop 9, $7 one-way; Westwood on the University of California at Los Angeles (UCLA) campus at UCLA Parking Structure 32, north side of Kinross Avenue one block west of Gayley Avenue, $5 one-way; and in the San Fernando Valley at the Van Nuys Airport FlyAway Bus Terminal, 7610 Woodley Ave., Van Nuys, $7 one-way, credit or debit cards only. LAX also is accessible via Los Angeles's Metrolink (www.metro.net), which provides easy access to downtown Union Station via the Metro Green Line Aviation Station and a short, free shuttle ride to LAX. Additional options include shared-ride vans* **SuperShuttle** *(800-258-3826 or 310-782-6600; www.supershuttle.com),* **Prime Time Shuttle** *(800-473-3743 or 310-342-7200; www.primetimeshuttle.com), and plentiful taxis and limousines.*

Musical styles are varied and can include jazz, funk, blues, reggae, rockabilly, salsa, and rock. Fisherman's Village connects with the Ballona Creek and South Bay Bicycle Trails, which combine more than 26 miles of coastal beach riding—you can find rentals available on the wharf as well.

Mother's Beach. Admiralty Way; there is no direct phone, but the visitor center has all the info at (310) 305-9545; www.beaches.co.la.ca.us/bandh/marina/mothersbeach .htm. So named because this wide, flat beach has no surf and is safe for kids, Mother's Beach is great for families. It has a children's area with play equipment, a lifeguard on duty, and rental bikes and skates. The calm waters also make it popular for kayaking and windsurfing.

Burton W. Chace Park. This lovely ten-acre park juts out into the marina channel, providing an excellent viewpoint to watch the boats and the sunset. It has picnic tables, barbeque facilities, and a cafe. If you're visiting during a holiday, Chase Park is the prime, free viewing location for the Marina's Christmas boat parade and July 4th boat parade and fireworks display. Just get there early.

Hornblower Cruises & Events. 13755 Fiji Way; (310) 301-6000 or (888) 467-6256; www .hornblower.com. This company offers a variety of sailing excursions at a variety of prices starting at $11 for a 45-minute narrated harbor cruise, where you'll see and learn about the magnificent yachts, quaint houseboats, and waterfront mansions throughout the Marina. More choices are weekend dinner-dance, jazz, and Sun champagne brunch cruises, all of which include drinks, three-course meals, and live music. These begin at $54.95. Reservations required.

Paradise Bound Yacht Charters. 4375 Admiralty Way; (800) 655-0850 or (310) 578-7963; www.the-calculating-lady.com/captalex. Private harbor cruises, dinner cruises, day sailing, and seasonal whale watching (Feb to Apr) for up to six people are offered onboard this company's luxury sailing yacht *Silver Eagle,* a 42-foot Catalina sailboat. Check the website for hourly rate specials.

Gondola D'Amore. 14045 Panay Way; (310) 736-7301; www.gondolasdamore.com. Experience the romance of Italy with a sail through the Marina in a 32-foot Italian gondola. Pillows, candles, Italian music, and appetizers are included; you provide the beverages. Sunset is a perfect time. The cruises are 1 or 2 hours. Prices begin at $100 for one person for an hour, up to $375 for six people for 2 hours. Reservations are necessary.

Marina del Rey Boat Rentals. 13719 Fiji Way; (310) 574-2822; www.boats4rent.com. The Marina's quiet waters are ideal for smooth sailing, and this company offers an array of watercraft including sail, power, and electric boats; kayaks, Jet Skis, and stand-up paddle boards. Hourly rentals begin at $15 for a kayak, up to $125 an hour for a 90-foot power boat.

Marina del Rey Sportfishing. Fiji Way; (800) 822-3625 or (310) 822-3625; www.marina delreysportfishing.com. This company offers half-day and three-quarter-day fishing excursions, departing from Dock 52 in the morning and afternoon. Advance reservations are recommended.

where to shop

Waterside at Marina del Rey. Admiralty Way; (818) 222-3444; www.shopwaterside.com. This Mediterranean-style outdoor shopping plaza offers high fashion to basics including a U.S. post office and grocery store among its twenty-seven shops and nine restaurants. You'll find Chico's, BCBGMAXAZRIA, Brighton Accessories, swimwear, and jewelry. For relaxed people watching, take a seat under a shady umbrella and enjoy a Pinkberry frozen yogurt. Hours are 10 a.m. to 7 p.m. Mon through Fri; 10 a.m. to 8 p.m. Sat; and 11 a.m. to 6 p.m. Sun.

where to eat

Cafe del Rey. 4451 Admiralty Way; (310) 823-6395; www.cafedelreymarina.com. This is one of the Marina's most sophisticated restaurants, and it attracts diners from throughout L.A. It features California-Mediterranean cuisine served in a sleek and contemporary setting—inside dining only—but huge picture windows look out on the marina. Fish is the specialty, and it's so fresh that the menu includes the name of the captain, the name of the boat, and location where it was caught. The mahi mahi is fresh from Kauai and served with white and green asparagus, celery root ravioli, wild mushrooms, and lemon caper sauce is a tasty example. The menu is diverse, offering a delicious variety from bone-in rib eye steak to *jidori* chicken breast, soups, salads, and starters. Open nightly for dinner, lunch is served Mon through Sat, and brunch on Sun. Reservations are recommended. $$$.

Cafe Mermaids. 14045 Panay Way; (310) 306-3883. This small quick-service eatery is a local favorite for everything from coffee, protein shakes, and lemonade to wraps, toasted sandwiches, quesadillas, salads, and pies—apple being the most frequent "pie of the week." The waterfront deck overlooks the boats and Mother's Beach, and it is always filled with resident boaters and condo dwellers enjoying the good food and view. Open Mon to Fri from 7 a.m. to 6 p.m., Sat and Sun from 7 a.m. to 5 p.m. $.

Shanghai Red's. 13813 Fiji Way; (310) 823-4522; www.shanghairedsrestaurant.com. A Marina landmark, this waterfront eatery has a decor mix of Tiki-style Polynesian—you enter by crossing a bridge over a koi pond—and Victorian-style funk that makes having a mai tai almost mandatory. You can dine inside or outside; most people prefer outside on the deck, which has one of the best views in the Marina overlooking the main channel. The food is classic American waterfront fare from crab-stuffed mushrooms and clam chowder to shrimp scampi and salmon, plus turf favorites including prime rib and filet mignon. Dinner is served nightly, lunch is Mon through Fri., and brunch is served Sat and Sun. Reservations are recommended but are essential for brunch. $$.

where to stay

Jamaica Bay Inn. 4175 Admiralty Way; (888) 823-5333; www.jamaicabay-inn.com. A long-time favorite, this is the only beachfront hotel on the sand in the Marina. At press time, it was closed for an expansion and is expected to re-open in late 2011.The redo will give it a West Indies–style look, including a stone fireplace in the lobby, an indoor/outdoor restaurant overlooking Mother's Beach, and new guest room decor and amenities. Call or check the website for opening rates.

Marina del Rey Hotel. 13534 Bali Way; (310) 301-1000; www.marinadelreyhotel.com. This full-service hotel offers the true feel of the Marina, located on a small peninsula, with boat slips and docks on three sides. The decor is casually elegant, with marina views from the pool, waterfront restaurant, and many guest rooms. Amenities include on-site assistance with tours, free wireless, and a 24-hour business center. $$–$$$.

Ritz-Carlton, Marina del Rey. 4375 Admiralty Way; (310) 823-1700; www.ritzcarlton .com. This is the Marina's most luxurious hotel, located on the water with its own dock, and it is popular with leisure and business travelers. It features a waterfront pool with private cabanas and a raised-patio event area with stellar views of the marina, a full-service waterfront spa, two lighted tennis courts, limo and car rental services and a 24-hour business center. Every room has a marina or city view along with goose-down pillows and the expected high-end services and amenities. Dine poolside or in the Jer-ne Restaurant + Bar. $$$.

venice beach

Set along the Pacific Ocean just north of Marina del Rey, Venice is famous for the colorful cast of characters who perform daily along Ocean Front Walk and the tanned bodybuilders who work out along its 2-mile stretch of wide golden sands. Established in 1905 as a seaside replica of its Italian namesake, picturesque canals still wind through several neighborhoods, and its bohemian vibe makes it home to Hollywood stars as well as struggling musicians and artists.

where to go

Ocean Front Walk. Known locally as the Venice Boardwalk, this beachfront walkway extends between Venice Boulevard and Rose Avenue, providing a people-watcher's dream, with its daily crowd of street performers, from chainsaw jugglers to freaky fortune tellers, sand sculptors to collage artists, and mimes to musicians. Watch for impromptu disco roller skating at the Skate Dancing Plaza, exotic drummers in the Venice Beach Drum Circle, and buffed-out bodybuilders—both male and female—working out on legendary Muscle Beach. Homey to hip eateries line the east side of Ocean Front Walk, providing ringside views of the action alongside souvenir shops, residences, and tattoo parlors. Weekends draw the most street performers.

Gold's Gym. 360 Hampton Dr.; (310) 392-4661; www.goldsgym.com. Nicknamed "the mecca of body building," this gym is credited with starting the workout craze when it opened here in 1965, and it's where Arnold Schwarzenegger was discovered. You can work out for $20 a day, take a class for $10, or simply buy a T-shirt or any number of Gold's Gym items in the gift shop. Hours are 4 a.m. to midnight on weekdays and 5 a.m. to 11 p.m. on weekends.

Venice Canals. The last remaining mile of Venice's original 16 miles of canals (founded in 1905 by local developer Abbot Kinney) winds through a neighborhood across from the beach near Washington Boulevard. This provides a picturesque stroll, with boats and ducks gliding through the water, arched bridges, and quaint residences lining the waterways.

where to shop

Abbot Kinney. www.abbotkinneynow.com. This 5-block stretch of trendy shops built into the hundred-year-old buildings along Abbot Kinney Boulevard between Main Street and North Venice Boulevard is one of Los Angeles's favorite shopping destinations. More than one hundred high-end stores sell everything from handmade furniture and jewelry to vintage clothing, art, and books, and some twenty-four cafes, bars, and restaurants offer a perfect perch for people watching. Stay for the Abbot Kinney 1st Friday (of each month) celebration, when many shops are open until 9 p.m. and feature live entertainment, special sales, and food or drink. Hours are from 10 a.m. to 6 p.m. or a bit later.

where to eat

Abbot's Habit. 1401 Abbot Kinney Blvd.; (310) 399-1171; www.abbotshabit.com. This popular hangout for coffee, sandwiches, bagels, and pastries is a great place to enjoy good food, rub elbows with the eclectic locals, and enjoy the Abbot Kinney scene—if you can find space at one of the few sidewalk tables and chairs. Fri and Sat night from 7 to 10 p.m. the Habit Jam features music by local musicians. Open daily from 6 a.m. to 10 p.m. $–$$.

Joe's Restaurant. 1023 Abbot Kinney Blvd.; (310) 399-5811; www.joesrestaurant.com. Serving fine California-French cuisine under the direction of chef-owner Joseph Miller, this restaurant is consistently rated among L.A.'s top ten restaurants in the Zagat Survey. Menu selections include Hudson Valley foie gras parfait with melba toast for starters, and inspired entrees such as New Zealand red snapper with potato scales, wild rice salsify, crispy spinach and red wine sauce; and equally wonderful meat and chicken dishes. The Dessert for Two is a heavenly chocolate soufflé cake, with crème fraîche ice cream, caramel rice candy, and passion fruit curd served with two half-glasses of port. There is a three-course prix-fixe menu for $45 and a daily Chef's Tasting Menu. Open for dinner Tues through Sun; lunch Tues through Fri, and brunch on Sat and Sun. Closed Mon. $$$.

On the Waterfront Cafe. 205 Ocean Front Way; (310) 392-0322; www.waterfrontcafe .com. Add a little Euro fun and cuisine to your boardwalk watching at this German beer garden–style eatery. The extensive German beer selection, served by the pitcher, is a main draw, along with Swiss cheese fondue, Bavarian pretzels, bratwurst, and other German-Swiss specialties. Pool tables are in the back. Open daily at 10 a.m. The kitchen closes at 9:30 p.m., and closing time depends on how busy they are. $$.

The Sidewalk Cafe. 1401 Ocean Front Way; (310) 399-5547; www.thesidewalkcafe.com. Located on the corner of Ocean Front Way and Horizon Avenue, this iconic patio restaurant offers great people watching. The large covered patio sports tables with red-checkered tablecloths, and a huge menu of American, Italian, and Mexican favorites, everything from burgers—they grind their own meat—to fajitas, soups, salads, sandwiches, and pastas. Breakfast is served all day. The bar features fun California disaster–inspired specialty drinks: Wild Fire is a delicious concoction of Southern Comfort, Amaretto, berry liqueur, and pineapple and orange juices. Open daily from 8 a.m. to midnight. Validated weekday parking is available 1 block south at Market Street. $–$$.

where to stay

Cadillac Hotel. 8 Dudley Ave.; (310) 399-8876; www.thecadillachotel.com. Painted pink with turquoise trim, this four-story boutique hotel is a Venice landmark, located on the boardwalk in the heart of the action. Built in 1914, it was once the residence of Charlie Chaplin and is still popular with visiting entertainment industry members. The newly remodeled rooms include flat-screen TVs and refrigerators. Other amenities include 24-hour concierge service, a rooftop patio, and limited parking. $$–$$$.

Hotel Erwin. 1697 Pacific Ave.; (424) 214-0046 or (888) 797-1651; www.hotelerwin.com. As a member of the Joie de Vivre boutique hotel chain, this property offers an upscale kitschy style, about 1.5 blocks from the Venice Boardwalk. Its in-room amenities include a media hub, iHome docking station, free Internet, and pillow-top mattresses. Some suites have walk-in showers and balconies with ocean views. The largest suite has a retro circular bed. The restaurant serves breakfast and dinner, and sunset cocktails and light fare are served on the rooftop lounge, which offers sweeping beach and boardwalk views. The hotel also has valet parking, a business center, and meeting space for small gatherings. $$–$$$.

Venice Beach Suites. 1305 Ocean Front Walk; (310) 396-4559; www.venicebeach suites.com. This hotel also is on the boardwalk in the center of activity, with twenty-eight studio and oceanfront suites, some with fully equipped kitchens. The style is turn-of-the-nineteenth-century funky, with hardwood floors and exposed brick walls. Amenities include high-speed Internet access, parking, and beach toys and lounge chairs that you can check out. $–$$.

worth more time

California State Route 1 (Pacific Coast Highway or just PCH). No matter what you call it, just taking a drive along any section of this famous California road is likely to bring you some excellent adventures and astonishing scenery you'll relish for a lifetime. Technically speaking, you will see it listed on maps as CA-1 or SR-1 with a green shield-shaped emblem. It travels along much of the Pacific coast of California, but also runs together with other roads and Highway 101—and just to make it more confusing, it is not signed SR 1 in many places! Here in Southern California, we generally just call it PCH.

Let's start at the southern end of PCH and work our way northward. Officially, PCH starts south of Los Angeles in Orange County in Capistrano Beach at the junction of I-5.

Then it runs northwesterly through the beach communities of Laguna, Newport, Huntington, Long, Redondo, Hermosa, and Manhattan, passing LAX (Los Angeles International Airport); then it is called Lincoln Boulevard and goes through the Los Angeles County neighborhoods of Westchester, Playa Vista, Marina del Rey, Venice Beach, and Santa Monica.

One of the most dramatic views on this part of PCH comes as you travel northbound, passing through the McClure Tunnel, emerging along Santa Monica's bodacious beachfront, and hugging the curving coast more than 30 miles through Malibu. PCH is the main drag through Malibu, spanning the entire 21 miles of the city. Be sure to stop and enjoy any number of famous beaches, dining, shopping, vibes, and surf breaks here before cruising by Mugu Rock. Here PCH leaves the coast and meanders into the Ventura County city of Oxnard, where it unceremoniously joins up with Highway 101. After traveling through the city of Ventura, PCH does briefly separate from Highway 101 for a few miles to track right along the ocean (feel the spray) from Emma Wood State Beach to the Mobil Pier Undercrossing, where it rejoins Highway 101 about 3 miles south of the Santa Barbara County line near La Conchita. Once again, PCH merges with Highway 101 (signage totally nonexistent) for 54 miles and passes through greater Santa Barbara, only to split again into Highway 101 and PCH (with signs for both) again just north of the Gaviota Tunnel. From here PCH veers through the cities of Lompoc (home of Vandenberg Air Force Base), Guadalupe, and Grover Beach before joining Highway 101 again in San Luis Obispo County near Pismo Beach. Confused yet?

SR 1 splits from Highway 101 again at San Luis Obispo and resumes as Cabrillo Highway. It continues north as a freeway through Morro Bay past Cayucos until it again becomes a winding, two-lane road with occasional passing lanes. This is probably the most popular and famous part of the road—where it hugs the oceanside through San Simeon (Hearst Castle), past the elephant seal colony at Piedras Blancas Lighthouse, and to the cliffs of Big Sur, over Bixby Bridge, and into Carmel and Monterey. After this, PCH enters Santa Cruz and the San Francisco Bay area, crossing the Golden Gate Bridge and continuing through Marin County to Fort Bragg before reaching its northern California endpoint in Leggett.

We recommend that you take any portion of PCH for a quintessential California road trip, particularly in a convertible to soak up the sensations!

west

day trip 01

west

 **the best of westside:**
beverly hills, westwood

beverly hills

Famous as the epicenter of mansions, movie stars, and designer shopping, Beverly Hills is all of that and more. In fact, the city calls itself the "province of Beverly Hills." Dining out is a way of life here, be it in sidewalk cafes, bistros, or tony restaurants. The see-and-be-seen climate permeates the city and its dynamic architecture along its palm-lined avenues, chic hotels, overly manicured gardens, and celebrity-infused attractions.

getting there

Drive west on the I-10 Freeway, exiting on Robertson Boulevard north. Continue for several miles; turn left on Wilshire Boulevard and drive until you see the landmark Beverly Wilshire Beverly Hills hotel on your left. Look right, and you'll see posh Rodeo Drive. Welcome to the heart of Beverly Hills. Put on your sunglasses, act like you own the world—and enjoy.

where to go

Beverly Hills Trolley Tours. Catch these trolleys on the southeast corner of Rodeo Drive and Dayton Way; (310) 285-2442; www.beverlyhills.org. These 40-minute narrated tours are a great way to get your bearing of the downtown center while learning about the city's architecture, history, and renowned areas. The trolleys run from 11 a.m. to 4 p.m. year-

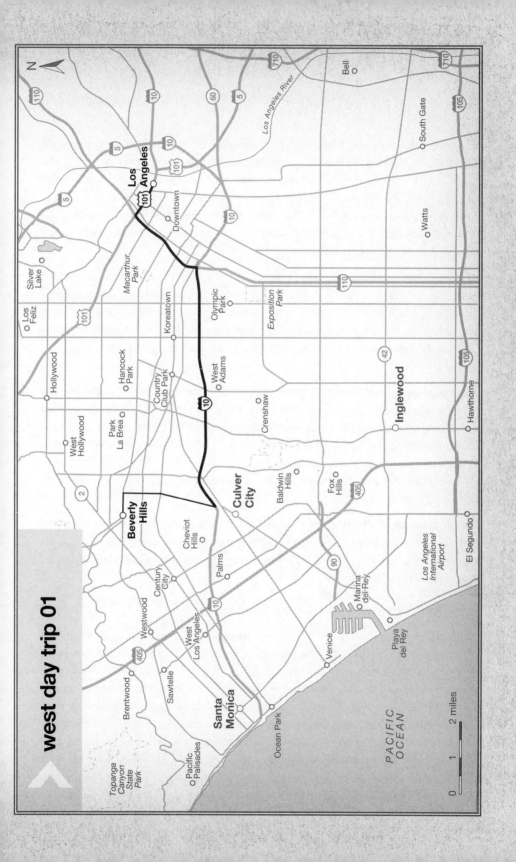

round on Sat and Sun; Tues to Sun from July 7 through Aug 31. The fare is $10 for adults and slightly less for kids.

Greystone Mansion and Park. 905 Loma Vista Dr.; (310) 550-4654; www.beverlyhills .org. View the fabulous fifty-five-room mansion built in 1928 by the son of oil tycoon, and Beverly Hills's founder, Edward Lawrence Doheny, and stroll around the grounds, which are now a city park. The Tudor-style mansion was the site of the untimely death of his son, Edward "Ned" Lawrence Doheny, at the hands of Hugh Plunkett, who then turned the gun on himself. The estate has appeared in numerous movies including *Ghostbusters* and *Spi-derman III.* The park is open daily from 10 a.m. to 6 p.m.

Virginia Robinson Gardens. 1008 Elden Way; (310) 276-5367; www.robinson-gardens .com. Built for the heir to the Robinson's department store fortune, this opulent Mediter-ranean-style villa is surrounded by six acres of gardens, including the largest collection of king palm trees in the nation. Advance reservations are required for a guided tour of the gardens and home—call at least two days ahead. Tours are at 10 a.m. and 1 p.m. Tues through Fri.

The Paley Center for Media (formerly the Museum of Radio and Television). 465 North Beverly Dr., on the corner of South Santa Monica Boulevard; (310) 786-1070; www .paleycenter.org. Come watch your favorite sitcoms from *The Honeymooners* and *I Love Lucy* to *The Mod Squad* and even *The Beverly Hillbillies.* With a library of more than 140,000 TV and radio programs, different footage is shown daily, as well as clips from current celeb-rity events. Guided tours are available, inquire at the front desk. Open noon to 5 p.m. Wed to Sun. Suggested donation is $10. Parking is free.

Rodeo Drive Walk of Style. As you stroll along Rodeo Drive look down to spot the plaques set in the sidewalk featuring the names and memorable quotes of fashion legends including movie costume designer Edith Head, designer-to-the-stars James Galanos, and Italian stylista Donatella Versace.

where to shop

Rodeo Drive. www.rodeodrive-bh.com. This shopping district extends for 3 long blocks between Wilshire and Santa Monica Boulevards and the cross streets. World famous for haute couture and designer boutiques, architecture and style combine at boutiques such as Prada, where visitors walk across a transparent Lucite floor with mannequins posed underneath; Gucci; Jimmy Choo; Georgio Armani; Fendi; Louie Vuitton; Bulgari jewelry—all the fashionista favorites are represented. But don't think you have to spend the big bucks. Check the side streets for stylish shops with lower prices, and even the top boutiques have seasonal sales. You won't see any sale signs in the windows, but check at the back for sale racks. Take time out to relax and people watch at ice cream shops, coffee bars, cafes, and restaurants along the way. Look for the public parking structures on the side streets and metered street parking. The first two hours are free in the public lots, then it's $3 each half-hour, with a $20 per day maximum.

Two Rodeo. Corner of Wilshire Boulevard and Rodeo Drive; www.tworodeo.com. Designed in the likeness of a European cobblestone lane, Two Rodeo features Versace, Tiffany & Co., and other high-fashion and gift boutiques and sidewalk cafes.

Wilshire Boulevard. Look for more shops along Wilshire Boulevard on either side of Rodeo Drive. Famous names include St. John, Niketown, Sak's Fifth Avenue, and Barneys.

where to eat

Brighton Coffee Shop. 9600 Brighton Way; (310) 276-7732. This is a regular old coffee shop smack in the heart of ritzy Rodeo Drive. It's been in the same spot since 1934—you may think some of the customers have been coming since it opened. A friendly atmosphere, waitstaff who call the locals by name, and the expected selection of breakfast and lunch items make it a simple pleasure. Breakfast is served all day. Open 7 a.m. to 5 p.m. Mon to Sat, and 7 a.m. to 3 p.m. Sun. $–$$.

Mastro's Steakhouse. 246 North Canon Dr.; (310) 888-8782; www.mastrosrestaurants .com. An ambience of upscale people enjoying good food and good times permeates this chic two-level restaurant. It's open for lunch, but dinner is the best time to enjoy its full-flavored cuisine and atmosphere. Ask for a table upstairs—that's where the Piano Bar Lounge attracts celebrities and fun lovers—with nightly live entertainment and dancing. The sizable menu ranges from caviar to iceberg-wedge salads, prime steaks to sea bass and chicken, and delicious forget-the-calories desserts. The Lounge is open daily 4:30 p.m. to 1 a.m. Dinner only 5 to 11 p.m. Sun to Thurs, and 5 p.m. to midnight Fri and Sat. $$$.

Spago Beverly Hills. 176 North Canon Dr.; (310) 385-0880; www.wolfgangpuck.com. This is the flagship of celebrity chef Wolfgang Puck's restaurant empire and a top spot for star sightings—Sir Paul McCartney was even seen here—and other people watching among its hip decor of original art, jeweled details, and garden patio. Chef Puck himself frequently works the crowd. You'll find all his California cuisine classics from sweet corn agnolotti with mascarpone to the grilled prime *cote de boeuf* for two. But don't ask for foie gras. Chef Puck supports humane food practices, and he's eliminated foie gras and other not-so-kindly produced fare from his menus. If you only have a minute, sip a drink at the bar and gaze at the dining room action. Lunch is noon to 2:15 p.m. Mon to Thurs and Sat, and 11:30 a.m. to 2:15 p.m. Fri. Dinner is 6 to 10 p.m. Sun to Fri, and 5:30 to 11 p.m. Sat. Valet parking is available. $$$.

Sprinkles Cupcakes. 9635 South Santa Monica Blvd.; (310) 274-8765; www.sprinkles .com. This is the store that started the cupcake phenomena, when maven Candace Nelson opened her first cupcake-only bakery here in 2005. Pull up a chair at the cupcake bar and enjoy any of the myriad of hand-crafted, freshly iced flavors, from banana to lemon coconut—and, of course, chocolate! You'll find this sleek little shop 2 blocks west of Rodeo Drive on "little" Santa Monica Boulevard; locals call it "little" because it's the smaller of the two Santa Monica–named streets that run parallel to each other through Beverly Hills. Open 9 a.m. to 7 p.m. Mon to Sat, and 10 a.m. to 6 p.m. Sun. $–$$.

where to stay

Beverly Wilshire Beverly Hills, A Four Seasons Hotel. 9500 Wilshire Blvd.; (310) 275-5200; www.fourseasons.com/beverlywilshire. Familiar to the world as the setting for the movie *Pretty Woman,* starring Julia Roberts, this landmark hotel is at the intersection of Rodeo Drive and Wilshire Boulevard. The preferred address of visitors from heads of state to Hollywood's elite, it features sumptuous decor, luxurious appointments, and all the twenty-first-century technology. Enjoy cocktails or a meal in The Blvd restaurant that looks out onto Rodeo Drive, or experience CUT, celebrity chef Wolfgang Puck's award-winning steakhouse. Valet parking only, $40 a night. $$$.

Hotel Beverly Terrace. 469 North Doheny Dr.; (310) 274-8141 or (800) 842-6401; www .hotelbeverlyterrace.com. Located a short distance from Rodeo Drive, this hotel has been a fixture for years due to its good location and value. The rooms are simple and artistically decorated in a retro mood and include free wireless and mini refrigerators. Complimentary continental breakfast is served poolside. On-site parking is $6 a night. $$.

Luxe Hotel Rodeo Drive. 360 North Rodeo Dr.; (310) 273-0300; www.luxehotelrodeo drive.com. You're in the heart of the action right on Rodeo Drive at this boutique hotel, surrounded by chic shops and restaurants. It offers a hip minimalist vibe; some rooms have Rodeo Drive views while others feature sun decks, and the penthouse suite (a favorite with celebrities) has wraparound views of it all. Sip cocktails in the lounge, enjoy breakfast, lunch, and dinner in the cafe. Valet parking only at $28 a night, but parking sometimes is included—so check when you make reservations. $$$.

Montage Beverly Hills. 225 North Canon Dr.; (310) 860-7800; www.montagebeverlyhills .com. This is Beverly Hills's newest hotel, opened in November 2008. Located a block from Rodeo Drive, it features a Spanish Mediterranean–style exterior and an opulent Europe-anesque interior. Guest room sizes begin at 500-square-feet, and the amenities include a luxurious spa, three restaurants, a lounge for drinks and afternoon tea, and a sunny rooftop pool. It's one of the country's first Gold LEED-certified hotels for eco-friendly practices. Valet parking only, $30 per night. $$$.

The Mosaic Hotel. 125 South Spaulding Dr.; (310) 278-0303; www.mosaichotel.com. This small smoke-free boutique hotel is set in a quiet residential neighborhood near Rodeo Drive. Understated affordable luxury is the theme with room amenities including Frette bath-robes, down quilts, and Bulgari bath products. A restaurant and a pool with cabanas add to the comfort. Valet parking is free. $$–$$$.

westwood

Bordered by Beverly Hills, Bel-Air, and Brentwood, Westwood is an affluent center of culture, entertainment, and, as home to the University of California at Los Angeles (UCLA), higher learning. If you love museums and theater—and coffee houses, cinemas, and artsy shops that cater to the lively, liberal UCLA student body—you'll love Westwood. You may even run into a movie premier or opening night at one of its many live theaters.

getting there

This one's easy: Just take a short ride down Route 2 from Beverly Hills and voilà—you're in the heart of Westwood.

where to go

The Getty Center. 1200 Getty Center Dr.; (310) 440-7300; www.getty.edu. For a day or evening of art, architecture, and breathtaking views of the Pacific Ocean and all Los Angeles—when the weather is clear—this can't be beat. Perched on a hilltop, the Getty displays Western art from the Middle Ages to the present including paintings, sculpture, decorative arts, manuscripts, and furnishings. The grounds feature serene gardens and a lovely restaurant with a view. Open 10 a.m. to 5:30 p.m. Tues to Fri and Sun; and 10 a.m. to 9 p.m. Sat. Closed Mon. Admission is free. Parking is $15 per car; parking is free after 5 p.m.

Skirball Cultural Center. 2701 North Sepulveda Blvd., Los Angeles; (310) 440-4500; www.skirball.org. This museum is great for families, especially the crowd-pleasing "Noah's Ark at the Skirball," a one-of-a-kind interactive exhibit that takes kids of all ages through a fanciful re-creation with whimsically crafted animals of the biblical story of the ark. The exhibits explore 4,000 years of Jewish heritage and American culture. Open noon to 5 p.m. Tues to Fri, and 10 a.m. to 5 p.m. Sat and Sun. Closed Mon. Admission is $10. Advance reservations for "Noah's Ark" are strongly recommended.

Fowler Museum at UCLA. 405 Hilgard Ave.; (310) 825-4361; www.fowler.ucla.edu. In addition to enjoying the museum's exceptional Asian, Oceania, African, Native American, and Latin American art, the Fowler makes a great excuse to visit the lovely UCLA campus, which is dotted with outdoor sculpture and red brick buildings. To get there, enter the UCLA campus at Sunset Boulevard and Westwood Plaza and park in the automated pay-by-space Lot 4. Open noon to 5 p.m. Wed to Sun, and noon to 8 p.m. Thurs. Admission is free. Maximum parking is $10.

Museum of Tolerance. 9786 West Pico Blvd.; (310) 772-2505; www.museumoftolerance .com. This institution confronts the dynamics of intolerance in history and the present with interactive exhibits, arts, and lectures. Open 10 a.m. to 5 p.m. Mon to Fri (early closing at

3:30 p.m. on Fri, Nov through Mar), and 11 a.m. to 5 p.m. Sun. Closed Sat. Admission is $15. Advance reservations are recommended

Westwood Village. Encompassing several blocks between UCLA and Wilshire Boulevard, this is L.A.'s original "village," created as a shopping and entertainment enclave in 1929. Take a stroll and discover diverse restaurants, seven cinemas, and impressive cultural venues. **The Hammer Museum** (10899 Wilshire Blvd.; 310-443-7000; www.hammer.ucla .edu) is known for impressionist, historic, and current art. The museum's also home to the **Billy Wilder Theater,** which along with the nearby **Geffen Playhouse** (10886 Le Conte Ave.; 310-208-5454; www.geffenplayhouse.com), presents wide-ranging original and famil- iar productions.

where to shop

Westside Pavilion. 10800 West Pico Blvd.; (310) 474-6255; www.westsidepavilion.com. For pure shopping pleasure, this three-story mall is where the locals go to find high fashion in all price ranges. It's anchored by Nordstrom and Macy's—with nearly one hundred mostly chain retailers from the Disney Store to Planet Funk. Open 10 a.m. to 9 p.m. Mon to Fri, 10 a.m. to 8 p.m. Sat, and 11 a.m. to 6 p.m. Sun.

Westwood Village. www.westwoodblvd.com. Dozens of eclectic shops make this a great area to discover those one-of-a-kind gems including clothing boutiques, stationers, jewelry stores, game shops and book shops. Bel Air Camera has been here for fifty years and is one of L.A.'s top camera stores, preferred by paparazzi and amateurs alike. Stores' hours are generally 10 a.m. to 6 p.m.

where to eat

Elysee Bakery & Café. 1099 Gaylee Ave.; (310) 208-6505; www.elyseebakery.com. If you like to people watch, this is a prime pick, located on one of Westwood's busiest cor- ners at Gaylee and Kinross Avenues. Don't worry if you can't get a sidewalk table—there are only a few—the view is equally good from inside this cozy, French-style cafe. Popular first for fresh-baked pastries, breads, and fabulous cookies, it also serves delicious salads, sandwiches, and made-to-order pastas. Open 6:30 a.m. to 11 p.m. daily. Metered or paid lot parking. $$.

Emporium Thai Cuisine. 1275 Westwood Blvd.; (310) 478-2838; www.ethaicuisine.com. This popular spot is proof that good food doesn't have to be expensive. It consistently garners foodie raves and has been voted "best Thai cuisine on the Westside" by various publications. In addition to the expected Thai and Asian fare, recommended specialties include the melt-in-your mouth Thai honey ribs, fresh salmon sautéed in chili and coconut sauce, and—believe it or not—traditional Thai-style country fried chicken. Open 11:30 a.m.

to 10:30 p.m. Mon to Thurs, 11 a.m. to 11 p.m. Fri and Sat, and 5 to 10:30 p.m. Sun. Metered street parking. $–$$.

Factor's Famous Deli. 9420 West Pico Blvd.; (310) 278-9175; www.factorsdeli.com. A favorite gathering place for Westsiders since 1948; take a seat in a booth or in the garden patio and enjoy all the traditional deli fare, including homemade soups and salads, and people watch to your heart's content. Open 7 a.m. to midnight daily. Free wireless. Valet parking is $3, or you can try to find a metered space on the street. $–$$.

where to stay

W Los Angeles–Westwood. 930 Hilgard Ave.; (310) 208-8765; www.starwoodhotels .com/whotels. Considered the hippest hotel in the area, the W is in a residential neighborhood near UCLA. It features uber-chic decor, lavish services, and cool public-area names— WET is the heated pool and cabana area—which attract an entertainment-industry clientele. Creative cuisine is served in three restaurants and the bar, where the people watching is excellent day and night. You'll find accommodations beginning with 400-square-foot studios up to a wide variety of suites. Dogs and cats are welcome and even get a nightly turn-down gift. People perks include complimentary rides around town in a chauffeur-driven Acura MDX. Valet parking only, $32 a night. $$$.

Hotel Palomar Los Angeles–Westside. 10740 Wilshire Blvd.; (310) 475-8711; www .hotelpalomar-lawestwood.com. Located 2 blocks from UCLA, this stylish smoke-free boutique hotel is on a hill, which provides sweeping views of Westwood and all of Los Angeles from many of the guest rooms. It also features a nightly complimentary wine hour with varying California vintages. Other amenities include a pool, 24-hour fitness center (with a personal trainer on request); a 24-hour business center, free wireless, and free overnight shoe shines. $$$.

Hilgard House Hotel & Suites. 927 Hilgard Ave.; (310) 208-3945; www.hilgardhouse .com. This is one of those terrific insider finds—a small hotel located at the edge of UCLA and within walking distance of Westwood Village and the Fowler Museum. You'll find traditional European decor, free parking, free continental breakfast, and free wireless in every guest room. For extended stays, one- and two-bedroom suites with full kitchens are available. $$.

day trip 02

west

beyond the pier:
santa monica

santa monica

Santa Monica's hip, forward-thinking vibe—it's the preferred address for screenwriters and other Hollywood creative types and wannabes—makes it more than just a day at the beach. Chic Art Deco hotels, trendy restaurants, and shops-to-the-stars, a sizable British community with the pubs to match, and quirky attractions such as the Camera Obscura, which recalls Santa Monica's late-nineteenth-century popularity with tourists, provide much to see and do. Keep your camera handy; public art is everywhere from murals on the sides of buildings to avant-garde sculptures in the sand. Suntanned in-line skaters and frequent celebrity sightings add to the scene.

getting there

Situated on Santa Monica Bay, it is surrounded on three sides by the city of Los Angeles— the neighborhoods of Pacific Palisades on the northwest, Brentwood on the north, West Los Angeles on the northeast, Mar Vista on the east, and Venice on the southeast. Santa Monica lies on the Pacific Ocean at the westernmost origin of I-10. From downtown L.A., take the I-10 west, exit at the 4th Street/5th Street ramp and turn right onto 5th Street. Turning left (west) on Colorado Avenue brings you to the Santa Monica Pier, the beach, and scenic Ocean Avenue.

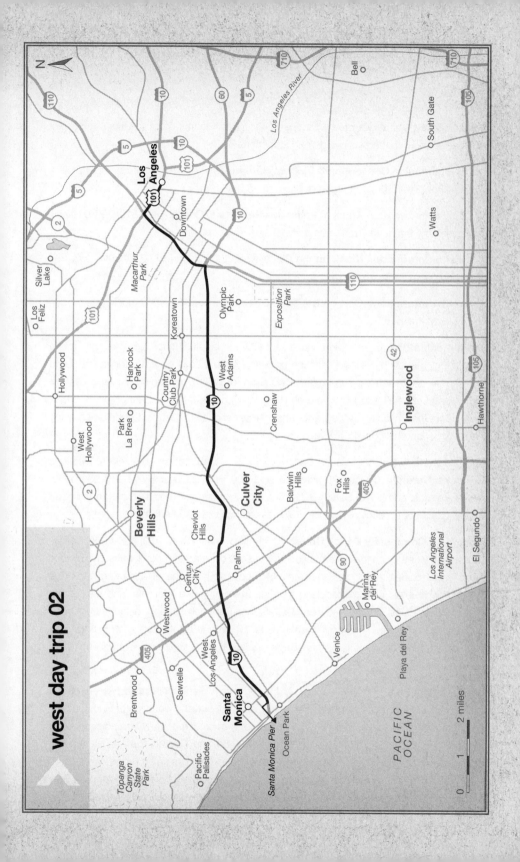

west day trip 02

where to go

Santa Monica Visitor Center. Visit any of the visitor center's four locations for useful information about that area's events and attractions.

> **Santa Monica Convention & Visitors Bureau.** 1920 Main St., Suite B; (800) 544-5319 or (310) 393-7593; open daily 9 a.m. to 5:30 p.m.
>
> **Visitor Information Kiosk in Palisades Park.** 1400 Ocean Ave.; (310) 393-0410; open daily 9 a.m. to 5 p.m. summer; 10 a.m. to 4 p.m. winter.
>
> **Visitor Information Kiosk on the Pier.** 322 Santa Monica Pier; (310) 804-7457; open daily 11 a.m. to 4 p.m.
>
> **Visitor Information Cart on the Third Street Promenade.** 1300 block, open daily 11 a.m. to 4 p.m.

Santa Monica Beach. This wide, white sandy beach, stretching for 3.5 miles, has made Santa Monica a favorite seaside escape since the 1890s. Located at the center of Santa Monica Bay, the beach is a sun-kissed playground for swimming, surfing, sunning, cycling, and playing volleyball. Lifeguards are on duty during daylight hours. Santa Monica Beach sports more than just sand: volleyball courts, whimsical public art, surfside cafes, beach-toy rental shops, and historic attractions.

For an upscale experience, Beach Butler service is available at two beachfront locations of **Perry's Café** (2400 Ocean Front Walk and 930 Pacific Coast Hwy.; 310-939-0000; www.perryscafe.com). The Beach Butler package includes two beach chairs, a table, an umbrella, and set up beginning at $50, plus assistance with food and beverages.

Annenberg Community Beach House. 415 Pacific Coast Hwy.; (310) 458-4904; beachhouse.smgov.net. Once the opulent beachfront estate of actress Marion Davies, this historic compound includes the original intricately tiled pool, lounge chairs, a viewing deck, the Splash Pad fountain area for toddlers, garden, changing lockers, a cafe, and the historic Marion Davies Guest House. The view deck, Splash Pad, garden, and restaurant are open daily. Admission is free. The pool is open June 21 through Sept. Admission is $10. Free docent-led tours through the Marion Davies Guest House are offered at varying times throughout the year.

Santa Monica Pier. 200 Pier Ave.; (310)458-8900; www.santamonicapier.org. This is the West Coast's oldest pleasure pier, built in 1909, and probably the world's most famous pier, since its landmark sign has appeared in dozens of movies. It's actually two adjacent piers and includes a historic 1922 carousel (310-394-8042); the **Pacific Park** family amusement center (310-260-8744; www.pacpark.com) with the world's first solar-powered Ferris wheel, a small roller coaster, miniature golf, and other games; and the **Santa Monica Pier Aquarium** (1600 Ocean Front Walk; 310-393-6149; www.healthybay.org/smpa), located underneath the pier. You can even take flying trapeze and aerial silks lessons at the pier with the **Trapeze School New York** (310-394-5800; www.trapezeschool.com). Restaurants, shops, and a bait-and-tackle shop—no license needed for fishing from the pier—round out this wooden wonderland. Admission to the pier and Pacific Park is free.

Palisades Park. Perched on a cliff overlooking the Pacific Ocean, this narrow twenty-six-acre greenbelt extends north from Colorado Avenue and the Santa Monica Pier for 2.1 miles and features stunning views, benches, winding paths under swaying palms, and access to the beach below. Take a stroll, cycle, enjoy a picnic, and visit the **Camera Obscura** (1450 Ocean Ave., inside the Palisades Park Senior Recreation Center), an optical device built as a tourist attraction in 1898.

South Bay Bicycle Trail. Known to the locals as "The Strand," this paved bikeway parallels the beach and is the in spot to see and be seen in-line skating, cycling, and just hanging out. It has several rental shops for bikes and in-line skates and inviting beachfront eateries. The Strand begins north of Santa Monica at Will Rogers State Beach in Pacific Palisades and runs for 22 miles south to Torrance.

The Cove Skatepark. 1401 Olympic Blvd.; (310) 485-8228; www.smgov.net/comm_progs/skatepark/index.htm. Santa Monica is the recognized birthplace of modern skateboarding, and the 20,000-square-foot Cove Skatepark has been featured in numerous skateboarding videos. Watch the action or test your personal best on its state-of-the-art ramps, half-pipes, and bowls. $16.50 registration fee includes one free day; $5.50 entry each day thereafter.

Self-guided Art Tour. With more than forty public art installations on the streets and beaches and in the parks, and some ninety art galleries and art museums, Santa Monica is an art-lovers dream. For a self-guided tour, download the Santa Monica Art Trek guide at www.santamonica.com/includes/media/docs/art-trek-map.pdf or pick one up—along with other Santa Monica maps and guides—at one of four walk-in information centers (see p. 154).

where to shop

Third Street Promenade. Third Street between Wilshire Boulevard and Broadway; (310) 393-8355; www.thirdstreetpromenade.com. People watching is as much fun as shopping along this famous open-air pedestrian mall. Crowds come from throughout L.A. to peruse its 3 blocks of stylish shops—including many preferred by celebrities, such as Rafinity jewelers, which makes custom bling for Hollywood's hottest stars—and to relax in one of the many outdoor cafes and coffeehouses. Live street entertainment often adds to the fun. From A/J Armani Exchange to Skechers and Banana Republic, doggie boutiques, and home and office shops, this mall has it all. Hours average from 10 a.m. to 10 p.m.

Santa Monica Place. 395 Santa Monica Place; (310) 393-8355; www.santamonicaplace .com. Opened in 2010, this three-story indoor mall on Broadway adjacent to the Third Street Promenade includes Bloomingdale's, Nordstrom, and other high-end chain and independent retailers.

Montana Avenue. From 6th Street north to 17th Street; www.montanaave.com or www .montanamerchants.com. This cosmopolitan retail strip is famous for upscale shops: high fashion for men, women, and children; interior design and home furnishing studios; antique galleries; fine jewelry; and stationers. Yet you'll also find medium-priced boutiques like Chico's and even luxury knitting supplies at L'Atelier. Numerous bistros, cafes, and bakeries offer tasty repasts and stylish people watching. Hours average 10 a.m. to 6 p.m.

Main Street. www.mainstreetsm.com. Housed in old-fashioned storefronts, this collection of out-of-the-ordinary shops stretches for a mile along Main Street from Pico Boulevard south to the Santa Monica city line. If you're into unique finds, this is a great spot, with one-of-a-kind stores including Ritual Adornment, a jewelry crafts shop featuring millions of beads from ivory Asian zodiac animals to blown glass fish; Ten Women, an artists' co-op with beautiful handcrafted gifts; and Papillon baby boutique. New concept apparel by up-and-coming L.A. designers (often worn by Hollywood stars), antiques, handmade bath and body products, Indonesian collectibles, books, eye wear, and activewear are all represented. Relax and recharge at quaint sidewalk cafes or cuisine boutiques such as the irresistible ZenBunni raw chocolate shop. Hours vary between 10 a.m. to 6 p.m., or later on weekends.

where to eat

The Lobster. 1602 Ocean Ave.; (310) 458-9294; www.thelobster.com. At the corner of Ocean Avenue and the Pier, this is one of Santa Monica's landmark restaurants and the unofficial entrance to the Pier. You'll find great seafood—live Maine lobster is the specialty—and amazing views of Santa Monica Beach and Santa Monica Bay. While the inside dining area has floor-to-ceiling windows, for the best sunset views in town, grab a seat at the outside bar. From here, you're looking straight onto the beach, the Pacific Ocean, and the sunset. You can have dinner at the bar as well. To insure a seat, get there around 5:30 p.m. Lobster cocktail, a lobster melt sandwich, and pan-roasted lobster with whipped potatoes and Jim Beam sauce are among the specialties, plus a full variety of dishes from sautéed Pacific sole to Caesar salad, soups, meat, chicken, and vegetarian choices. Open 11:30 a.m. to 10 p.m. Sun through Thurs, 11:30 a.m. to 11 p.m. Fri and Sat. Valet parking is available. Reservations are highly recommended. $$$.

Big Dean's Oceanfront Cafe. 1615 Ocean Front Walk; (310) 393-2666; www.bigdeans oceanfrontcafe.com. Tucked below the Pier, this is a rustic locals' favorite that looks as if it were straight out of a '50s movie—not surprising since it's been in the same spot since 1902. Burgers, beer, sports TV, and a *Cheers* kind of friendliness make it a memorable find.

Open noon to 9 p.m. Mon; 11 a.m. to 9 p.m. Tues through Thurs; and 10 a.m. to 10 p.m. Fri through Sun. $–$$.

Ye Olde Kings Head. 116 Santa Monica Blvd.; (310) 451-1402; www.yeoldkingshead .com. Reflecting Santa Monica's sizable British community, this English-style pub is a bit touristy, but it's been a Santa Monica fixture for more than thirty years and is enjoyed by Brits and visitors alike. You'll find dart boards, dark woods, and Guinness on tap along with great-tasting fish-and-chips, steak and kidney pie, and all the classic British fare, including English breakfasts. Open 9 a.m. to 10 p.m. Mon through Thurs; 9 a.m. to midnight Fri; 8 a.m. to midnight Sat; and 8 a.m. to 1 a.m. Sun. $$–$$$.

The Penthouse and Ultra Lounge. 1111 Second St.; (310) 393-8080; www.thehuntley hotel.com. This rooftop restaurant on the eighteenth floor of the Huntley Hotel offers a hip vibe inside and out. The view is amazing—a full 360 degrees looking out over the Pacific Ocean to Malibu beach and Santa Monica to Los Angeles and Hollywood. Inside, the white Hollywood Regency–style decor is a perfect match for the entertainment-industry crowd who gathers here and provides interesting people watching. The contemporary California cuisine is excellent and ranges from hamburgers to seared ahi tuna. Full dinner service is available at the bar, which makes a great perch for viewing both the panorama and the people. Open daily from 7 a.m. to 3 p.m. for breakfast and lunch; 6 p.m. to 10:30 p.m. for dinner. Sun brunch is served from 11 a.m. to 2:30 p.m. Happy hour is 4 to 7 p.m. Mon through Fri. Valet parking is available. $$$.

where to stay

Shutters on the Beach. 1 Pico Blvd.; (310) 458-0030; www.shuttersonthebeach.com. If you want to stay where the entertainment industry does, this is the place. It's likely you'll see a celebrity or two during your stay. It's also one of the few Santa Monica hotels that is right on the sand, providing effortless access to the ocean and fun-in-the-sun activities. The bike trail passes directly in front. Newly refreshed by the Obama White House designer Michael Smith, this hotel features an understated luxury. Its numerous amenities include a pool, spa, fitness center, and activities such as yoga on the beach. Enjoy fine dining at One Pico, which overlooks the beach and is ideal for sunset cocktails and dinner; it also serves brunch and lunch. For a casual setting, Coast cafe is also on the beach—and attracts an entertainment industry power-breakfast crowd. $$$.

Hotel Shangri-La. 1301 Ocean Ave.; (310) 394-2791; www.shangrila-hotel.com. Originally built in 1939, this luxury boutique hotel with views of the Pacific Ocean is in the heart of the action across from Palisades Park. Relive the Santa Monica movie-star glamour of yester-year amid its streamline Moderne architecture and Art Deco and Hollywood Regency decor. It offers fine dining and a poolside bar; the rooftop bar features incredible open-air views of the city, the beach, and Santa Monica Bay. Enjoy a pleasant walk to the Pier, Third Street Promenade, and countless cafes, bars, and boutiques. $$$.

The Georgian Hotel. 1415 Ocean Ave.; (310) 395-9945; www.georgianhotel.com. This distinctive turquoise and gold Art Deco gem, built in 1933 as a seaside getaway for the exclusive Hollywood set, has been beautifully restored and refurbished. Choose from fifty-six spacious rooms and twenty-eight suites overlooking the city and Santa Monica Bay. $$–$$$.

Seaview Motel. 1760 Ocean Ave.; (310) 393-6711; www.seaviewmotel.net. If you want to experience Santa Monica like a local—and on a budget—this small motel is tucked away on a side street just a block from the beach and a few blocks from the Pier. (It's actually in the same neighborhood as the luxurious Viceroy Santa Monica boutique hotel and Loews Santa Monica Beach Hotel.) You'll find clean, simple rooms here, a large sun deck, a laundry room, and—free parking. $.

worth more time

Bergamot Station Arts Center. 2525 Michigan Ave.; (310) 453-7535; www.bergamot station.com. Take Olympic Boulevard to Cloverfield and make a right to Michigan Avenue, where you will find the center's gated entrance. Dating back to 1875 when it was a stop for the old Pacific Red Line trolley running from Los Angeles to the Santa Monica Pier, the building is steeped in history and gets its name from bergamot—a flower of the mint family that once flourished in the area. Open Tues through Fri 10 a.m. to 6 p.m.; Sat, 11 a.m. to 5:30 p.m.; Closed Sun and Mon. Free admission and parking.

Now this enclave of forty eclectic art galleries exhibits a range of expression. This is a light industrial area, so galleries have metallic roofs, high ceilings, and lots of wall space. From sculpture and wearable art to paintings, photography, and prints, this is a wonderland of creativity. There is a schedule listing each gallery, openings, and current exhibits. **The Gallery Cafe** is a good place to stop first and take a moment to plan your stops. The **Santa Monica Museum of Art** (310-586-6488; www.smmoa.org) located in Studio G1 has changing exhibits as well, and was founded in 1984 by Abby Sher. SMMoA devotes its exhibition spaces—the main gallery and two project rooms—to presenting and advancing the work of contemporary local, national, and international artists whose work merits sustained inquiry and recognition. Hours are Tues through Sat 11 a.m. to 6 p.m. Parking is free (making Bergamot Station a great place to start your further exploration of Santa Monica).

day trip 03

west

twenty-seven miles of sun, sand & surf:
malibu

malibu

Famous as the land of movie stars and surfers, Malibu stretches north from Santa Monica along fabled beaches, but it also encompasses miles of rolling hills and rugged mountains inland. And while the gated Malibu Colony is off limits (unless you have a friend with a home in this star-studded seaside residential enclave), everything else is wide open. Don't be surprised if the landscapes look familiar; you've probably seen them on the big and small screens, since Malibu has been a favorite filming ground since moviemaking began in the early twentieth century. Although part of Los Angeles County, Malibu is actually a separate city—and a funny-shaped one at that. Because of the area's geography, Malibu is barely 1.5 miles wide but some 27 miles long. The Pacific Coast Highway (aka PCH or SR 1) is the lifeline of this seaside community and the commuting route to Hollywood.

getting there

From downtown Los Angeles, zip onto the I-10 heading west, and take it all the way to Santa Monica and the coastline where it veers north and becomes Pacific Coast Highway (SR 1). Continue on up PCH—as this highway is called by everyone who lives anywhere in Southern California—and enjoy the scenic drive into Malibu. The highway winds along the coast between steep brown bluffs and the sometimes calm, sometimes wild Pacific Ocean. Look to the right and you'll see gorgeous homes and wildflowers in the springtime, and to

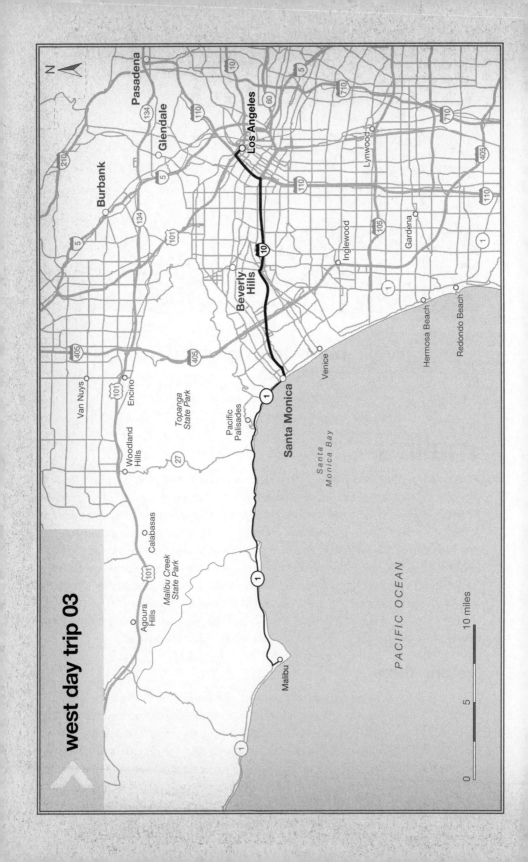

left surfers in dark wet suits bobbing on the sea in search of the perfect wave. At Topanga Canyon Boulevard look for the sign that says MALIBU—27 MILES OF BEAUTY. You've arrived.

where to go

The Getty Villa. 17985 Pacific Coast Hwy.; (213) 458-2003; www.getty.edu. Once the residence of millionaire art-collector J. Paul Getty, this museum not only showcases price-less Roman, Greek, and Etruscan antiquities from 6500 B.C. to A.D. 400, it puts you into the likeness of a first century A.D. Roman country house and gardens similar to the ones where ancient Romans frolicked before Mount Vesuvius snuffed out Pompeii and Herculaneum. Artifacts from monumental sculptures to jewelry and everyday utensils are arranged in gal-leries by theme, including "Gods and Goddesses" and "Dionysus and the Theater." The "Family Forum" features a hands-on experience for kids. Enjoy lunch in the cafe with tasty salads, sandwiches, and ocean views through the pine trees. Open 10 a.m. to 5 p.m. Wed to Mon. Closed Tues. Admission is free. Parking is $15 per vehicle. Each visitor must have an advance, timed ticket.

Weisman Museum of Art. 24255 Pacific Coast Hwy.; (310) 506-4851; www.pepperdine .edu/museum. Located on the picturesque private Pepperdine University campus, enjoy cutting-edge contemporary art and panoramic ocean views on the drive up to the hilltop institution. Open 11 a.m. to 5 p.m. Tues to Sun. Closed Mon. Admission and parking are free. As you enter the campus, tell the guard at the gate you're going to the art museum.

Adamson House. 23200 Pacific Coast Hwy.; (310) 456-8432; www.adamsonhouse.org. Before there were movie stars, there was Frederick Hastings Rindge, who owned most of Malibu from the mountains to the sea. See how his daughter lived in her 1930 Mediter-ranean mansion, which has the original furnishings. The renowned Malibu Potteries tile is the hallmark of this museum-home, with amazing tile floors designed to resemble Persian carpets, tile murals, fountains, and three-dimensional tile figureheads. Enjoy the beautiful views of Malibu Lagoon and the Malibu Pier. Afterward, if you're still in a museum mood, the **Malibu Lagoon Museum** (310-456-8432) is next door. It has artifacts tracing Malibu's history from the early Chumash Indians to the Malibu movie colony. The Adamson House is open 11 a.m. to 3:30 p.m. Wed to Sat. Admission is $5, cash only. The museum has similar hours and free admission. Parking is free on PCH, if you can find a spot. Nearby parking lots charge $6 to $8.

Ramirez Canyon Park. 5750 Ramirez Canyon Rd.; (310) 589-2850; www.lamountains .com. This 22.5-acre estate formerly belonged to Barbra Streisand, and she donated it to the Santa Monica Mountains Conservancy in 1993. It features four homes, including one in the Art Deco style, a Mediterranean-style villa, and the "Barn," her first and favorite house, a three-bedroom cottage covered inside and out with wood and stone, stained glass, lofts, and ladders. The estate is open for garden tours, with outside views of the houses and tea on the Barn patio. Tours are by appointment only. At press time, the public tours had been suspended, but the Conservancy hopes to resume them in the future.

Santa Monica Mountains National Recreation Area. The official Visitor Center is located at 401 West Hillcrest Dr., Thousand Oaks; (805) 370-2301; www.nps.gov/samo. The Santa Monica Mountains Conservancy (310-589-3200; http://smmc.ca.gov) will provide maps and information regarding attractions and hiking trails in the park's vast area. The park offers hiking, picnicking, fishing, horseback riding, mountain biking, seasonal wildflower viewing and many other outdoor options. Call for current park hours or more information. The Visitor Center is open daily from 9 a.m. to 5 p.m. It is closed on some federal holidays, as well as Thanksgiving, Christmas and New Year's Day.

where to shop

Malibu Lumber Yard. 3939 Cross Creek Rd.; (310) 465-7395; www.themalibulumberyard .com. This is where chic shopping meets creative cuisine, and puts strip malls to shame! Epitomizing the Malibu lifestyle, this one-of-a-kind architectural statement captures the sun and sea with its spacious decks on two levels. The casual ambience at the Lumber Yard goes deeper than you think, as the space has been designed to be green and sustainable. There is comfortable seating on both levels, and every square foot reflects the charismatic and cultural legacy that has made Malibu world famous. Here's the perfect place to spend an afternoon at leisure—there's even free Wi-Fi so you can surf next to the surf. Trendsetting boutiques dominate from **Kitson Malibu** (www.shopkitson.com) where the selection of hip, colorful fashions, souvenirs, and accessories for all—from babies to seniors—is mind boggling! Do you want to dress like the movie stars? Stop by **Intermix** (www.intermix.com) where celebrity-inspired fashionista favorites come in all sizes. **The Chocolate Box** (www.thechocolatebox.com) serves gelato inspired by their original family recipe from Verona, Italy, in flashy flavors from gianduia (milk chocolate and hazelnuts) to cinnamon. Hot chocolate beverages can be ordered in twelve different flavors, from caramel to chili pepper. **The Café Habana** (www.cafehabana.com), cousin to those in New York City and Brooklyn, serves Cuban specialties such as grilled corn with chili powder, lime and cheese as well as other Havana favorites. The Lumber Yard is open seven days; call for specific times of retailers.

where to eat

Dukes at Malibu. 21150 Pacific Coast Hwy.; (310) 317-0777; www.dukesmailbu.com. Named after Duke Kahanamoku, the father of surfing, this is the ideal place to get the feeling of the Malibu lifestyle, thanks to the magnificent stretch of windows overlooking the beach. The prices are fairly reasonable, and there's plenty of surfing memorabilia in case you get bored watching the waves (not likely). Lunch and dinner daily. $$.

malibu's beach scene

Malibu has an incredibly amazing variety of beaches—some packed with visitors, others much less populated. Public access to all the beaches is marked along PCH, and several have public parking. Parking is free on PCH itself—but it's almost a miracle when/if you find a space (particularly in the summer). Each beach has its own qualities and type of crowd; explore them all or head for your zone! Here are just a couple of our favorites.

Zuma Beach County Park. *30050 Pacific Coast Hwy.; (310) 305-9546; http:// beaches.co.la.ca.us/bandh/beaches/zuma.htm. Swimming, surfing, fishing, diving, major volleyball courts, snack bars, and more than 2,000 parking spaces on-site make this an extraordinarily busy and popular place to hang. Winter finds it a lot mellower yet still as beautiful.*

Point Dume State Beach. *Westward Beach Road at PCH (18 miles up the coast from Santa Monica; (818) 880-0363; www.parks.ca.gov. For a less crowded beach experience, this serene slice of sand is perfect. Watch rock climbers scramble up its steep cliffs then rappel down, or try it yourself. A paved path winds up to the cliff peak, offering an easy-to-medium trek and gorgeous views of the ocean and the Channel Islands. Tide pools and seasonal whale watching Feb to Apr make this beach a wonderful pleasure.*

Leo Carrillo State Park and Beach. *35000 Pacific Coast Hwy.; (818) 880-0350; www.parks.ca.gov. This beach draws raves from families, who love its kid-friendly activities including tide pools, surfing, snorkeling, fishing and hiking, bicycling, and other inland activities. It features campgrounds for overnight stays, but make reservations well in advance; many families have been camping here for years.*

Additional beaches. *With 27 miles of coast, other Malibu beach choices include: Topanga State Beach, Las Tunas State Beach, Las Flores Beach, Dan Blocker State Beach (also known as Corral Beach), Paradise Cove (private), El Matador, La Piedra and El Pescador State Beaches, Nicholas Canyon County Beach, and County Line Beach (bordering Ventura County to the north). For more information and descriptions visit www.ci.malibu.ca.us.*

Gladstone's. 17300 Pacific Coast Hwy., Pacific Palisades; (310) 454-3474; www.glad stones.com. While this eatery is technically in Pacific Palisades in Los Angeles County, it's a Malibu area landmark owned by former L.A. mayor Richard Riordan and restaurant/ nightclub entrepreneur Sam Nazarian. This is where Sunset Boulevard meets the Pacific Coast Highway at the beach. The happy hour at sunset is a tradition. Whether you order the fresh fish, Manhattan-style chowder, or peel-and-eat shrimp this is a Malibu tradition you shouldn't miss, especially with its million-dollar renovation featuring a bright, new airy feel. The white walls are draped with antique art, there is an open layout, huge ocean-view windows; and a patio covered with tables and chairs that are shaded by giant umbrellas (called Jumbrellas). There is a newer, fresher seafood menu to savor. Open daily; call for seasonal hours. $$.

The Reel Inn. 18661 Pacific Coast Hwy., Malibu; (310) 456-8221; www.reelinnmalibu.com. Casual to the max, this roadside dining marker has been reeling in seafood fans for years, and that's not a fish tale! The menu is on a blackboard, and folks wait in line to order fresh fish from halibut and mahimahi to ahi tuna and orange roughy. Appetizers are popular and mainly cost under $10 (the lobster tail is the exception); they range from fish tacos and steamed clams to raw oysters on the half shell and grilled scallops There is a respectable kids' menu, and for non–fish eaters there are chicken and pasta. The Reel Inn is adjacent to the famous Malibu beaches and north of where Topanga Canyon meets PCH. There is valet parking on the weekends. Open daily from 11 a.m. to 9 p.m. $–$$.

Paradise Cove Beach Cafe. 28128 Pacific Coast Hwy., Malibu; (310) 457-2503; www .paradisecovemalibu.com. This much-loved institution with captivating ocean views is home to casual dining with breakfast fare, "big" salads, soups and chowders, and the Gigantic Iced Seafood Tower. The menu is a miracle of comfort food and portions designed for sharing such as fish tacos, and shore dinners with specialties such as Parmesan-crusted halibut and free-range swordfish. Breakfast, lunch and dinner are served 'til closing, so you never have to rush through your meal. There is something for everyone on the menu—land- lubbers, too! Open daily from 8 a.m. to 10 p.m., but call for closing times as they can vary seasonally. $$.

Taverna Tony. 23410 Civic Center Way; (310) 317-9667; www.tavernatony.com. You may think you are in the Plaka in Athens, Greece, with authentic entrees from moussaka and dolmathes on the menu, but blink twice and you'll find it's this favorite Malibu establish- ment. The rotisserie and grill feature lamb-loin souvlaki and roast baby lamb *kleftiko* among other Grecian specialties, so go easy on the starters (such as spanakopita, feta and kal- amata olives, and calamari fried Athenian-style). Plan ahead for the "feast that Tony made famous on two continents," which is a selection of twelve different specialties—salads, hot appetizers, and dips—served on separate dishes. Open daily 11:30 a.m. to 11 p.m. Call for seasonal hours. $$$.

where to stay

Casa Malibu Inn on the Beach. 22752 Pacific Coast Hwy.; (310) 456-2219. This twenty-one-unit vintage inn is well located and has a marvelous view of the ocean plus stairs leading directly to the beach. Part of the pleasure of spending a night or two in Malibu is its disconnect to chain hotels and corporate-driven hospitality. The Casa is one of a few surviving inns that take pride in this style of welcome, and because of this it remains a haven for those who just want to get away. An added value is free parking and Wi-Fi. Loyal guests say this is a leftover jewel from Malibu's golden age and has survived because it hasn't changed much in generations. Low-rise, cozy, and value conscious, this is an ideal place to spend time exploring Malibu, especially the Getty Villa. $$.

Malibu Beach Inn. 22878 Pacific Coast Hwy.; (310) 456-6444; www.malibubeachinn .com. Look for the famous Malibu Pier and you have arrived at this irresistible forty-seven-room, nonsmoking inn where a real Malibu experience awaits you. Located on Carbon Beach (also known as Billionaire's Beach) this is the perfect getaway when you want to be lulled to sleep by calling seagulls after strolling along the mesmerizing beach. The inn is home to the Cure Spa, where massages and skincare you should experience are on the menu. Their popular restaurant, the Carbon Beach Club, has a patio for outdoor dining and an excellent selection of California-inspired cuisine and wines. If you are a night owl, you will find their 24-hour room service convenient. There are romantic extras here, such as a Rose Petal Turndown, among other creative options. Should you happen to be star gazing from your balcony, you never know when you might see a local reputed celebrity resident, such as Suzanne Somers, Robert Downey Jr., or Kurt Russell. Valet parking only for an additional charge. $$$.

Malibu Country Inn. 6505 Westward Beach Rd.; (310) 457-9622; www.malibucountryinn .com. Another Malibu hideaway, now nearly fifty years old, with sixteen comfortable guest rooms, free parking, and a loyal clientele. Known for the very private patios, this is a perfect place to have tea or coffee, or just relax and take in the lush ambience. There is a lovely landscaped garden plus a heated pool. There are six room categories to choose from—ocean or mountain view, a mini suite, two Jacuzzi rooms, a patio room, and eight garden-view accommodations. This is a casual place for laid-back beach lovers where you can take it easy and relax—and that's real California Dreamin'! $$.

northwest

day trip 01

northwest

funny names, friendly places:
oxnard, simi valley

oxnard

What could you possibly enjoy in a place with such a funny name? Plenty! The town got its moniker from nineteenth-century entrepreneur Henry T. Oxnard, an agriculture visionary who foresaw that the fertile plains just north of the Conejo Hills (Co-nay-hoe) would be an excellent place to raise sugar beets and process them into the nation's favorite sweetener. When the day came in 1903 to register the town's name with the clerk in California's state capital of Sacramento, Henry had a bad phone connection and settled for his surname (he was going to call his town Zachari, the Greek word for sugar). Sweet history aside, Oxnard has grown into a culturally and economically diverse community, with high-tech business parks, 7 miles of sandy beaches, and Channel Islands Harbor, a world-class marina, and a commercial/retail area. Often described as California's Strawberry Coast, Oxnard boasts fields of fresh fruit, roadside farm stands you should not miss, and the nationally recognized California Strawberry Festival (www.strawberry-fest.org) held the third weekend in May. In late July, make time for spicy foods and sizzling entertainment at the Oxnard Salsa Festival (www.oxnardsalsafestival.com) celebrating the area's extensive Latino cuisine and culture. So what would Henry Oxnard think of his city today? Here's what we think!

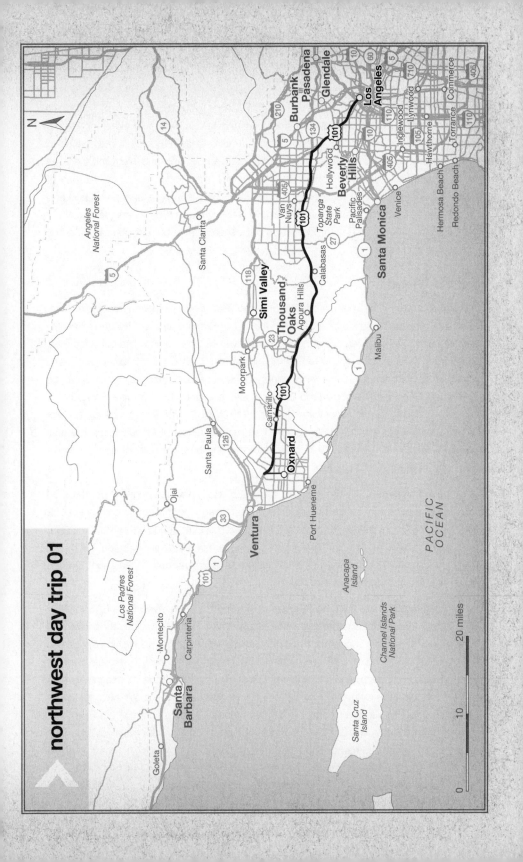

northwest day trip 01

getting there

Just cruise north up US Highway 101 from Los Angeles until you see signs for Oxnard around mile marker 60 and the Vineyard Avenue/Pacific Coast Highway 1 interchange to access most attractions. You can also reach Oxnard via Amtrak and Metrolink trains as well as Greyhound bus lines stopping at the Oxnard Transportation Center. As one of Southern California's major transportation hubs, there also is a regional airport (OXR) and Union Pacific freight lines, as well as two large U.S. Navy bases (Port Hueneme and Naval Air Station Point Mugu). The commercial Port of Hueneme is the busiest port between Los Angeles and San Francisco.

where to go

Heritage Square. 715 South A St.; (805) 483-7960; www.heritagesquareoxnard.com. The square reflects the area's past century, with its faithful restorations of a late-nineteenth-century church, water tower, pump house, and eleven vintage homes. The buildings were moved from various parts of Oxnard to this single block, which is combined with fresh twenty-first-century energy. Summer Fri night concerts delight audiences of all ages. It's also home to the Petit Playhouse and Oxnard's award-winning Elite Theatre Company as well as the nearby historic Woolworth Building (210 West Fourth St.; www.thewoolworth building.com/Museum.html), recently restored with a small museum. Check out all the cafes and retail shops in the vicinity. Guided tours of the district are usually offered on week-ends—call for the current schedule.

Carnegie Art Museum. 424 South C St.; (805) 385-8157; www.carnegieam.org. Housed in an imposing two-story structure built in 1906 as a library, the museum's permanent collection focuses on twentieth-century California painters. Ever-changing exhibits highlight photography, sculpture, oils, watercolors, and some humorous displays. In the vicinity, art galleries are scattered about like bonbons waiting to be unwrapped. Open Thurs through Sat 10 a.m. to 5 p.m., and Sun 1 to 5 p.m.

Channel Islands Harbor & Visitor Center. 2741 South Victoria Ave., Suite F; (805) 985-4852; www.channelislandsharbor.org. Fisherman's Wharf, Harbor Landing, and the Marine Emporium Landing have shopping, fine dining, and plenty of sailing and fishing options as well. Over 2,600 working and pleasure craft call this bustling area home. There are plenty of parks, a swimming beach, and the Maritime Museum. Throughout the year various events are held, including the Celebration of the Whales, visits by the tall ships, Fireworks by the Sea on July 4th, the Ventura County Boat Show, Ventura Vintage Rods Harbor Run Classic Car Show, and the annual Holiday Parade of Lights. Fresh fruits and vegetables plus arts and crafts are at the harbor's farmers' market held at the Marine Emporium Landing from 10 a.m. to 2 p.m. every Sun. The Channel Islands Water Taxi, with its painted-on smiling face, is the best way to see the seafront; call (805) 985-4677 for current schedule and fares.

Ventura County Maritime Museum. 2731 South Victoria Ave., just past Channel Islands Boulevard; (805) 984-6260. Free for all you mateys, discover a collection of ship models made with materials ranging from bone to wood to metals that reflects maritime history from ancient to modern times. Changing exhibits deal with maritime commerce, art, Channel Islands history, whaling, and shipwrecks. Open daily 11 a.m. to 5 p.m. Closed major holidays.

Gull Wings Children's Museum. 418 West Fourth St.; (805) 483-3005; www.gullwings .org. If you've got kids ages two to twelve, this is Ventura County's only kids' museum and worth a stop. Indoor sports abound at this innovative facility, from a variety of hands-on exhibits and a medical room with cutaway models to a simulated campground and farmers' market. It's located downtown, a bit off the beaten path in the old USO Hall. Hours are seasonal; call for times.

Murphy Classic Auto Museum. 2230 Statham Blvd.; (805) 487-4333; www.murphyauto museum.org This 16,000 square-foot facility contains a wide variety of vintage, milestone, and special interest vehicles, including a large collection of Packards dating from 1927 to 1958. Open Sat and Sun 10 a.m. to 4 p.m.

where to shop

Camarillo Premium Outlets. 740 East Ventura Blvd., Camarillo; (805) 445-8515; www .premiumoutlets.com/camarillo. Satisfy your shopping urges at 160 stores including the world's leading designers and brand names such as Banana Republic Factory Store, Coach, Kate Spade, Movado, Tommy Hilfiger, and more. Whether you are a bargain hunter or fashion seeker, this mall's Mission-style village setting is a shopaholic's dream destination, only 45 miles up the coast from L.A. Take Highway 101 to Camarillo, exit at Las Posas Road, go west then turn left on Ventura Boulevard. Regular hours are Mon to Sat from 10 a.m. to 9 p.m., and Sun 10 a.m. to 8 p.m., with holiday and special events promotions variable—call for details.

The Esplanade Shopping Center. 461 West Esplanade Dr. (Esplanade exit off Highway 101); (310) 314-5000. Home to Nordstrom Rack, Borders Books & Music, TJ Maxx, Home Depot, Old Navy, In-n-Out Burger, BJ's Brewery and Restaurant, La Salsa, Starbucks, Jamba Juice, Party City, Cost Plus, Staples, Golfsmith, and other major names. Call for current hours.

Marine Emporium Landing. 3600 South Harbor Blvd.; (805) 985-5828; www.marine emporiumlanding.com. This is the best place to start for waterfront fun in Oxnard, with dozens of restaurants and specialty shops as well as kayak rentals and tours; fishing charters; dive trips; jet ski, electric boat, and Segway rentals; walking paths; and excursions to **Channel Islands National Park.** (See listing in Northwest Day Trip 03). Hard to miss, it's the dock for the tall ship *Bill of Rights*—a 129-foot double-mast, gaff-rigged, topsail schooner built in 1971, offering 3-hour coastal cruises via concessionaire **Island Packers** (805-642-1393; www.islandpackers.com/ipco_general_news.html).

where to eat and stay

Embassy Suites Mandalay Beach Resort and Capistrano's Restaurant. 2101 Mandalay Beach Rd.; (805) 984-2500; www.mandalaybeach.embsuites.com. This resort is right on the sand, with its own beach, just off Channel Islands Boulevard, and you can rent boogie boards, bicycles, beach chairs, snorkeling gear, or just kick back in the spacious serpentine pool. All 249 units here are two-room, two-bath suites, so you can really spread out and relax. Check out the deluxe amenities in every suite—fridge, microwave, coffeemaker, two TVs, plus a free cooked-to-order hot breakfast every morning and free beverages and refreshments every evening in the garden courtyard. Dine with an ocean view at **Capistrano's** (www.capistranos.com/index-mbr-news.htm) on fresh seafood and pasta for lunch and dinner or stop by for the award-winning Sun brunch. $$$.

Herzog Wine Cellars and Tierra Sur Restaurant. 3201 Camino Del Sol; (805) 983-1560; www.herzogwinecellars.com. The largest kosher winery/restaurant/gift shop in the United States, Herzog produces fine kosher wines here in this 77,000-square-foot facility that hosts many special events and offers tastings and tours. The gift shop stocks a variety of stylish serving pieces and wine ware, naturally. Mediterranean-inspired kosher cuisine is served for lunch and dinner at the impressive Tierra Sur Restaurant on the premises. Menu items such as pomegranate-marinated lamb, aged rib eye steak, and wild king salmon are cooked outdoors over an open flame. The menu also includes house-made organic corn tortillas with exotic fillings such as *birria* (chili-braised lamb) with salsa cruda and grilled achiote-marinated red snapper with tomatillo salsa. Open Sun thru Fri afternoon; closed Sat. $$$.

simi valley

The Simi Valley (pronounced "see-me") lies on a plateau at around 800 feet above sea level, about 20 minutes inland from Oxnard. SR 118 (also known as just "the 118" or the Ronald Reagan Freeway) bisects the valley, connecting it to SR 23 (known as the 23) with access to Highway 101 along the coast. With a population of more than 100,000, this area is a popular bedroom community for adjacent Los Angeles County.

where to go

Ronald Reagan Presidential Library & Museum and Air Force One Pavilion. 40 Presidential Dr., Simi Valley; (805) 522-2977 or (800) 410-8354; www.reaganlibrary.com. Located in a Spanish Mission–style building constructed around a courtyard and set on a hilltop, this site provides you with an incredible view of the rolling hills leading down to the Pacific Ocean, including the late president's memorial site and final resting place. The Library houses over fifty-five million pages of gubernatorial, presidential, and personal papers, and over 40,000 gifts and artifacts chronicling the lives of Ronald and Nancy Reagan. Within the library's museum are photographs and memorabilia of President Reagan's

port hueneme

*Yet another unusual name in this area, it's pronounced "Why-nee-me." Why should you be interested? In 1941, the U.S. Navy took advantage of the only natural deep-water harbor between Los Angeles and San Francisco to build its Construction Battalion (known as CB or Seabee) in Port Hueneme (named after a native Chumash Indian settlement, Weneme, that occupied the site). This town of 22,000 actually was plotted in 1869, but its prominence today is due to its military importance as the home base of the U.S. Navy Civil Engineer Corps (CEC). These skilled construction experts have actively fought in military engagements around the world. Visit the **CEC/Seabee Museum (**1000 23rd Avenue, Building 99, Port Hueneme; 805-982-5165 or 805-982-5167; www.seabeehf.org), located at the U.S. Naval Construction Battalion at Ventura Road and Sunkist Avenue, within the gates of the Naval Base Ventura County. Free tours there let you see models of equipment, actual weapons, and uniforms of the CEC and Seabees. Call ahead to confirm hours and current civilian accessibility.*

Additionally, Port Hueneme is also the only commercial port for international shipping between Los Angeles and San Francisco, employing more than 4,000 and boasting niche markets of cars and fruit cargoes. Public educational tours of the port are offered. For schedules, call (805) 488-3677 or visit the website at www.portofhueneme.org.

entire life (1911–2004), gifts of state he received during his administration, a replica of the Oval Office, and a piece of the crumbled Berlin Wall. This facility provides a compelling look at "the Great Communicator" and his legacy as the fortieth U.S. president. The Air Force One Pavilion houses the former president's Boeing 707 airplane, available for boarding and tours, along with exhibits about presidential travel. From US 101, exit at Simi Valley, drive 5 miles inland from Highway 101 and exit on Highway 118, then follow the signs. Open daily 10 a.m. to 5 p.m.; closed New Year's Day, Thanksgiving, and Christmas.

where to eat and stay

Grand Vista Hotel. 999 Enchanted Way, Simi Valley; (805) 583-2000 or (800) 455-7464; www.grandvistasimi.com. Very spacious 195-room, full-service hotel with two swimming pools (one heated) and the Vistas Restaurant. Complimentary full breakfast buffet (Mon through Sat) will get you ready for touring! Located only 2 miles from the Reagan Library, exit at First Street off Highway 118. $$$.

day trip 02

northwest

spiritually inclined:
ojai

ojai

To master the most difficult part of this daytrip, just say "Oh-high." That's how you pro-
nounce the city's moniker used by original Chumash Indian inhabitants believed to mean
"Valley of the Moon," a spiritually inclined enclave (home to the Krotona Institute of The-
osophy as well as a retreat dedicated to the teachings of Jiddu Krishnamurti) nestled in a
verdant, peaceful valley. Surrounded by the Topa Topa Mountains, Ojai is portrayed as the
mythical paradise of Shangri-La by filmmaker Frank Capra in his classic 1937 movie *Lost
Horizon*.

In 1917, the rustic village was discovered by Edward Drummond Libbey, early owner of
the Libbey Glass Company. After a devastating fire, he re-created downtown Ojai with distinctive Colonial Revival architecture, including a Spanish-style arcade, a bell tower reminiscent
of Havana's Campanile, and an outdoor amphitheater (Libbey Bowl—home to the Ojai Music
Festival) still very much part of the town's charm today. The same things that Libbey loved
back then, you'll still love about Ojai today—a Mediterranean climate with hot, dry summers
and mild winters with unique topography. Ojai is surrounded by an east/west mountain range,
one of few places in the world to have a "pink moment" occur as the sun is setting: Look to
the east over the Topa Topa Mountains and you'll see a brilliant shade of pink reflected at
that end of the valley. Try to time your visit here for this phenomenon; it never fails to aston-
ish. Conversely, the rising moon over Ojai's mountain ranges creates a gorgeous lunar glow.

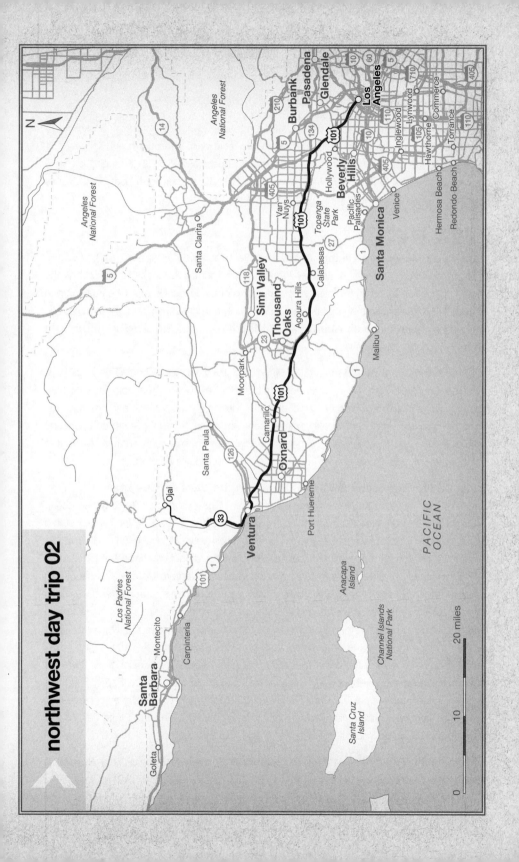

northwest day trip 02

getting there

The drive here alone is worth the trip because of the scenic mountain vistas and lakes you'll encounter around practically every turn in the two-lane road. Head north on Highway 101 to Ventura, then turn inland on either Highway 33 (technically SR 33) through Oak View (about 13 miles) or take Highway 150 (technically SR 150) further north past Lake Casitas (for about 17 miles) to reach the Valley of the Moon.

where to go

Ojai Valley Museum of History & Art. 130 West Ojai Ave.; (805) 640-1390; www.ojai valleymuseum.org. Located downtown in the historic Thomas Aquinas Church chapel, the museum houses changing exhibits of art, natural history, and local lore. A Chumash garden (a local Native American tribe that designs eco-friendly gardenscapes) and gift shop provide interesting diversions. Open Wed through Fri 1 to 4 p.m., and Sat and Sun 10 a.m. to 4 p.m. $ (under six free).

Ojai Theatre. 145 East Ojai Ave.; (805) 646-1011; www.ojaitheatre.com. This circa-1910 building, beautifully restored in 2008, now features the best viewing technologies with classic Hollywood charm including Art Deco–style chandeliers, movie posters, and luxe curtains. First-run features, matinees, weekly independent film series, special events, and concerts are featured—and the theater is home to the Ojai Film Festival each autumn. No matter what's playing, you'll have a blast from the past with all today's comforts here.

Lake Casitas Recreation Area. 11311 Santa Ana Rd., Ventura; reservations: (805) 649-1122 or info: (805) 649-2233; www.lakecasitas.info. Open year-round for day use during daylight hours, there are 400 overnight campsites subject to availability; fees vary. Set in a valley of its own off Highway 150, approximately 3 miles west of the junction of Highway 33 (about 15 minutes from downtown Ojai), this 35-mile-long, irregularly shaped lake is actually a human-made reservoir that provides drinking water for Ventura County. Consequently, there is no swimming in the lake, but the fishing for trout, bass, crappie, and catfish is renowned. Powerboats, canoeing, and sailing are fun here, too, year-round. There is a basic snack bar, small grocery store, boat rental, bait shop, and a large kids' playground. Open only in the summertime, the Water Adventure Area offers two distinctly wet playgrounds—an 18-inch-deep pool or the Lazy River tube-float pool (separate admission fee). There are plenty of special events happening here that add even more fun, such as Family Fun Fishing Day in Mar; the annual Ojai Wine Festival in June (forty-plus wineries in a scenic tasting environs; visit www.ojaiwinefestival.com for more information); and the Pirate Faire & Fall Renaissance Festival. You could easily just spend your day trip here.

Krishnamurti Foundation of America Library & Bookstore/Pepper Tree Retreat & Education Center. 1130 McAndrew Rd.; (805) 646-4773 or (805) 646-2390 for library info; www.kfa.org and www.peppertreeretreat.com. Located on eleven acres of quiet, natural beauty in the east end of the Ojai Valley, explore Pine Cottage, the historic landmark home of world renowned philosopher Jiddu Krishnamurti (who resided here from 1922 to 1986), now the **Krishnamurti Library & Bookstore,** open Thurs through Sun from 1 to 5 p.m. Also on the grounds is the **Pepper Tree Retreat,** the former guest house (built in 1910) that is now a vegetarian bed-and-breakfast with eight guest suites. During his sixty-four years in Ojai, Krishnamurti welcomed thousands of visitors from around the world—including Aldous Huxley, John Barrymore, Greta Garbo, Dr. Jonas Salk, D. H. Lawrence, Jackson Pollack, Igor Stravinsky, even the Beatles—who were challenged by his penetrating inquiries into the fundamental questions of life. A very spiritual and thought-provoking place to visit, no matter what your philosophy.

where to shop

More than two dozen art galleries and artists' studios are located throughout the Ojai Valley. Stop by the Chamber of Commerce at 201 South Signal St. for a current list of exhibitions and locales. Strolling the Arcade on East Ojai Avenue in the center of the village is always a shopper's delight.

Bart's Books. 302 West Matlija St.; (805) 646-3755; www.bartsbooksojai.com. Home of the largest independently owned and operated outdoor bookstore in the United States and nestled under a 400-plus-year-old coastal live oak tree since 1964, Bart's was founded by Richard Bartinsdale when his collection of books got so overwhelming that he constructed bookcases along the sidewalk so that passersby could peruse the titles. Instead of a cash register, "Bart" left coffee cans atop the bookcases so patrons could make their selections and leave their payment in the can—giving rise to the world famous tradition of selling books via the honor system. Yes, there are books indoors, too—an incredible selection of dime novels to first editions (they're locked up). Located downtown at the corner of Canada Street, every reader and book junkie needs to make a trek to Bart's. Call for hours.

SoulCentered: A Metaphysical Shoppe. 311 North Montgomery St.; (805) 640-8222; www.soulcentered.com. Enhance your spiritual journey with incenses from around the world, books, CDs and DVDs, a world-class selection of crystals and stones, gift cards, candles, divination decks, and art and jewelry by local artisans. There's even a children's area with books, puppets, musical instruments, and toys. Check out the events in the 1,000-square-foot geodesic dome. Generally open daily; call for hours.

where to eat

Boccali's. 3277 Ojai-Santa Paula Rd., at the corner of Reeves Road; (805) 646-6116; www.boccalis.com. Casual, fun dining inside or outside on the patio featuring tasty pizzas and loads of pastas. Family owned and operated since 1986 with a casual, friendly atmosphere. Takeout is available and always popular. Serving dinner seven nights a week and lunch Wed through Sun. $.

The Ranch House. 500 South Lomita, at Besant Road; (805) 646-2360; www.theranch house.com. If you seek a completely romantic, California-continental cuisine experience for dinner or Sunday brunch, this is it: intimate garden dining tables amongst meandering streams or on the wooden porch; bakery and herb garden on premises; winner of the *Wine Spectator* Award of Excellence for a wine list with over 500 selections available. Closed Mon; call for hours; reservations recommended. $$$.

where to stay

Ojai Valley Inn & Spa. 905 Country Club Rd., just west of town off Highway 150; (805) 646-5511 or (800) 422-6524; www.ojairesort.com. This magnificent AAA five-diamond-rated resort was founded in 1923 by Edward D. Libbey as his private country club and golf course. Situated on 220 landscaped acres, the resort offers 308 first-class rooms and suites overlooking gardens, woods, pools, and a PGA-rated championship golf course. Warm up on the putting green, or perhaps try tennis (four courts), horseback riding, a jogging course, hiking, and biking (rentals available). Kids and teens programs change with the season, plus there's tours of the small-animal farm and pony rides.

Do not miss experiencing the **Spa Ojai** facility—named the number-one spa by *Shape* magazine and one of the top-ten best spas by *USA Today.* You'll experience the full complement of deluxe services such as hydrotherapy, massage, facials, manicures, and more (try the Kuyam—the only treatment of this type in the United States, combining the therapeutic effects of cleansing mud, dry heat, inhalation therapy, and guided meditation).

Dining options include the **Maravilla,** serving breakfast daily from 6:30 to 11:30 a.m. and featuring regionally grown fruits, house-made granola, and organic egg dishes; dinner is served nightly from 5 to 10 p.m. with a focus on prime steaks, chops, and the freshest seafood. **Jimmy's** offers an authentic pub experience from 11 a.m. to midnight daily with boutique beers on tap, along with California wines by the glass, all complemented by bountiful sandwiches, burgers, and crusty brick-oven pizzas. The **Oak Grill** serves lunch on the terrace overlooking the golf course and mountain vistas. The **Café at the Spa** serves lighter fare with a Mediterranean flair.

worth more time

The Oaks at Ojai. 122 East Ojai Ave.; (805)646-5573; www.oaksspa.com. This is a destination health spa founded in 1977 by world-renowned fitness expert, author, and former professional figure skater Sheila Cluff. The Oaks is a truly delightful, stress-free place that still focuses on healthy weight loss and wellness along with a wide array of relaxing spa treatments. The clientele come here to embrace a healthy lifestyle. Day programs are available, such as the Fitness Spa Day that includes your choice of sixteen fitness classes, full use of the facility plus the spa sanctuary with eucalyptus steam room, whirlpool, sauna, locker room, and three healthy spa cuisine meals—all for only $117 per day (in 2010).

day trip 03

northwest

the way california was:
ventura, channel islands
national park

ventura

Wend your way 70 minutes northwest of Los Angeles to reach historically revitalized downtown Ventura—one of the few remaining classic California districts along the coast with its eclectic Art Deco, Craftsman, Neoclassical, and Victorian architecture all lovingly preserved in storefronts, offices, and residences. The city is home to more than 125 antique dealers in thirty-nine locations, earning a well-deserved reputation as a mecca for hard-core enthusiasts as well as casual buyers. (A free Antique Guide & Map is available from the Ventura Visitors Bureau.) Downtown includes the restored Mission San Buenaventura as well as boutiques, restaurants, wine bars, and nightlife. Galleries stay open late on the first Friday of each month—a great time to wander in/out/around to meet featured artists and greet locals. Approximately 6 blocks from historic downtown, discover the Ventura Pier, beaches, and promenade as well as the Ventura County Fairgrounds. Area beaches—stretching from Surfer's Point to Ventura Harbor—include surf breaks, San Buenaventura State Beach, the Seaward Avenue Beach District, several county parks, and miles of scenic bike paths. Ventura's warm, sunny climate and value-priced accommodations and attractions make this a very affordable getaway up the coast from L.A.

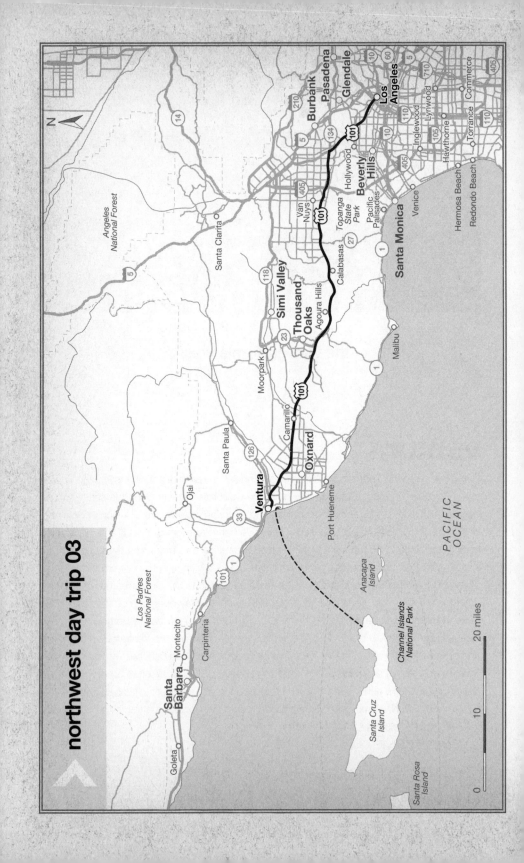

northwest day trip 03

getting there

Popularized in the 1970s hit song by America, the mighty Ventura Highway, officially known as US 101, continues to wend its way north of Los Angeles, and at mile marker 70, you can take the California Street exit to reach the city of Ventura. Ventura wraps around the east/west ribbons of US 101 here (even though the signs say North–South, don't be confused!) You can also take Amtrak's Pacific Surfliner to the Ventura train platform immediately adjacent to the beach and Ventura County Fairgrounds.

where to go

Albinger Archaeological Museum. 113 East Main St.; (805) 648-5823; www.albinger museum.org. Free admission to this museum is just one reason to explore its artifacts, spanning 3,500 years and all excavated from a single dig site next to the Mission San Buenaventura. Fascinating audiovisual programs describing the labor-intensive process of excavation are available on request. Open Wed through Sun 10 a.m. to 4 p.m.

Mission San Buenaventura. 211 East Main St.; (805) 648-4496; www.sanbuenaventura mission.org. Founded in 1782 and completed in 1809, ninth in the chain of twenty-one California missions, the present mission includes a small museum and a restored church that continues to be an active parish. It's the only mission in the United States with bells made of wood; the reason still remains a mystery. Open Mon through Fri 10 a.m. to 5 p.m., Sat 9 a.m. to 5 p.m., and Sun 10 a.m. to 4 p.m.

Ventura County Museum of History and Art. 89 South California St. (temporary); (805) 653-0323; www.venturamuseum.org. Major expansion/construction of the original 100 East Main St. location began in April 2008; the museum is scheduled to return there some time in 2011. Its current home features attractive displays blending local chronicles and illustrations along with the popular George Stuart historical figures, changing exhibits, and a good research library detailing the city's origins: After a brief period of Mexican rule, following California statehood in 1850, Ventura became a bustling frontier town. Call for hours and event schedule.

Ventura Harbor Village. 1583 Spinnaker Dr.; (877) 89-HARBOR or (805) 642-8538; www .venturaharborvillage.com. Sailing, fishing, scuba diving, and sightseeing trips can all be arranged at this thirty-three-acre waterfront village located about 1 mile west of the Harbor Boulevard/Seaward exit from Highway 101. Rent a paddle boat or kayak, or simply enjoy a few hours by the sea. Be sure to check out the various modes of transportation that will take you to the Channel Islands. The thirty-six-horse carousel and arcade games are fun for the whole family—not to mention the specialty shops, cafe bakery, ice cream parlor, and restaurants serving the freshest locally caught seafood. Hours are seasonal, call for current opening/closing times.

perry mason

More than 150 Perry Mason novels written by Erle Stanley Gardner, a young Ventura lawyer, gained worldwide popularity in mid-twentieth century and remain so today. Many of Ventura's buildings, locations, and characters were used by Gardner in his novels and copied later in the Perry Mason radio show and the TV series, which starred Raymond Burr. About two or three times each year, walking tours of the famous sites are held downtown, including city hall (in the 1920s, it was the courthouse); the old sheriff's office; Gardner's law office, now called the Perry Mason Building; Gardner's favorite lunch spot; the shoe store where he purchased his wing tips; and the site of his first Ventura home. Tour leader Richard Senate remarks, "Salinas has Steinbeck and Sonoma has London and Gardner's Perry Mason is Ventura's gift to the world." To unlock the mystery of Perry Mason tours, schedules, and fees, give a call to the City of Ventura at (805) 658-4726.

where to shop

From downtown's plethora of antique emporiums and unique boutiques to the full spectrum of modern retailers at the **Pacific View Mall** (3301-1 East Main St.; 805-642-5530; www.shoppacificview.com) you've got plenty of shop-'til-you-drop options in greater Ventura. If you're feeling a vintage vogue, check out more than three dozen consignment and thrift stores found in midtown and downtown. In fact, the Visitors Bureau has compiled a comprehensive list entitled "Vintage Ventura" for your edification. Perennial faves are **B on Main Gifts and Antiques** (337 East Main St.; 805-643-9309; www.b-onmain.com) and **Blue Moon** (600 East Main St.; 805-643-2553; www.bluemoonfashion.net) for women's clothing and accessories. Ventura is home to one of the most environmentally conscious outdoor retailers in the world, so be sure to check out the main store of **Patagonia-Great Pacific Ironworks** (235 West Santa Clara St.; 805-643-6074; www.patagonia.com); it's open daily for your every outdoor, hiking, surfing need and/or desire.

where to eat

Andria's Seafood Restaurant & Market. 1449 Spinnaker Dr., #A, in Ventura Harbor Village; (805) 654-8228; www.andriasseafood.com. For a relaxed, casual, family-friendly atmosphere, this is your seafood place. Since 1982, the food's always fresh off the nearby boats, cooked to order—grilled, fried, baked, or broiled—and served with a smile. Open seven days a week from 11 a.m. $–$$.

Jonathan's at Peiranos. 204 East Main St.; (805) 648-4853; www.jonathansatpeiranos .com. Located in Ventura's oldest commercial building, Jonathan's offers alfresco patio and art gallery dining as well as J's Tapas, a martini bar featuring live jazz and a superb appetizer menu, plus an extensive wine list with more than thirty-five selections offered by the glass. For lunch and dinner, savor owner/executive chef Jason Collis's creative menus of fine and affordable Mediterranean-styled eclectic fare. Call for hours and specials. $$–$$$.

Rocket Fizz. 105 South Oak St.; (805) 641-1222; www.rocketfizzstore.com. Check out this crazy candy shop! To fit in with Ventura's classic California vibe, you need the sweets to match! Discover more than 500 different bottled soda pops manufactured from all corners of the United States plus an enormously awesome candy selection. Call for hours. $.

where to stay

Pierpont Inn & Spa and Austen's Restaurant. 550 Sanjon Rd.; (805) 643-6144 or (800) 285-4667; www.pierpontinn.com. This attractive seventy-seven-unit property was established in 1928 and has been renovated and restored over the ensuing years. Some rooms have fireplaces, and most rooms have ocean views with balconies. We like the cottages the best. Even through you are across the highway from the Pacific Ocean, this property has two heated pools (one indoor). It also has twelve lighted tennis courts and a friendly, helpful staff. The ocean-view restaurant, Austen's, serves classic California cuisine for lunch and dinner daily as well as Sun brunch. It's adjacent to US 101; northbound exit is Sanjon Road, southbound exit is Seaward Avenue. $$$.

channel islands national park

Less than 20 miles off the coast of Ventura and Santa Barbara Counties, the Channel Islands National Park comprises five of the eight offshore Channel Islands: Santa Barbara, Anacapa, Santa Cruz, Santa Rosa, and San Miguel. These islands provide an unparalleled introduction to the flora and fauna of the local marine environment. Nature, unspoiled and unsullied by us humans, is the main attraction here; quite honestly, it's the only attraction!

Because the balance of nature on these islands and their surrounding waters is so fragile, visitors' activities are strictly regulated. For instance, there are no snack bars or RV campgrounds, and when you tour the area, you must bring (and take back what remains of) your own food, water, and other supplies. Rangers conduct guided hikes on San Miguel and Santa Rosa. Private concessionaires' boats or charter craft provide transportation across the channel to specific embarkation points.

getting there

From Los Angeles, follow the directions under "getting there" in the Ventura section, above, then head to Ventura Harbor Village to start arranging your visit to the Channel Islands. The key word here is "islands" . . . the only way to get to the park is to kayak, hop on a boat run by a private concessionaire or charter craft to specific embarkation points; or take a plane (use your own boat or plane if you happened to bring it along).

where to go

The Channel Islands National Park Robert J. Lagomarsino Visitor Center (1901 Spinnaker Dr.; 805-658-5730; www.nps.gov/chis) is located in Ventura Harbor Village. The waterfront visitor center houses quality exhibits that graphically describe the entire park, including its ecosystem, mammals, and birds. Plus the center has an indoor tide pool, great for learning about the sea creatures you'll see en route. There is also a movie and video about the islands shown here. A stairway and elevator lead up to the observation tower that will give you a 360-degree view of the harbor and, on most clear days, all the way to the islands themselves. Taking a day to visit our fortieth national park is well worth the effort and will be a sea journey to another dimension you certainly won't forget.

Ventura Harbor Village. 1583 Spinnaker Dr.; (877) 89-HARBOR or (805) 642-8538; www.venturaharborvillage.com. After getting filled up on information at the visitor center, make arrangements in the Village to visit the Channel Islands (unless, of course, you own a plane). Take part in all those outdoor and water activities you've been totally wanting to try since, like, forever! For more information on options for getting to the Islands, call or visit the website.

Island Packers Company. 1691 Spinnaker Dr., Suite 105 B; (805) 642-1393; www.island packers.com. Adjacent to Channel Islands National Park Visitor Center, this tour operator has been based here since 1968 and offers scheduled charters to all the islands year-round, as well as whale-watching trips and cruises; it's the home dock for the *Islander* and the *Island Adventure.* Call for special packages and itineraries. (The nearby satellite office, and the home dock for the *Vanguard,* is located in Channel Islands Harbor, 3600 South Harbor Blvd., Oxnard.) Open daily; call for hours.

day trip 04

northwest

>>> **america's riviera revealed:**
santa barbara

santa barbara

Magnificent palm trees swaying against a sensuous beach with a backdrop of golden mountains; red-tile-roofed buildings with whitewashed adobe walls—is this Cannes or Monaco? No, *mes amis,* this is the American Riviera—the destination resort of Santa Barbara only 90 miles up the coast (northwest) of Los Angeles. The city of Santa Barbara was first hailed as a prime tourist destination in 1872 by East Coast travel writer Charles Nordhoff, who opined, "Santa Barbara certainly is the most pleasant place throughout the state." Santa Barbara is an extraordinarily popular year-round getaway—for a day, week, and often a lifetime. Ask Oprah Winfrey and hundreds of other celebrities why they have homes here now. Many will cite the potent blend of Chumash Indian, Spanish, Mexican, and American cultures that gives Santa Barbara an extremely rich and well-preserved heritage, plus the extraordinarily protected natural beauty of the region, bounded by the Santa Ynez Mountains to the north and Pacific Ocean to the south. Yes, all Santa Barbara's beaches face south along the Pacific (the only place in the United States where this happens), so when you want to check out the magnificent sunsets, be sure you face the beach and look over your right shoulder!

You'll find from Sunday to Thursday there's fewer crowds and better deals, especially in the winter months, yet year-round the weather is generally sunny and mild, averaging 62

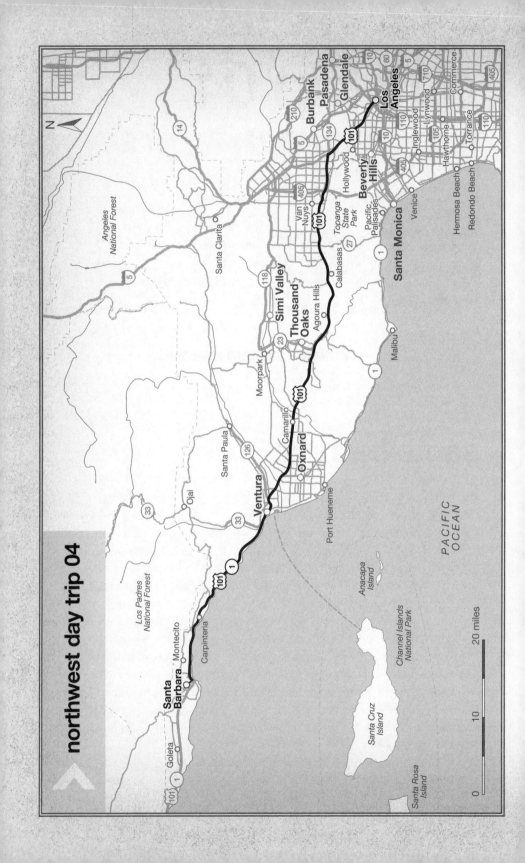

northwest day trip 04

degrees Fahrenheit. Laura is a bit biased about Santa Barbara since she's lived in the area since 1985 (and Pamela lived here for several years as well)—so come see for yourself the scenery, stars in the sky and in the vicinity, shopping, museums, art, culture, great restaurants, and trendy places to hang out on America's Riviera.

getting there

Via vehicle, head north on Highway 101 and exit at Garden Street—turn left toward the waterfront or right into the downtown area. (To avoid the Sunday afternoon Highway 101 mess of southbound stop-and-go traffic, stay for dinner and the sunset or really relax and stay the night!)

where to go

Stearns Wharf. Cabrillo Boulevard and State Street (look for the dolphin fountain statue at the beachfront); (805) 564-5518; www.stearnswharf.org. Built in 1872 to serve cargo and passenger ships, this Santa Barbara historic landmark is now the site of specialty shops, some amazing-view restaurants, the Ty Warner Sea Center, a boat charter dock, and fishing spots. You can actually drive and park as well as stroll onto this historic wharf, but parking is limited so try one of the city lots to the east and then meander while enjoying the magnificent views of the Pacific and looking back at the city.

Ty Warner Sea Center. 211 Stearns Wharf; (805) 962-2526; www.sbnature.org/sea center. Owned and operated by the Santa Barbara Museum of Natural History, you'll really see sea life—such as sea stars, urchins, limpets, and sharks—up close here. When you enter the two-story glass foyer, you'll be greeted by an impressive thirty-nine-foot life-size model of a California gray whale. Many interactive exhibits, including live encounters with tide-pool animals, let you experience the wonders of oceanography. Open daily 10 a.m. to 5 p.m.; closed major holidays.

Chase Palm Park stretches east from Stearns Wharf along the waterfront on both sides of beachfront Cabrillo Boulevard. On the park's sandy/grassy south side, there are bike paths, plenty of lawn to stretch out on under the palm trees, and if you're ready to roll, discover **Skaters Point,** a popular, free 12,000-square-foot concrete mecca for skateboarders that is open dawn to dusk. On the ten-acre north side of the park, check out the restored antique **Carousel** (enclosed in its own pavilion, it's open daily for kids of all ages at a nominal fee); a kids-only **Shipwreck Playground** with a rubberized deck; grassy knolls, picnic tables; restrooms; a snack bar; and an intimate amphitheater where free live concerts take place all summer long.

Ask for schedules, free maps, and coupons at the nearby **Santa Barbara Region Chamber of Commerce Visitor Center** (1 Garden Street at Cabrillo Boulevard; 805-965-3021; www.sbchamber.org).

Santa Barbara Zoological Gardens. 500 Ninos Dr.; (805) 962-5339; www.santabarbara zoo.org. Located on a former estate overlooking the glittering Pacific, 2 blocks off Cabrillo Boulevard near East Beach, this thirty-acre zoo is a special treat for any age. Start your visit with a ride on the minitrain that circumnavigates the zoo's beautiful gardens. Discover 500 animals, including condors, big cats, roaring elephants, gangly giraffes, and a flight-full aviary. Morning visits are favored, capped with a picnic or lunch in the Ridley-Tree House Restaurant or the Wave featuring seafood at the zoo's hilltop. Open daily 10 a.m. to 5 p.m. except Christmas.

Santa Barbara Yacht Harbor, Marina, and Breakwater. West of Stearns Wharf, the motor entrance is along Cabrillo Boulevard just past the Castillo Street intersection. Harbor master's office is located at 132-A Harbor Way; (805) 564-5520; www.santabarbaraca.gov. We just love to stroll along the quarter-mile-long concrete breakwater (avoiding the ocean wave spray) and contemplate the extraordinary views of the city rising into the mountains beyond framed by the masts of 1,000 sailboats, as well as powerboats, and trawlers. Every

take a vacation from the gas pump

Santa Barbara is so easy to visit from Los Angeles without your car—in fact, we highly recommend the experience! Founded in 1998, the **Santa Barbara Car Free Project** *is an award-winning ecotourism partnership sponsored by the Santa Barbara County Air Pollution Control District (recipient of the 2009 EPA National Clean Air Excellence Award), committed to alternative transportation for cleaner air and a healthier planet. Check out www.santabarbaracarfree .org for comprehensive information about enjoying the beauty of this area and reducing your carbon footprint. You can download maps and get incredible deals on forty-plus hotels, activities, and attractions just for making a car-free pledge. Discover free walking tours, bike maps, bus routes, Amtrak train schedules, maps, and vacation packages/hotel discounts. Eleven Amtrak trains daily leave Los Angeles Union Station (www.amtrak.com) including the Pacific Surfliner and the Coast Starlight for Santa Barbara. Tracks run right along the ocean in parts, and Santa Barbara's historic train station is at 209 State St., only 2 blocks from the beach. When you get tired of walking, hop aboard the nifty electric shuttle buses operated by the Metropolitan Transit District (www.sbmtd.gov) or take a pedicab or hybrid taxi, or rent a bicycle or surrey cycle! To receive info by mail, call (805) 696-1100 or write P.O. Box 60436, Santa Barbara, CA 93160. Viva Car Free-dom!*

Sat morning, there's a **Fishermans' Market,** a great place to see the fruits of the sea including sea urchin, rock cod, halibut, spiny lobster and crab.

Sea Landing. 301 West Cabrillo Blvd.; (805) 963-3564; www.sealanding.net. Hook your own seafood on a half- or full-day fishing expedition charter boat that docks here, or sign up for a dive trip or whale watching excursion. There is a full-service tackle shop, dive shop, and rental department available for all your angling needs. Sea Landing is the home dock of the award-winning *Condor Express,* a 75-foot, 149-passenger high-speed jet-powered catamaran run by **Condor Cruises** (805-882-0088 or 888-77-WHALE; www.condor cruises.com). Call for current schedules and fares. This custom-designed boat is specifically designed for naturalist-led whale-watching trips (all year-round) and one of the best ways to see the majesty of the Pacific on a very stable vessel. **Truth Aquatics** (805-962-1127; www.truthaquatics.com) arranges popular sea kayaking, scuba, and diving charters and also acts as official concessionaire for boat trips to the Channel Islands National Park, some 20 miles offshore. (Refer to Northwest Day Trip 03 for more details on the park.) Call for seasonal times, schedules, and fares.

Santa Barbara Sailing Center. Near the public boat launch in the marina; (805) 962-2826 or (800) 350-9090; www.sbsail.com. Rent a sailboat—there are more than forty to choose from (with or without a skipper). This is the home dock of the *Double Dolphin* catamaran, a forty-nine-passenger sailboat that runs whale-watching trips, sunset cruises, and private charters. The ASA-certified sailing school here offers beginning through advanced instruction if the lure of sea captures you!

Santa Barbara Maritime Museum. 113 Harbor Way; (805) 962-8404; www.sbmm.org. Located in the former Naval Reserve Building in the center of the marina, the museum illustrates the evolution of nautical technology, starting with local origins in the Chumash culture up to modern-day boats and submarines. Highly interactive exhibits, and great for kids. Call for hours and admission fees.

Heading into downtown, do not miss a visit to the **Santa Barbara County Courthouse** (1100 Anacapa St.; 805-962-6464; www.sbcourts.org/general_info/cthouse_info.htm). We understand that you probably are skeptical about spending any time in the criminal justice system, but this 1929 National Historic Landmark building is the exception. You can climb the 80-foot clock-tower stairs (or take the elevator) for a stunning panoramic view of the city, all the way to the bright Pacific. The award-winning Spanish Moorish design is one of the most-photographed and admired settings—and the sunken gardens, perfect for picnicking, host concerts and festivities throughout the year. Building is open Mon through Fri 8 a.m. to 5 p.m., Sat and Sun 10 a.m. to 5 p.m.; gardens are open 24/7.

Santa Barbara Historical Museum and Covarrubias Adobe. 136 East de la Guerra St.; (805) 966-1601; www.santabarbaramuseum.com. Learn the region's story from the age of the Chumash Indians to the Space Age via this downtown museum's permanent exhibits of documents, furniture, decorative and fine arts, and costumes. Representing an easier, slower lifestyle, the Casa Covarrubias Adobe, circa 1817, may have served briefly as the headquarters of Pio Pico, the last Mexican governor of California. Open Tues through Sat 10 a.m. to 5 p.m.

To stay in the historic mode, also visit **El Presidio de Santa Barbara State Historic Park** (123 East Canon Perdido St.; 805-965-0093; www.sbthp.org/presidio.htm). Not your traditional recreational type park, this place is a piece of living history. Santa Barbara's El Presidio was the last military outpost built by Spain in the New World, dedicated in 1782. A continuous, ongoing project restores the actual structures, including El Cuartel, the padre's quarters; the chapel; and the commandant's office. Open daily 10:30 a.m. to 4:30 p.m., except for major holidays.

Santa Barbara Museum of Art. 1130 State St.; (805) 963-4364; www.sbmuseart.org. Collections encompass more than 27,000 works by American and European artists, including Monet and other Impressionists. Displays include American, Asian, and nineteenth-century French art, plus Greek and Roman antiquities and major photographic works. Special exhibits rotate throughout the year. Open Tues through Sun 11 a.m. to 5 p.m.

Karpeles Manuscript Library Museum. 21 West Anapamu St., one-half block off State Street; (805) 962-5322; www.rain.org/~karpeles. Free admission always to see an original engraver's copy of the Declaration of Independence, handwritten scores by a dozen leading composers, and the computer guidance system used on the first Apollo lander flight to the moon. Rotating exhibits show fascinating glimpses into antiquity. Open Wed through Sun; call for hours.

Mission Santa Barbara. 2201 Laguna St., at the corner of Laguna and East Los Olivos Streets, approximately five minutes from downtown; (805) 682-4149; www.sbmission.org. Founded on December 4, 1786, the feast day of Saint Barbara, and finally completed in 1820, this is one of the best-preserved among California's renowned chain of twenty-one missions. You will definitely want to tour "the Queen of the Missions," still the longest continuously operating parish of the chain. A fascinating self-guided walking tour that includes artworks, fountains, a courtyard, and a cemetery is recommended. Open daily from 9 a.m. to 5 p.m. except Easter, Thanksgiving, and Christmas.

Santa Barbara Museum of Natural History and Gladwin Planetarium. 2559 Puesta del Sol Rd., just around the corner from the Mission Santa Barbara; (805) 682-4711; www.sbnature.org. The museum has exhibits on early Native American tribes as well as animals, birds, insects, plants, minerals, marine science, and geology. The planetarium hosts impressive star shows. Open daily (except major holidays); call for seasonal schedules and special exhibits.

Santa Barbara Botanic Garden. 1212 Mission Canyon Rd., just north of the Natural History Museum, about 2 miles into Mission Canyon; (805) 682-4726; www.sbbg.org. Seventy-eight exquisite acres devoted only to California species are a delight to wonder and wander through. Self-guided and guided tours available. Open daily except for major holidays; call for seasonal hours and special exhibits. $.

where to shop

Primary shopping districts in Santa Barbara are along **State Street,** the main thoroughfare that runs from the beach (starting at Sterns Wharf) and curves inland at the 2900 block (29 blocks from the beach) to run parallel along the mountains. Major national retailers from Abercrombie & Fitch to Saks to Nordstrom are adjacent to independent retailers, art galleries, antique malls, and bohemian emporiums. Adjoining Santa Barbara's tony suburb of Montecito, **Coast Village Road** is like a mini Rodeo Drive shopping-and-dining enclave with high-end boutiques, jewelers, and art dealers.

El Paseo (from the Spanish word *pasear,* "to walk"; essentially a walkway for pedestrians) is considered one of California's first shopping centers, built in the 1920s and still home to unique shops, jewelers, offices, and restaurants (including the award-winning Wine Cask). Discover the main entrance in the 800 block of State Street near De la Guerra Street downtown.

Paseo Nuevo. 651 Paseo Nuevo; (805) 963-7147; www.paseonuevoshopping.com. Opened in 1989, this charming open-air Mediterranean-style mall has a collection of exclusive local and national shops, restaurants, and cinemas as well as the Contemporary Arts Forum and Center Stage Theater—all within walking distance to the beach. If you bring your out-of-town driver's license to the Paseo Nuevo Management Office, you'll receive a complimentary Shopping & Dining Visitor Rewards Book filled with special savings and offers. It's located 1 block west, parallel to State Street, between Haley and Canon Perdido Streets.

Santa Barbara Sunday Arts & Crafts Show. Cabrillo Boulevard from Stearns Wharf to Calle Puerto Vallarta. (805) 897-1982; www.sbaacs.com. Established in 1965 by area artists and inspired by the sidewalk art shows of Europe, this is the only continuous, nonjuried arts festival of original drawings, paintings, graphics, sculpture, crafts, and photography in the world. From 10 a.m. to dusk every Sun and most holidays, meet over 200 Santa Barbara County resident artists and purchase their wares direct.

where to eat

Chuck's Waterfront Grill. 113 Harbor Way; (805) 564-1200; www.chuckswaterfrontgrill .com. For lunch and dinner daily starting at 11 a.m., their moniker is true: "Experience Stunning Food & Delicious Views." There's casual, surf-inspired decor on two levels plus outdoor decks and a patio overlooking the harbor. Full bar, outstanding seafood and steaks. Hawaiian Poke Ahi Salad is a personal favorite. $$–$$$.

Sambo's on the Beach, 216 West Cabrillo Blvd., 2 blocks from Stearns Wharf; (805) 965-3269. If you're a boomer, this restaurant may sound familiar—it is the original and only remaining Sambo's, founded here on June 17, 1957, by two Santa Barbara friends (Sam Battistone and Newall "Bo" Bohnett), now owned and operated by Sam's grandson Chad Stevens. Make it your stop for hearty breakfasts featuring its famous pancakes and syrup, and all-American lunches, served seven days a week from 6:30 a.m. to 3:30 p.m. $.

McConnell's Ice Cream & Yogurt Shop. 201 West Mission; 805-569-2323; www.mcconnells.com. Delicious if not nutritious, don't leave Santa Barbara without having some of this super-premium (17 percent butterfat) ice cream with no artificial ingredients or stabilizers. Since 1949, this family-owned midtown business also supplies grocery stores and area restaurants and attracts celebs like Barbra Streisand and Kelsey Grammer for a luscious fix. Open daily at 10:30 a.m.; call for closing closing hours as they do vary. $.

The Palace Grill. 8 East Cota St., just off State Street; (805) 963-5000; www.palacegrill.com. Authentic Cajun, Creole, and Caribbean cuisine for lunch and dinner daily at 11:30 a.m. Savor the crawfish étouffée, New Orleans Pan Bar-B-Que Shrimp, or blackened filet mignon accompanied by potent drinks, jovial team servers, and a festive party atmosphere. $$$.

where to stay

Fess Parker's Doubletree Resort. 633 East Cabrillo Blvd.; (805) 564-4333 or (800) 879-2929; www.fpdtr.com. Once owned in part by the late actor/vintner (famed for his Davy Crockett and Daniel Boone roles), this Spanish Mission–style property has all the amenities to suit any and every type of guest, with rooms and suites featuring ocean, mountain, or courtyard views—many with patios or decks—great for enjoying the fresh sea breezes. Located on twenty-three acres across from East Beach, this 360-room resort (Santa Barbara County's largest) has a heated outdoor swimming pool, whirlpool, fitness center, new spa, beauty salon, gift shop, putting green, tennis courts, bicycle and skate rental shop, game room, and full concierge services. Try the California cuisine of Cafe Los Arcos for breakfast, lunch, and dinner; Rodney's Steakhouse for dinner; and Barra Los Arcos for happy hour and live entertainment. Call for seasonal specials and package plans. $$$.

Inn of the Spanish Garden. 915 Garden St.; (805) 564-4700; www.spanishgardeninn.com. Located in the historic Presidio District, just 3 blocks from State Street's fine dining, shops, museums, and art galleries of downtown, this establishment has consistently ranked number one on TripAdvisor.com since opening in 2001. The hotel's traditional Spanish Colonial architecture of white adobe walls, red-tile roofs, courtyard fountains, and vaulted ceilings is updated with all the modern amenities (Wi-Fi, flat screen TVs, deep soaking tubs, luxury linens). Choose from twenty-three rooms and suites and enjoy complimentary breakfast, no-host wine bar, and underground parking complemented by a friendly, can-do-anything-for-you staff. $$$.

Upham Hotel & Garden Cottages. 1404 De La Vina St., just 2 blocks off State Street; (805) 962-0058 or (800) 727-0876; www.uphamhotel.com. Located downtown on an acre of eye-catching gardens, choose from fifty different Victorian-style rooms or cottages, filled with comfortable, not stuffy, antiques. Built and opened in 1871, the Upham is Santa Barbara County's oldest continuously operating hotel. Enjoy complimentary afternoon wine and cheese, a deluxe continental all-you-can-eat breakfast buffet, plus Oreo cookies and milk in the evening. The hotel has always been independently owned and operated and feels like a family home. Call and inquire for current rates and packages. Louie's Restaurant on premises serves delicious California cuisine for lunch Mon through Fri and dinner nightly on the historic veranda. $$.

worth more time

Santa Barbara's Wine Country: Santa Ynez Valley. Located in northern Santa Barbara County, the Santa Ynez Valley is just 35 miles from the beaches of Santa Barbara and 125 miles up the coast from Los Angeles via Highway 101 to Highways 154 and 246. Six distinctive communities are encircled by the Santa Ynez and San Rafael mountain ranges: **Buellton,** home of the original Pea Soup Andersen's Restaurant, is the commercial gateway to the Valley; **Ballard,** with its continuously operating one-room school and 4-diamond award-winning inn and restaurant; **Los Alamos** (Spanish for "the cottonwoods"), located at the northern entry to the region at the junction of Highway 101 and SR 135, is surrounded by vineyards and ranches and has an old-time rustic sensibility; **Los Olivos,** where dozens of tasting rooms, artists, and galleries reside; **Santa Ynez** itself, a thoroughly western burg; and the largest town, **Solvang,** truly another world, is Southern California's little bit of Denmark founded in 1911 by adventurous Danish-Americans and nationally recognized by Orbitz Travel as one of the top-five "U.S. destinations with international flair."

The 2004 Academy Award–winning movie *Sideways* was filmed on location in the Santa Ynez Valley and continues to bring worldwide recognition to the region. Starring Paul Giamatti, Thomas Haden Church, Virginia Madsen, and Sandra Oh, it is a tale of two middle-aged men and the women they meet while on a weeklong wine-tasting adventure. Take the *Sideways* tour using the map available at www.santabarbaraca.com/sideways.

More than 23,000 acres of vineyards annually produce more than a million cases of wine in Santa Barbara County. Not only Chardonnay, Pinot Noir, and Syrah, but also superior Riesling, Sauvignon Blanc, Cabernet Sauvignon, Viognier, and dozens of other varietals are planted and nurtured in more than one hundred vineyards and then crafted into world-class wines enjoyed around the globe. This region's east/west coastal mountains form valleys opening directly to the Pacific Ocean. This unique topography allows the flow of sea breezes to shape distinct microclimates, perfect for the cultivation of classic grape varietals resulting in award-winning wines. The vast majority are small, boutique operations run by individuals or families that welcome visitors year-round either at the winery or in tasting rooms located throughout the valley—all within a 20-minute drive. It is easy and fun to do self-directed wine tours or to enjoy guided tours in limousines, jeeps, vans, or private sedans provided by local tour companies—most leaving from Santa Barbara hotels and the train station for easy and safe accessibility. For maps and complete information on current vintners, events, winemaker dinners, and festivals, contact **Santa Barbara County Vintners Association** (805-688-0881; www.sbcountywines.com) or the **Santa Ynez Valley Wine Country Association** (800-563-3183; www.santaynezwinecountry.com).

After satisfying your wine-tasting urges, satisfy every shopping desire in art galleries, clothing boutiques, and specialty gift and antique stores. Savor delicious meals—from gourmet wine-country cuisine to Danish specialties as well as international and classic American favorites—perfect for any palate. Pick apples, walnuts, and berries direct from the branch. Discover the area's rich multicultural heritage at prominent Native American, Spanish, Mexican, and Danish museums and the 1804 **Old Mission Santa Inés,** a National Historic Landmark. Bicycle, golf, hike, fish, and see wildlife. Tour a lavender farm or horse ranch, an ostrich or alpaca farm. Take a horseback ride or soar over it all in a glider. Enjoy a picnic lunch in a vineyard, or waterside at **Cachuma Lake** or **Nojoqui Falls** parks. Refresh and rejuvenate at a day spa. Experience year-round 24/7/365 gaming and live entertainment at **Chumash Casino Resort.** At night, do some dancing, take in a live concert or see PCPA (Pacific Conservatory of Performing Arts) Theaterfest's professional summer performances under the stars. At the end of the day, there are thirty-four comfortable inns, lodges, luxury resorts, or full-service hotels—each offering rates, amenities, and seasonal or themed packages for every budget. This is one destination that is definitely worth a longer day trip from L.A. For detailed information, visit www.santaynezvalleyvisit.com or www.solvangusa.com.

regional information

north

day trip 01

Hollywood Chamber of Commerce
7018 Hollywood Blvd.
Hollywood, CA 90028
(213) 469-8311
www.hollywoodchamber.net

The Hollywood Visitor Information Center
6801 Hollywood Blvd.
Hollywood, CA 90028
(323) 467-6412
www.discoverlosangeles.com

West Hollywood Marketing and
Visitors Bureau
8687 Melrose Ave., Suite M-38
West Hollywood, CA 90069
(310) 289-2525 or (800) 368-6020
www.visitwesthollywood.com

day trip 02

Burbank Chamber of Commerce
200 West Magnolia Blvd.
Burbank, CA 91502
(818) 846-3111
www.burbankchamber.org

day trip 03

Universal City/North Hollywood Chamber
of Commerce
6369 Bellingham Ave.
North Hollywood, CA 91606
(818) 508-5155
www.noho.org

Santa Clarita Valley Tourism Office
23920 Valencia Blvd., Suite 235
Santa Clarita, CA 91355
(661) 255-4318 or (800) 868-7398
www.visitsantaclarita.com

northeast

day trip 01

Pasadena Convention and Visitors Bureau
171 South Los Robles Ave.
Pasadena, CA 91101
(626) 795-9311 or (800) 307-7977
www.visitpasadena.com

day trip 02

Lake Arrowhead Communities Chamber
of Commerce
P.O. Box 219
Lake Arrowhead, CA 92352
(909) 337-3715
www.lakearrowhead.net

Lake Arrowhead Village
P.O. Box 640, 28200 SR 189
Suite F-240
Lake Arrowhead, CA 92352
(909) 337-2533
www.lakearrowheadvillage.com

day trip 03

Big Bear Chamber of Commerce
630 Bartlett Rd., Big Bear Village
Big Bear Lake, CA 92315
(909) 866-4607
www.bigbearchamber.com

Big Bear Lake Resort Association and
Visitor Center
630 Bartlett Rd., Big Bear Village
Big Bear Lake, CA 92315-1936
(909) 866-6190 or (800) 4-BIG BEAR
www.bigbearinfo.com or www.bigbear.com

east

day trip 01

California Welcome Center,
San Bernardino-Inland Empire
1955 Hunts Lane, Suite 102
San Bernardino, CA 92408
(909) 891-1874
www.cwcinlandempire.com

day trip 02

Desert Hot Springs Chamber of Commerce
11711 West Dr.
Desert Hot Springs, CA 92240
(760) 329-6403

Palm Springs Visitors Center
2901 North Palm Canyon Dr.
Palm Springs, CA 92262
(760) 778-8418 or (800) 347-7746

day trip 03

Palm Springs Desert Resorts Convention
and Visitors Authority
70-100 Highway 111
Rancho Mirage, CA 92270
(760) 770-9000 or (800) 41-RELAX
www.giveintothedesert.com or
www.palmspringsusa.com

day trip 04

Joshua Tree National Park Headquarters
74485 National Park Dr.
Twentynine Palms, CA 92277-3597
(760) 367-5500 (visitor information line)
www.nps.gov/jotr

southeast

day trip 01

Anaheim/Orange County Visitor and
Convention Bureau
800 West Katella Ave.
Anaheim, CA 92802
(714) 765-8888 or (888) 598-3200
www.anaheimoc.org

day trip 02

Buena Park Convention and Visitors Office
6601 Beach Blvd., Suite 200
Buena Park, CA 90261-2904
(714) 562-3560 or (800) 541-3953
www.visitbuenapark.com

day trip 03

City of Orange Chamber of Commerce
439 East Chapman Ave., Suite A
Orange, CA 92866
(714) 538-3581 or (800) 938-0073
www.orangechamber.org

Santa Ana Chamber of Commerce
2020 North Broadway, Second floor
Santa Ana, CA 92702
(714) 541-5353
www.santaanachamber.com

Costa Mesa Conference and Visitor Bureau
P.O. Box 5071
Costa Mesa, CA 92628-5071
(866) 918-4749 or (714) 435-8530
www.travelcostamesa.com

Irvine Chamber of Commerce
Visitors Bureau
2485 McCabe Way, Suite 150
Irvine, CA 92614
(949) 660-9112 or (877) IRVINE-7
www.irvinecvb.org

day trip 04

Huntington Beach Conference and
Visitors Bureau
301 Main St., Suite 208
Huntington Beach, CA 92648
(714) 969-3492 or (800) 729-6232
www.surfcityusa.com

Laguna Beach Visitors and
Conference Bureau
252 Broadway (SR 133)
Laguna Beach, CA 92651
(949) 497-9229 or (800) 877-1115
www.lagunabeachinfo.org

Newport Beach Conference and
Visitors Bureau
110 Newport Center Dr., Suite 120
Newport Beach, CA 92660
(949) 722-1611 or (800) 94-COAST
www.visitnewportbeach.com

south

day trip 01

Long Beach Area Convention and
Visitor's Bureau
1 World Trade Center, Third floor
Long Beach, CA 90831
(562) 436-3645 or (800) 452-7829 or
(800) 452-7829
www.visitlongbeach.com

Port of Los Angeles
425 South Palos Verdes St.
Los Angeles, CA 90731
(310) SEA-PORT
www.portoflosangeles.org

San Pedro Peninsula Chamber
of Commerce
390 West Seventh St.
San Pedro, CA 90731
(310) 832-7272 or (888) 447-3376
www.sanpedro.com

day trip 02

Catalina Island Visitors Bureau and
Chamber of Commerce
P.O. Box 217
Avalon, CA 90704
(310) 510-1520
www.visitcatalina.org or
www.catalinachamber.com

Santa Catalina Island Company
P.O. Box 737
Avalon, CA 90704
(310) 510-2000 or (800) 626-1496
www.visitcatalinaisland.com

southwest

day trip 01

Marina del Rey Convention and
Visitors Bureau
4701 Admiralty Way
Marina del Rey, CA 90292
Visitor information line: (310) 305-9545
www.visitmarinadelrey.com

west

day trip 01

Beverly Hills Chamber of Commerce
239 South Beverly Dr.
Beverly Hills, CA 90212
(310) 248-1000
www.beverlyhillschamber.com

Beverly Hills Conference and
Visitors Bureau
239 South Beverly Dr.
Beverly Hills, CA 90212
(800) 345-2210
www.beverlyhillsbehere.com

day trip 02

Santa Monica Convention and
Visitors Bureau
1920 Main St., Suite B
Santa Monica, CA 90405
(310) 319-6263 or (800) 544-5319
www.santamonica.com

day trip 03

Malibu Chamber of Commerce
23805 Stuart Ranch Rd., Suite 100
Malibu, CA 90265
(310) 456-9025
www.malibu.org

northwest

day trip 01

Oxnard Convention & Visitors Bureau
1000 Town Center Dr., Suite 130
Oxnard, CA 93036
(805) 385-7545 or (800) 2-OXNARD
www.visitoxnard.com

California Welcome Center-Oxnard
1000 Town Center Dr., Suite 120
Oxnard, CA 93036
(805) 988-0717
www.visitcwc.com/oxnard

Simi Valley Chamber of Commerce &
Visitors Center
40 West Cochran St., Suite 100
Simi Valley, CA 93065
(805) 526-3900
www.simichamber.org

day trip 02

Ojai Valley Chamber of Commerce
201 South Signal St.
Ojai, CA 93023
(805) 646-8126
www.ojaichamber.org

day trip 03

Ventura Convention and Visitors Bureau
89-C South California St.
Ventura, CA 93001
(805) 648-2075 or (800) 333-2989
www.ventura-usa.com

day trip 04

Santa Barbara Conference & Visitors
Bureau and Film Commission
1601 Anacapa St.
Santa Barbara, CA 93101
(805) 966-9222, (800) 927-4688, or (800)
676-1266
www.santabarbaraca.com

Santa Ynez Valley Visitors Association
P.O. Box 1918
Santa Ynez, CA 93460
1-800-742-2843 or (805) 686-0053
www.santaynezvalleyvisit.com

Solvang Conference & Visitors Bureau
1639 Copenhagen Drive
P.O. Box 70
Solvang, CA 93464
(805) 688-6144 or (800) 468-6765
www.solvangusa.com

festivals & celebrations

NOTE: Contact information can change from year to year. Your best bet is to call tourism offices for the cities or areas listed in Regional Information to determine the most current and detailed information. Keep in mind that dates are always subject to change.

january

Bob Hope Chrysler Classic. Palm Desert; (888) MR B HOPE (672-4673); www.bhcc .com. A prestigious PGA Tour Golf Tournament featuring top pros and big-name celebrities. The Classic provides millions to charities.

Dr. Martin Luther King Day Parade and Festival. Long Beach; (562) 570-6816. Parade, entertainment, and celebrities. Free. Call parade founder/coordinator councilmember Dee Andrews.

Dr. Martin Luther King Jr. Celebration. Santa Monica; (310) 434-8101. Sponsored by Santa Monica Community College, this interfaith celebration has music, dramatic readings, and inspirational messages. Free.

Palm Springs International Film Festival. Palm Springs; (760) 778-8979; www.psfilm fest.org. More than 200 international films with a special awards gala honoring industry greats.

Tournament of Roses Parade. Pasadena; (626) 449-4100; www.tournamentofroses .com. World-class parade of flowers features music and fantasy. The annual Rose Bowl collegiate football game follows.

february

Golden Dragon Parade. Los Angeles; (213) 617-0396; www.lagoldendragonparade .com. Chinese New Year parade with colorful floats, multicultural performances, arts and crafts. Free.

International Film Festival. Santa Barbara; (805) 963-0023; www.sbfilmfestival.org. Premieres and screenings of independent U.S. and international films; gala opening, celebrity awards, panels, and seminars by film professionals. Admission fees vary.

Riverside County Fair and National Date Festival. Indio; (760) 863-8247 or (800) 811-FAIR; www.datefest.org. The festival features exhibits of dates and produce; fine arts; floriculture; gems and minerals; a livestock show; and pig, camel, and ostrich races.

march

BNP Paribas Open Tennis Tournaments. Indian Wells; (800) 999-1585; www.bnpparibas open.com. BNP Paribas, the global leader in banking and financial services, sponsors the ATP World Tour Masters 1000 and Sony Ericsson WTA Tour Premier tennis tournaments, drawing 30,000-plus visitors per day for ten days to the Palm Springs area.

Celebration of the Whales. Oxnard; (805) 985-4852; www.channelislandsharbor.org. Festivities on Harbor Boulevard, near the Marine Emporium Landing Channel Islands Harbor farmers' and fishermen's market, in conjunction with the Channel Islands Harbor, celebrate the migration of the Pacific gray whales. Free.

Free Museum Day. Santa Ynez Valley; (800) 742-2843 or www.SantaYnezValleyVisit.com. All eight museums in the area offer free admission on the first Sat of Mar each year.

La Quinta Arts Festival. La Quinta; (760) 564-1244; www.lqaf.com. Takes place at Center for the Arts (south of SR 111). It all takes place 30 minutes from downtown Palm Springs in a dramatic desert setting at the base of the Santa Rosa Mountains, as it has annually since 1982. Live entertainment and tastes of Coachella Valley's great restaurants abound, and showcase stunning art creations from more than 270 juried artists.

Taste of Solvang. Solvang; (805) 688-6144 or (800) 458-6765; www.solvangusa.com. This annual weekend food and wine event features a Friday evening dessert reception, Saturday afternoon walking smorgasbord with 40 taste stops, Saturday evening wine tasting room tour as well as free entertainment throughout. Fees vary.

Kraft Nabisco Golf Championship. Rancho Mirage; (760) 324-4546; www.kncgolf.com. The top women golfers in the world play in the first major on the LPGA tour at Mission Hills Country Club. The competition is fierce for the $2 million-plus purse and the coveted Dinah Shore Trophy.

april

Glory of Easter. Garden Grove; (714) 971-4069; www.crystalcathedral.org. This annual Easter play features special events, live animals, and a cast of more than 200 in the dramatic presentation of the last seven days of Christ on earth.

Joshua Tree National Park Art Festival. Twentynine Palms; (760) 367-5522; www.joshua tree.org/artfestival.html. Exhibits and sales by more than twenty artists.

Los Angeles Times Festival of Books. Los Angeles; (213) 237-5000; www.latimes.com. More than 800 exhibitors and 600 authors, speakers, and celebrity presentations, plus a giant children's area, all take over the UCLA campus for the weekend. For the love of reading, don't miss this! Free.

Presidio Day, Santa Barbara; (805) 966-1279; www.sbthp.org. Celebration of early California arts, crafts, and music at historic 1782 Presidio Park. Free.

Toyota Grand Prix. Long Beach; (562) 981-2600; www.gplb.com. International field of world-class drivers and high-performance race cars negotiate the tight turns of the city in heated wheel-to-wheel competition.

may

Cinco de Mayo. Los Angeles; (213) 485-8372; www.olvera-street.com/html/fiestas.html. Celebrate Mexico's 1862 victory over French forces in Pueblo, Mexico, with popular and traditional music, cultural presentations, dancing, and ethnic cuisine on Olvera Street, the center of Mexican culture in Los Angeles. Free.

California Strawberry Festival. Oxnard; (805) 385-4739; www.strawberry-fest.org. Strawberry foods, contests, music, and arts and crafts.

I Madonnari Street Painting Festival. Santa Barbara; (805) 964-4710; www.imadonnari festival.com/im.html. More than 200 local artists and children create chalk paintings in front of the Old Mission; Italian market and entertainment. Free.

May Trout Classic. Big Bear Lake; (909) 585-6260 or (800) 4-BIG-BEAR; www.bbmwd .org/eventspg3-maytrout.html. This fishing competition is fun for all ages.

National Orange Show Festival, San Bernardino; (909) 888-6788; www.nosevents.com. This festival includes a fabulous carnival, petting zoo, live circus, commercial exhibitors, a juried art exhibition, strolling entertainment, and much more.

Old Pasadena Summer Fest. Pasadena; (626) 797-6803. Festival includes Taste of Pasadena, arts and crafts, children's activities, jazz festival, and entertainment. Free.

Spring Air Arts and Crafts Faire. Big Bear Lake; (909) 585-3000; www.bigbear.com /specialevents. The show features more than one hundred artists, crafters, and home-improvement specialists from throughout the West Coast offering everything from hand-made jewelry to hand-carved wooden decor and signs to homemade jams and jellies.

june

International Film Festival. Burbank; (818) 438-4736; www.burbankfilmfestival.org. Capturing its home city's rich history and moviemaking magic by promoting fresh pieces of cinematic art by up-and-coming filmmakers from around the world.

Seafest. Ventura; (805) 644-0169; www.venturaharborvillage.com. Celebrate the beginnings of summer with entertainment booths, environmental instruction, a chowder cook-off, and children's activities galore.

Summer Solstice Celebration. Santa Barbara; (805) 965-3396; www.solsticeparade .com. Annual celebration featuring a 100 percent non-motorized parade; music and arts-and-crafts festival in Alameda Park downtown. Celebrating the arrival of summer attracts more than 50,000 people each year. Free.

Theater and Arts Festival. North Hollywood; (818) 508-5115 or (818) 508-5156; www .nohoartsdistrict.com. More than fifteen theaters host two days of live theater and entertainment, arts and crafts, food booths, and a children's court. Free.

july

Catalina Island Fourth of July Celebration. Avalon; (310) 510-1520; www.catalina.com. Golf cart parade, dinner, and fireworks over Avalon Bay.

Celebration on the Colorado Street Bridge. Pasadena; (626) 441-6333; www.pasadena heritage.org. Bands, local restaurants, classic autos and motorcycles, art exhibits, and performance groups.

Festival of Arts and Pageant of the Masters. Laguna Beach; (949) 494-1145 or (800) 487-3378; www.pageanttickets.com. Colorful exhibit of fine, strictly original creations by 160 South Coast artists; includes the world-famous Pageant of the Masters "living pictures" performances.

Fireworks by the Sea. Oxnard; (805) 385-7545 or (800) 269-6273; www.visitoxnard.com. Family-oriented daytime activities (arts and crafts, entertainment, and more), concluding with a fireworks display over the water. Free.

Fireworks Extravaganza. Long Beach; (562) 435-3511; www.visitlongbeach.com. Features strolling entertainment and fireworks display. Free.

Fourth of July Celebration. Huntington Beach; (714) 536-5496; www.surfcityusa.com. Red, white, and blue bash with a 5K run, parade, and fireworks. Free.

Fourth of July Celebration. Ventura; (800) 333-2989; www.ventura-usa.com. Parade and street fair with 8 blocks of arts and crafts, food, and entertainment; fireworks in the evening. Free.

July 4th Fireworks over the Lake. Big Bear Lake; (909) 866-2112 or (800) BIGBEAR; www.bigbear.com. Barbecue, entertainment, and spectacular fireworks.

Lotus Festival. Los Angeles; (213) 485-8745; www.lotusfestival.org. Experience a variety of Asian cultures, entertainment, art exhibits, ethnic cuisine, and children's activities.

Orange County Fair. Costa Mesa; (949) 708-3247; www.ocfair.com.This rural fair in an urban setting offers livestock, a carnival, a rodeo, commercial wares, themed attractions, and fiber arts.

Sawdust Art Festival. Laguna Beach; (949) 494-3030; www.sawdustartfestival.org. The city becomes a magical village created by artists. The two-month (July and Aug) festival includes handcrafted treasures, entertainment, jugglers and storytellers, and jazz, country, rock, and contemporary musicians. Become an artist yourself by attending one of the many hands-on workshops.

august

Catalina Ski Race. Long Beach; (714) 994-4572; www.catalinaskirace.net. World's largest water-ski race involving 110 boats pulling skiers from Long Beach's Belmont Pier to Catalina.

Old Spanish Days (Fiesta). Santa Barbara; (805) 962-8101; www.oldspanishdays-fiesta .org. Community-wide five-day celebration of Spanish and Mexican heritage beginning with La Fiesta Pequena musical/dance showcase on the steps of Old Mission Santa Barbara; plus El Desfile Historico (largest equestrian parade in the western United States); Children's Parade; La Noches de Ronda musical shows at the Courthouse Gardens; *mercados* (marketplaces) and much more. Free.

Salsa Festival. Oxnard; (805) 483-4542; www.oxnardsalsafestival.com. Salsa-making contest, 5K run, arts and crafts, dancing, music, and a carnival for children. Free.

Taste in San Pedro. San Pedro; (310) 832-7272; www.tasteinsanpedro.com. San Pedro restaurants present their signature entrees. Arts and crafts and a vintage car show are other highlights.

U.S. Open of Surfing. Huntington Beach; (714) 366-4584; www.usopenofsurfing.com. Watch the best surfers in the world compete for a large sum. Free.

Ventura County Fair. Ventura; (805) 648-3376 or (800) 333-2989; www.venturacountyfair .org. Traditional county fair features top-name entertainment, exhibits, livestock, motor sports, rodeo, food, and fireworks. Admission fees vary.

september

Aloha Beach Festival. Ventura; (805) 200-8674; www.alohabeachfestival.com. Three stages of entertainment, food, a surfing contest, and beach volleyball.

Catalina Festival of the Arts. Avalon; (310) 510-2700; www.CatalinaArtAssociation.org. Exhibits include mixed media, photography, crafts, and sculpture. Free.

Danish Days. Solvang; (805) 688-6144; www.solvangusa.com. Celebration of Solvang's rich Danish heritage features Danish folk dancing, music, food, *aebleskiver*-eating contests, three parades, and live entertainment. Free.

Los Alamos Old Days. Los Alamos; (805) 344-1717; www.losalamosvalley.org. Founded in 1876, this three-day weekend celebrates the town's western heritage with entertainment, barbeques, dances, peddler's mart, classic car show, and Sunday morning parade. Free.

Los Angeles County Fair. Pomona; (909) 623-3111; www.lacountyfair.com. California's sensational county fair you can't miss! It takes at least a full day to visit the flower and garden exposition, midway, and various entertainments. Kids can participate in educational activities.

Simi Valley Days. Simi Valley; (805) 581-4280; www.simivalleydays.com. Fair features a carnival, hoedown, barn dance, horse show, parade, 5K and 10K runs, food, and entertainment. Admission fees vary.

Stater Bros. Route 66 Rendezvous. San Bernardino; (909) 388-2934; www.route-66 .org. Join in the celebration of the historic Mother Road as 1,900 pre-1975 classics, muscle cars, hot rods, trucks, and Corvettes of any year will cruise for an audience of 500,000 during the four-day event. Experience the contests such as the Neon Light, Poker Run, Open Header, and Model Car.

Taste of the Town. Santa Barbara; (805) 563-4685; www.tasteofthetownsantabarbara .com. More than eighty local restaurants and wineries provide tastes of their best fare in the beautiful Riviera Research Park overlooking the city. Always held the first Sunday after Labor Day as a benefit for the local branch of the Arthritis Foundation. Ticket prices vary.

Book Fair. West Hollywood; (323)848-6515; www.westhollywoodbookfair.org. Founded by the City of West Hollywood as a means of encouraging reading, writing, and literacy and to heighten the community's awareness of books. More than 300 authors, 100 exhibitors, and 25,000 guests attend the event.

october

California Avocado Festival. Carpinteria; (805) 684-0038; www.carpinteriachamber.org. This bountiful avocado celebration includes food, arts and crafts, music, and a flower show. Don't miss the world's largest bowl of guacamole. Free.

Catalina Jazz Festival. Avalon; (818) 347-5299; www.jazztrax.com/jazz/catalina.html. Since 1987, contemporary jazz musicians and instrumentalists perform in the renowned Catalina Casino ballroom and local venues over three consecutive weekends.

Lemon Festival. Goleta; (805) 967-4618; www.lemonfestival.com. Family event featuring a lemon pie-eating contest, food, arts and crafts show, children's activities, farmers' market, and entertainment. Free.

november

Doo Dah Parade. Pasadena; (626) 795-9311; www.pasadenadoodahparade.info. Eccentric parade features unique performing groups and artist teams; includes wacky costumes and cars. Free.

Sawdust Art Festival Winter Fantasy. Laguna Beach; (949) 494-3030; www.sawdustart festival.org/winter-details. Unique holiday arts-and-crafts festival features 150 artists and craftspeople from around the country, with artist demonstrations, hands-on workshops, children's art activities, continuous entertainment, Santa Claus, and a snow playground. Continues through Dec.

december

Christmas Boat Parade. Newport Beach; (949) 729-4400; www.christmasboatparade .com. More than 200 illuminated and decorated boats cruise the harbor. Free.

Festival of Lights Parade. Palm Springs; (760) 325-5749; www.paradesofpalmsprings .com. Illuminated bands, floats, and automobiles make this one of the area's top holiday events.

Festival of Lights. Riverside; (909) 683-7100 or (909) 683-2670; www.riversideca.gov/fol. Holiday lighting of the historic Mission Inn and surrounding downtown locations. Entertainment and specialty booths. Free.

Glory of Christmas. Garden Grove; (949) 544-5679; www.crystalcathedral.org. Live Nativity scene includes animals, flying angels, holiday music, and pageantry.

Holiday Boat Parade of Lights. Santa Barbara; (805) 897-1962; www.santabarbaraca .gov/Visitor/Things/Waterfront/Annual_Parade_of_Lights.htm. Colorful parade of decorated lighted boats on Santa Barbara waterfront plus free festival on Stearns Wharf.

Julefest, Solvang; (805) 688-6144; www.solvangusa.com. Month-long Danish-American village celebration features thousands of twinkling lights, carolers around town, tree lighting with ballerinas, Sat morning parade. Free.

Torchlight Parade. Big Bear Lake, (800) 4-BIG-BEAR or (909) 866-6190; www.bigbear info.com. Snow Summit hosts this spectacular sight of skiers and snowboarders gliding down the mountain holding torchlights on New Year's Eve.

index